Software Development with Z

A Practical Approach to Formal Methods in Software Engineering

INTERNATIONAL COMPUTER SCIENCE SERIES

Consulting editors	**A D McGettrick**	University of Strathclyde
	J van Leeuwen	University of Utrecht

SELECTED TITLES IN THE SERIES

Distributed Systems: Concepts and Design *G Coulouris and J Dollimore*

Software Prototyping, Formal Methods and VDM *S Hekmatpour and D Ince*

High-Level Languages and their Compilers *D Watson*

Elements of Functional Programming *C Reade*

Software Development with Modula-2 *D Budgen*

Interactive Computer Graphics: Functional, Procedural and Device-Level Methods *P Burger and D Gillies*

Program Derivation: The Development of Programs from Specifications *R G Dromey*

Program Design with Modula-2 *S Eisenbach and C Sadler*

Parallel Processing: Principles and Practice *E V Krishnamurthy*

Real Time Systems and their Programming Languages *A Burns and A Wellings*

Prolog Programming for Artificial Intelligence (2nd Edn) *I Bratko*

Introduction to Expert Systems (2nd Edn) *P Jackson*

Logic for Computer Science *S Reeves and M Clarke*

Computer Architecture *M De Blasi*

The Programming Process: an Introduction using VDM and Pascal *J T Latham, V J Bush and D Cottam*

Analysis of Algorithms and Data Structures *L Banachowski, A Kreczmar and W Rytter*

Handbook of Algorithms and Data Structures in Pascal and C (2nd Edn) *G Gonnet and R Baeza-Yates*

Algorithms and Data Structures *J H Kingston*

Principles of Expert Systems *P Lucas and L van der Gaag*

Discrete Mathematics for Computer Scientists *J K Truss*

Programming in Ada plus Language Reference Manual (3rd Edn) *J G P Barnes*

Software Engineering (4th Edn) *I Sommerville*

Software Development with Z

A Practical Approach to Formal Methods in Software Engineering

J. B. Wordsworth

IBM United Kingdom Laboratories Ltd

ADDISON-WESLEY PUBLISHING COMPANY

Wokingham, England · Reading, Massachusetts · Menlo Park, California · New York
Don Mills, Ontario · Amsterdam · Bonn · Sydney · Singapore
Tokyo · Madrid · San Juan · Milan · Paris · Mexico City · Seoul · Taipei

Cover designed by Chris Eley and
printed by The Riverside Printing Co. (Reading) Ltd.
Typeset using BookMaster™ and the IBM 3816 Page Printer.
Printed in Great Britain by T. J. Press (Padstow) Ltd, Cornwall.

First printed 1992.

British Library Cataloguing in Publication Data
A catalogue record for this book is available from the British Library.

Library of Congress Cataloging in Publication Data
Wordsworth, J. B.
Software development with Z: a practical approach to formal methods in software engineering / J.B. Wordsworth.
p. cm.
Includes bibliographical references and index.
ISBN 0-201-62757-4
1. Z (Computer program language) 2. Computer software--Development. I. Title
QA76.73.Z2W67 1992
005.1′2--dc20 92-15874
CIP

Preface

This book has two principal aims. The first is to encourage software developers in industry to explore the use of formal methods in perfecting their craft. The second is to give students of formal methods an insight into the practical problems of applying mathematics to real software development. One audience for this book is experienced in the practical problems, but has limited time for study, and probably a fast-fading knowledge of logic and discrete mathematics. The other has access to mathematics teaching, plenty of time for (or at least incentive to) study, but only a vague understanding of the possible applications of the subject. These two audiences might be thought to need separate treatment, but I believe that this is not necessary. Almost every chapter in this book is open to dual interpretation. The software developer will see how familiar procedures and decisions can be made precise and enriched by the use of mathematics. The student will see how the mathematics can be applied to novel problems of specification and design.

Some reviewers of this book have doubted the wisdom of introducing a complete Z specification in Chapter 2, before dealing with the necessary mathematics. I feel that a preview of this kind is very valuable, since it sets the scene for where we are going. The mathematics used is very simple, and the specification contains much informal text, including diagrams, to explain what is being made precise.

Chapters 3 and 4 cover the necessary discrete mathematics and logic. The student of computer science, for whom these chapters might not be a primary text, should study the technical vocabulary and the choices that have been made in the presentation. For instance, we use a typed rather than an untyped set theory, and this choice affects the scheme of reasoning about sets presented in Chapter 3. The software developer will use these chapters as a primary source in discrete mathematics and logic, and will find there not a complete account, but enough for application to software development.

Chapter 5 deals with schemas and the notion of a specification as a precise document on which a software development can be based. This chapter places emphasis on the devices of the schema calculus that allow large and complex specifications to be built from small ones. In particular, the marshalling of conjunction and hiding into the technique called promotion is considered in detail. The influence of non-functional requirements on the progress of a design, and the recording of design decisions using Z and Dijkstra's guarded command language are covered in Chapters 6 and 7. The book thus contains a complete development method from specifications to programs.

Some of the material in this book has appeared in print before. A tutorial 'Specifying and refining programs with Z' published in *Software Engineering 88*, IEE Conference Publication 290, forms the basis of Chapter 7, and material from that tutorial is reproduced by kind permission of the Institution of Electrical Engineers. Other material prepared by me and used in courses on Z specifications and refinement methods at IBM's Hursley Park laboratory and elsewhere is reproduced by kind permission of IBM United Kingdom Laboratories Ltd. IBM also provided facilities for storing, editing and drafting the manuscript during its preparation. Various reviewers have done their best to prevent me from making too many mistakes in the general approach and in the details of the mathematics, but I am afraid they might not always have succeeded. In particular I should like to thank Mandy Chessell, Sylvia Croxall, Jonathan Hoare, Peter Lupton, Keith Mantell, Glyn Normington, Mark Pleszkoch and Martin Tucker of IBM, Professor C. A. R. Hoare, Mark Josephs, Steve King, John Nicholls and Jim Woodcock of Oxford University, Mark Ardis of AT&T, David Garlan of Carnegie-Mellon University, Andy Gravell of Southampton University and Richard Wallace of Digital Equipment Corporation. All these people made contributions to the improvement of the book. There are many things I should like to have added, or done differently, but a line must be drawn for the presses to roll.

John Wordsworth
February, 1992

Contents

Chapter 1
Introduction

Summary: Why the book was written – subjects covered – how to use the book – a view of software development – what formalization means – software development phases – relation model – state machine model – encapsulation – design – verification – testing – summary of the role of formal methods.

1.1 Why this book was written

This book is intended to provide practical guidance about the use of Z in the development of software. Z is a notation developed at the Programming Research Group at Oxford University for recording in a precise way some of the many decisions that are made in the course of the development of a piece of software. The author has been associated over a number of years with the development of Z as a teacher of programming languages and software engineering, and as a designer of software. The book is therefore the fruit of a considerable amount of thought in and around the subject, and of enthusiasm for formal methods tempered by practical experience. Having said that this is a practical guide, I should advise readers that for the theory of Z, its semantics, and its formal mathematical basis they should look elsewhere, in Spivey (1987) for instance.

1.2 Subjects covered

A glance at the contents will show that the book contains a certain amount of mathematics and mathematical notation. Happily, the mathematics that is appropriate to recording the decisions of software development is not very difficult. The notions of elementary set theory are of prime importance, and these are covered in some detail in Chapter 3, but always in the context of their relevance to software development. We shall need to be familiar with the notions of sets, relations, functions and sequences, and these will provide the basis for making precise the things that we perceive in a software system. This kind of mathematics is usually called **discrete mathematics** to distinguish it from the continuous mathematics of real numbers that includes differential and integral calculus. The other facility we need is to make statements about the things we perceive and to express the required or possible relationships between them, and for this we need predicates on sets etc.

Z is a method of presenting mathematics in a readable framework. Z documents consist principally of English text in which are to be found small pieces of mathematics that make precise what is described informally in natural language, pictures etc. The main Z construct is the **schema**, in which we draw to the attention of the reader some things of importance in the software system, and make some statements about the relations of those things to one another.

We shall explore the use of Z for recording software specifications, data design decisions and (in conjunction with a programming notation) algorithm design decisions. A later section of this introduction describes in detail one kind of software development process in which these decisions are embedded. The reader will find that the use of Z for writing specifications of software systems is covered more fully than its use in the later phases of the development process. This is mainly due to the fact that there is much more experience in the use of Z for specification than for design. Chapters 6 and 7 have been written in the hope of encouraging experimentation in the use of Z in the later parts of the process. They are based on ideas developed at IBM's laboratory at Hursley Park, UK, in the course of a formal methods project reported in Collins *et al.* (1987).

Not all the mathematics that is available to writers of Z is covered here. Readers should consult some of the books in the Bibliography on p. 321 for more mathematical notations, and for aspects of Z not covered here. My aim has been to cover such basic notations as occur frequently in specifications and designs, introducing them in the context of software specification and development problems.

1.3 How to use this book

The book can be read as a tutorial on Z and its use in software development, and can be used for reference afterwards. Industrial users of a new technology often have difficulty in getting started on their own. Although this book cannot replace expert on-the-spot guidance, it will advise on some of the pitfalls, and give examples of good practice and precept in using Z. There are examples of common techniques for presenting specifications and examples of the use of common data structures for refinement. Academic users will find a source book for examples on the application of mathematics to practical problems. Teachers, whether in industry or in academic institutions, will find plenty of exercises in the mathematical and practical parts of Z.

Solutions are provided for most of the routine examples, and to some of the longer ones, but the solutions to some of the longer exercises are left for group discussion. Using formal methods should be seen as part of the social process of software development in which the exposition of a specification or design by one or more people to a group of critical listeners is an important part.

1.4 A view of software development

Software development is an important activity in our civilization, one likely to play a big part in the future. It is software that looks after our money in the bank, pays our salaries, books our holidays, flies us about in aircraft from place to place, and controls the nuclear power stations that generate electricity to light and heat our homes. There is a need to develop new software faster and at less cost than ever before, and there is a need to adapt existing software to new circumstances.

Much of software development is a cooperative activity involving many developers. Although software can be developed by one person working alone, the future is not likely to lie with the one-man band. Where people work together to create a large piece of software, they need to come to some understanding of their roles. The idea that software can be constructed in separate pieces or modules is an old one, and much of the division of labour of traditional software development was based on the idea that one more experienced developer would decide how the system was to be decomposed, and then give the specifications of the modules to the less experienced to implement. As the requirements for systems get more complex, the work of decomposition gets more arduous and error-prone. Many a system has been modularized, coded and unit tested, and then come to grief at integration when fundamental misunderstandings about the nature of the interfaces between the modules have come to light. One of the duties of the software engineer is to undertake such a decomposition of a system, and to ensure that those responsible for the parts of it are in no doubt as to what is required of them. The relation of the software engineer to the developers is much like that of a customer to suppliers – the customer fixes the requirements and the suppliers furnish program material to meet them. If the pieces to be constructed are very large, then the decomposition of those requirements might be the responsibility of another software engineer.

The software engineer's research into how a requirement is to be met might conclude that the system can be built from existing parts. The notion that software components can be reused is one that has often been mooted, but not much acted on. It is a principal recommendation of object-oriented development systems. To reuse a previously written software component, the software engineer must have a precise description of the function of that component. This precision is essential, as a misconception about the function of a component imported from elsewhere might not become apparent until late in the development process, when changes are difficult and expensive.

Software developers make assumptions about what the user will be satisfied with. The user has some say in what those assumptions are, but not usually enough. A significant function of a software engineer is to ensure that the customer's requirements are well understood and well documented, so that the initial decomposition is soundly based. Customers present two problems: they do not know what they want, and they frequently change their minds about what they thought they wanted. The software engineer's skill here lies in seeing which of the customer's requirements can be made precise, and in using precision to explore and illuminate the requirements.

Software developers makes decisions about how the user's requirements are to be implemented. These decisions are conditioned by many things such as the available hardware, the available programming skills, the available programming languages, the need for future modification, the need for finding and fixing bugs, the users' guesses about how they will use the system, and the users' requirements for performance.

The philosophy of formal methods of software development is that we should use mathematics to record as much of the development as is practical. Mathematics arose from the need to take control of certain intuitive ideas that appeared to have practical value, and the goal of mathematics has been to make these ideas precise. This activity has a long history, and the notions of arithmetic and Euclidean geometry were well known in the classical period. More recently, notions like rate-of-change, stimulated by the astronomical and dynamical researches of the sixteenth and seventeenth centuries, gave rise to differential calculus. More recently still, the notion of precision has been made precise in mathematical logic. The process of making a vague notion precise is called **formalization**, and there seems good reason to suppose that this process can be applied to various parts of software development just as well as to other fields of applied mathematics. We look now at a software development process, examining some of the places where formalization is possible and seeing what benefits it might bring.

There are many models used to describe software development processes, but most have the following phases in common.

- Requirements analysis, in which we find out what the users of the software want.
- Specification, in which we decide what the software developers are going to provide.
- Design, in which decisions are made about how the requirements are to be met.
- Programming, in which the decisions are embodied in the statements of a programming language and some module-level testing is done.
- Testing, in which the system is built and put through its paces.
- Maintenance, in which errors reported by users are fixed.

In many software development organizations this process is repeated to produce successive releases of a product, each built on its predecessor.

Requirements analysis tries to find out what the users who are going to use the software actually want. The requirements should include function (what we want it to do), performance (how fast we want it to do it), operations (what we are prepared to do in order to make it work), implementation (what other hardware and software we need), serviceability (how we shall diagnose and fix its problems), availability (how much we are going to use it), cost (how much we are prepared to pay for it), time-scales (when we need it), and other things.

Specification is a process that sets out what the development organization is going to provide. The resulting specification document will often follow the broad lines of the requirement statement, addressing the same issues. A comparison of specification and requirements should give the users confidence that what they are going to get will help them solve the problems that prompted the requirements. It is in the specification of the function to be provided that formal methods are usually introduced into the development process. Much of this book is about formalizing the notions of functional requirements and recording the result in Z. Formal methods are not so easily applied to performance, operations etc., at least not at the specification stage. All the other requirements are brought to bear on the design decisions made later in the process.

In a specification we do not describe the intended programs and data structures in detail; indeed we probably do not know what they are going to be. Rather, we present an **abstract model**. The level of abstraction is such that a user not familiar with the details of programming and machines can assess the behaviour being specified, and agree that it is what is required. In this book it is suggested that certain parts of mathematics are suitable for expressing abstract models in specifications.

Sometimes the requirement is of the form

> I need a system that will accept certain information as input and produce certain other information as output according to a certain rule.

More specifically we might have

> I need a system that will accept a text file marked up with certain special signs, and produce formatted pages on a laser printer, the correspondence between the input and the output being given by the following rule ...

A suitable model for such a system is the **relation model**, based on the notion of a mathematical relation described in Chapter 4 and illustrated in Figure 1.1.

The **relation rule** must state clearly its **precondition**, i.e. the condition the inputs must satisfy if they are to be acceptable. The notion that only certain inputs might be acceptable is very important, and its acknowledgement is often missing from informal descriptions of

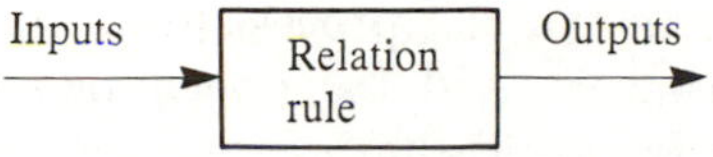

Figure 1.1 The relation model in specification.

systems. Vagueness in this area can cause developers much trouble and users much annoyance when the system is delivered to them. For acceptable inputs the rule must also state how the outputs are related to the inputs. The relation model allows different outputs to arise from the same input, and this property is called **non-determinism**. This is a valuable specification device, since it allows requirements that say 'In this circumstance I don't care whether ... or ...' to be made precise without forcing the issue at the specification stage. If there is no freedom in the choice of outputs for a given input the relation model becomes a **function model**, and the relation rule becomes a **function rule**. Forcing a function model where a relation model would be more appropriate is an instance of **over-specification**. Another kind of over-specification occurs when the user expresses a requirement that has a precondition, but the specification insists on fixing what is to happen in every circumstance. The user says 'In this circumstance I expect the following function ..., but in other circumstances I don't care what happens'. Constraining the behaviour in these other circumstance is over-specification.

The relation model is not suitable for many systems. Returning to the text processing example, we might wish to control the formatting by options that can be set independently of a formatting run. For such a system the **state machine model** is appropriate. In this model **persistent data** or **state** is retained in the machine, and used to affect its subsequent behaviour, as illustrated in Figure 1.2

A typical state machine model consists of an abstract model of the state, a description of the initial state, and relation or function rules for each of the operations on the state. Each rule relates the inputs of an operation and the starting state to the outputs of the operation

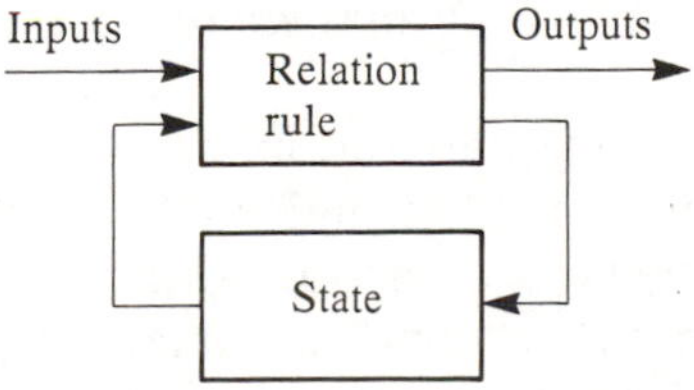

Figure 1.2 The state machine model in specification.

and the ending state. In the text processing example, the state would be the formatting controls, and the operations would be the interactions with the outside world that change the options, or perform a formatting run on a text file. A piece of data and operations that are the only means of accessing it constitute an **abstract data type**. The notion that data should be so protected is called **encapsulation**. Most of Chapter 5 is concerned with techniques of presenting abstract data types using appropriate abstract models and relation rules. The ideas of preconditions, non-determinism and over-specification apply to the relation rule in the state machine model in the same way as in the relation model.

Design is a process in which the developers make and record decisions about how the specification is to be implemented. There are two classes of design decisions to be made.

- How are the abstract models of the specification to be represented using hardware and software? This is **data design.**
- What programs do we need to construct to manipulate the hardware and software to provide the operations described in the specification? This is **algorithm design.**

These decisions are made in such a way as to satisfy the functional requirements embodied in the specification, and to meet the non-functional requirements of performance etc. In a formal method of development these decisions are recorded using mathematics. A precise design can be checked against a precise specification using mathematical proof techniques, a process called **verification**. Rules for verification, and examples of proofs, are to be found in Chapters 6 and 7.

In programming, the algorithm design is translated into a program in the chosen programming language. The amount of freedom the programmer has is determined by the degree of detail in the algorithm design and the capabilities of the language. Usually the algorithm designer and the programmer will be the same person, and the two activities go hand-in-hand. The programmer will do unit testing on each module he or she produces to check for gross errors in implementing the specification, but exhaustive testing is usually impossible, and the goal of formal methods is that code should be correct by design.

The testing phase integrates the modules into a system and tests for correctness of function. If formal methods have been used in the development, correctness of function is not likely to be the main focus of testing, but other non-functional properties like performance, operability and soundness of user publications will be scrutinized. However, function still has to be tested, and a formal specification gives the tester important insights into the kinds of ways that the function of the product can be exercised. As explained above, the specification gives a precise description of the preconditions of the various operations, and the observable behaviour of the product in every circumstance that meets the preconditions. On this basis functional test plans can be built to cover all the cases of the preconditions, and to provoke the various kinds of behaviour of which the system is capable. It is only for the behaviour that is non-deterministic that a plan cannot be made from the specification alone. For non-deterministic behaviour the tester must look into the design to find out the circumstances that must be set up to provoke the different cases. It is also necessary to test the design in the sense that there might be important points of operation in the design that are invisible to the user of the system.

In maintenance, the development organization responds to two kinds of pressures from users of the product. The first pressure is to correct errors in the product and its documentation, and the second is to add more facilities to the product and distribute another release of it. You might think that if a product has been built from a formal specification with a formally recorded design and all the verifications done then an error in the function should be impossible, but software production does not always follow the counsel of perfection. In the first place the proofs of correctness will probably only have been done informally. In the second place even those that have been done formally might have mistakes in them. So what is the point of a formally recorded development? It is important when an error is discovered to find out how it came to be introduced, and to do this a record of the specification and the design decisions that were based on it is invaluable. The point of introduction of each error can be determined, and corrective action taken to strengthen that part of the decision-taking process.

1.5 Summary of the role of formal methods

Formal methods are not methods for developing software without facing up to difficult decisions, but methods for recording those decisions once made. On the way, they allow us to explore the consequences of decisions before making them irrevocable, or very expensive to revoke, and they can suggest some decisions that might have been overlooked. They help us at each stage to ask what decisions have been made and what decisions have been deferred, and perhaps they will encourage us to record the reasons for making or deferring decisions. They provide a development organization with a complete record of the design decisions that led to the product being the way it is, and this record is a valuable asset in the continuing life of a product. The role of a formal record of development as a business asset is explored further in Wordsworth (1992).

1.6 Method of the book

The book proceeds by looking at specification, data design and algorithm design with a simple example that should be within the reader's experience. The example is discussed, and the techniques that it points to are enlarged in other examples. Hints and tips about practical applications and pitfalls are presented. The whole is liberally interspersed with exercises, some of a routine nature, and some pushing the work further.

Exercises

(1.1) Give informal descriptions of systems for which the relation model is appropriate.

(1.2) Give informal descriptions of systems for which the state machine model is appropriate.

(1.3) Consider any computer interfaces that you use in your daily work. Which models are appropriate for them?

(1.4) Consider the publications provided with a computer interface that you use for which the state machine model is appropriate.

- (a) How explicit is the abstract model of the state?
- (b) Does the documentation define the initial state?
- (c) How well does it define the precondition of each of the operations?
- (d) What questions of the form 'What happens if the situation is ..., and I try to do ...?' does it leave unanswered?

(Solutions are not provided for these exercises.)

Chapter 2
A simple Z specification

Summary: Informal statement of requirements – given sets and constants – abstract state – abstract initial state – simple operations – preconditions – error cases – the user interface – summary of responses – models – specifying operations – robust and partial interfaces – generic specifications.

In the view of software development advanced in the previous chapter, a specification is a statement about the nature of a software interface that is agreeable both to the prospective users and to the suppliers of the interface. The rest of this book is largely concerned with the functional part of the specification, i.e. the statement of what functions the interface will provide. That statement is to be made in language that is both precise and simple, and should be made in such a way that there can be no doubt that suppliers and customers are talking about the same thing. In order to get precision in our description we shall enlist the aid of a certain part of mathematics that is appropriate for formalizing the kinds of notions that are commonly found being used by users of computer systems. These notions are often not the same as those being used by technical people skilled in the development and supply of software systems, but in a specification we wish to enforce a proper separation of concerns between suppliers and customers.

2.1 A class manager's assistant

A specification that will be used from time to time in this book is based on an example in Jones (1980). It provides support for a class manager to admit students to a class, and to record who has done the midweek exercises. In later chapters we shall refer to the system specified here as the class manager's assistant. This specification exhibits many features common to Z specifications. It begins with an informal statement of requirements to set the scene in the problem area we are talking about. Next it presents fundamental sets from which the specification will be constructed; in this case there is only one: the set of all possible students. The class manager's view of a class is formalized in a data model presented as a schema called *Class*. The kinds of behaviour that the user of the system might see are presented next and related informally to the operations that the user requires in the interface. The normal aspect of each operation is presented first, then the errors. Finally, the complete operations of the interface are specified by combining the fragments of operations previously described.

The specification is presented much as it would be documented ready for an inspection of the kind described on p. 152. A few remarks of an explanatory nature have been added to help the reader unfamiliar with Z through the specification, but the reader should find the informal text and pictures sufficient to get an idea of what is meant. At this stage a detailed understanding of the formal text is not important.

Each piece of mathematics is surrounded by informal text. The purpose of the mathematics is to make precise what is written in the informal text. The purpose of the informal text is to explain the mathematics in relation to the problem domain. Each schema is surrounded by informal text. The style adopted here is to use the text before the schema to explain the declarations, and that following the schema to explain the predicates.

The formal text is presented in an italic typeface, different from that of the informal text, though whenever a formal name is referred to in the informal text the formal type face is used.

2.1.1 A note on the system of cross-references

Many of the examples in this book are spread over several chapters. A system of cross-references is used to help readers retrace their steps from a place where a name is used to the place where it is defined. On some lines of mathematical text, next to the right-hand margin, will be found one or more page numbers in parentheses. The page numbers show where the names used in the line are defined. Not all names are treated in this way, but only those beginning with a capital letter.

2.1.2 Informal statement of requirements

A computerized class manager's assistant is required to keep track of students enrolled on a class, and to record which of them have done the midweek exercises. When a student applies for a class, he or she will be enrolled on it, unless it is full. Such a student will be presumed not to have done the exercises. When a student completes the exercises, the fact is to be recorded. Students may leave a class even if they have not done the exercises, but only the students who have done the exercises are entitled to a completion certificate.

The operations required are as follows:

Enrol This operation enrols a student on a class, or issues a warning if the class is full, or if the student is already enrolled.

Test This operation records that a student has done the exercises, or warns if the student is not enrolled, or has already done the exercises.

Leave This operation removes a student from the class with an indication of whether the student is entitled to a completion certificate. Only students who have done the exercises are entitled to a certificate. If the student is not enrolled, a warning is given.

Enquire This operation shows whether a student is enrolled, and whether the student has done the exercises.

The screen layouts for these operations and the responses to them are yet to be decided.

2.1.3 The given sets for the specification

Some kind of identifier is required for students, so the notion of a student will be represented by a given set *Student*.

$[Student]$

We require the user of the system to specify a maximum class size, *size*, though at what stage this will be fixed is not yet decided.

$$\begin{array}{|l} size: \mathbb{N} \end{array}$$

The type definition for the responses to the operations is as follows:

$$\begin{aligned} Response ::= {} & success \\ & \mid notenrolled \\ & \mid nocert \\ & \mid cert \\ & \mid alreadyenrolled \\ & \mid alreadytested \\ & \mid noroom \end{aligned}$$

2.1.4 The abstract state data

The notion of a *Class* consists essentially of the notion that some students, possibly none, are enrolled on it; these we call *enrolled.* Some of those enrolled students, possibly none of them, have done the exercises; these we call *tested.* The abstract view of a class then is two sets of students, one a subset of the other. The larger set contains all those enrolled on the class, while the smaller contains those who have done the exercises.

$$\begin{array}{|l} \multicolumn{1}{l}{\_Class\_\_\_\_\_\_\_\_} \\ enrolled, tested: \mathbb{P}\ Student \\ \hline \#\ enrolled \leq size \\ tested \subseteq enrolled \\ \hline \end{array} \qquad (14)$$

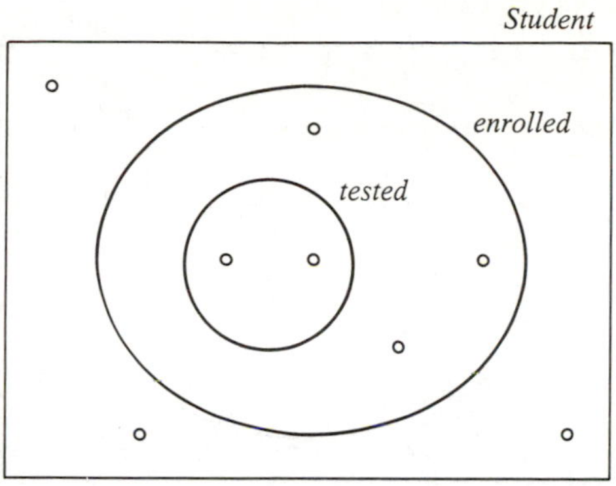

Figure 2.1 The abstract state data.

Not more than *size* students can be enrolled. The students who have done the exercises must all have been enrolled.

Figure 2.1 illustrates an instance of a class for which *size* is at least 5. The rectangle is supposed to contain all possible students past, present and future, though only a few of them are represented by dots. The circle labelled *tested* represents those students who have done the exercises (there are two of them in the diagram), and the ellipse labelled *enrolled* represents those students who have been enrolled, including of course the ones that have done the exercises. Diagrams of this kind will be used to give informal illustrations of the various operations on a class It should be understood that the diagrams can only illustrate instances of the operations, and are not definitive.

2.1.5 The abstract initial state

When the class manager's assistant is first switched on, no students will be enrolled.

$$ClassInit \mathrel{\widehat{=}} [Class' \mid enrolled' = \varnothing] \tag{14}$$

Since those who have done the exercises must all have been enrolled, it follows that there can be no students who have done the exercises, a fact expressed by the following theorem.

$$ClassInit \vdash tested' = \varnothing \tag{15}$$

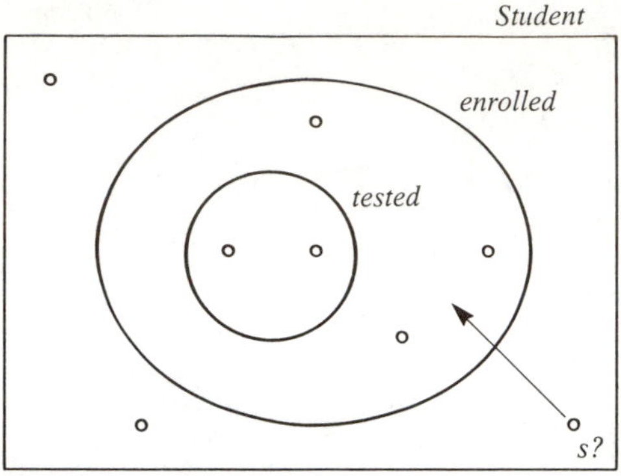

Figure 2.2 Enrolling a student.

2.1.6 Enrolling a student

To record the enrolling of a student, the class changes. The student *s?* must be supplied as input, and an output response *r!* will be generated.

Enrolok

$\Delta Class$	(14)
$s?: Student$	(14)
$r!: Response$	(14)

$$s? \notin enrolled$$
$$\# enrolled < size$$
$$enrolled' = enrolled \cup \{s?\}$$
$$tested' = tested$$
$$r! = success$$

For the moment we describe only the case in which the student is new. There must be room to add a new student. The student is added to the *enrolled* set. A newly enrolled student is not recorded as having done the exercises, so the *tested* set is unchanged. The output response is *success*. Figure 2.2 illustrates an instance of enrolling a student in a class for which *size* is at least 6.

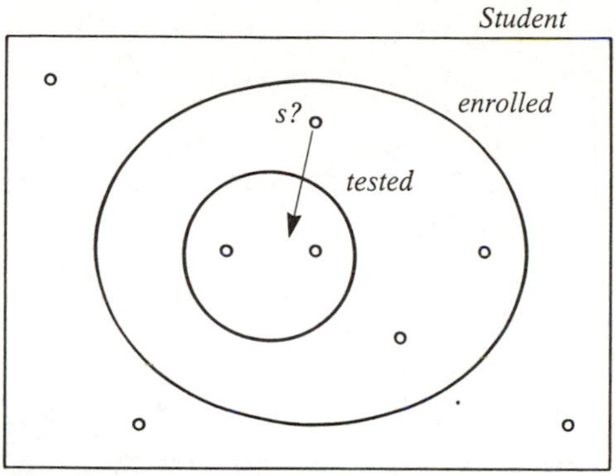

Figure 2.3 Testing a student.

2.1.7 Testing a student

To record that a student has done the exercises, the class changes. The student *s?* must be supplied as input, and an output response will be generated.

Testok

$$
\begin{array}{|l}
\Delta Class \qquad (14) \\
s?: Student \qquad (14) \\
r!: Response \qquad (14) \\
\hline
s? \in enrolled \\
s? \notin tested \\
tested' = tested \cup \{s?\} \\
enrolled' = enrolled \\
r! = success
\end{array}
$$

We describe the case in which the student has been enrolled, but is not yet recorded as having done the exercises. The student is added to the *tested* set, and the *enrolled* set is unchanged. The output response is *success*. Figure 2.3 illustrates an instance of testing a student.

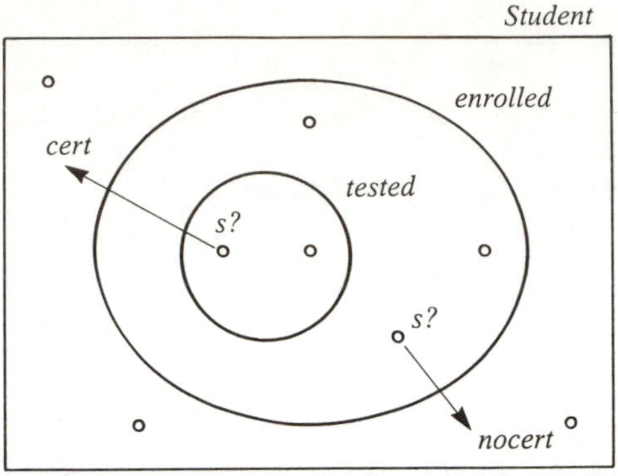

Figure 2.4 Discharging a student.

2.1.8 Discharging a student

To record that a student is leaving the class, the class changes. The student *s?* must be supplied as input, and an output response *r!* will be generated.

```
┌ Leaveok ──────────────────────────────
│ ΔClass                                     (14)
│ s?: Student                                (14)
│ r!: Response                               (14)
├───────────
│ s? ∈ enrolled
│ enrolled' = enrolled \ {s?}
│ ( ( s? ∈ tested ∧ tested' = tested \ {s?} ∧ r! = cert )
│ ∨ ( s? ∉ tested ∧ tested' = tested ∧ r! = nocert ) )
└───────────────────────────────────────
```

We describe the case in which the input student has been enrolled. The student is removed from the *enrolled* set. The output response depends on whether the student has done the exercises. If the student has done the exercises, the response is *cert*, but if not, then it is *nocert*. Figure 2.4 illustrates two instances of a student being discharged.

2.1.9 Enquiries

There is an enquiry operation to report whether a student is enrolled, and to indicate whether the student has done the exercises. This operation does not change the class, it merely reports on it. The student *s?* must be supplied as input. An output response *r!* will be generated.

Enquire

$\Xi Class$ (14)
$s?: Student$ (14)
$r!: Response$ (14)

$$((s? \notin enrolled \wedge r! = notenrolled)$$
$$\vee (s? \in (enrolled \setminus tested) \wedge r! = alreadyenrolled)$$
$$\vee (s? \in tested \wedge r! = alreadytested))$$

If the student is not enrolled, the response is *notenrolled.* If the student is enrolled, but has not done the exercises, the response is *alreadyenrolled.* If the student has done the exercises, the response is *alreadytested.*

2.1.10 Preconditions

We document the preconditions of the operations so far specified in Table 2.1.

Table 2.1 Preconditions of partial operations.

Schema	Input	Precondition
Enrolok	*s?*	$s? \notin enrolled$ $\# enrolled < size$
Testok	*s?*	$s? \in enrolled$ $s? \notin tested$
Leaveok	*s?*	$s? \in enrolled$
Enquire	*s?*	true

In each case it is assumed that the starting state satisfies the state invariant of the *Class* schema.

2.1.11 Errors

Sometimes the user will attempt to enrol a student who is already enrolled. The class must not change as a result of this behaviour. The student *s?* must be supplied as input. An output response *r!* will be generated.

```
─AlreadyEnrolled──────────────────────
│ ΞClass                                  (14)
│ s?: Student                             (14)
│ r!: Response                            (14)
├──────────
│ s? ∈ enrolled
│ r! = alreadyenrolled
└─────────────────────────────────────
```

This behaviour is observed only when the input student is already enrolled, and the response is *alreadyenrolled.*

Sometimes there will be no room to enrol another student. The class must not change as a result of this behaviour. There is no input, but an output response *r!* will be generated.

```
─NoRoom───────────────────────────────
│ ΞClass                                  (14)
│ r!: Response                            (14)
├──────────
│ # enrolled = size
│ r! = noroom
└─────────────────────────────────────
```

This behaviour is observed only when the class is full, and the response is *noroom.*

Sometimes an attempt will be made to record that the exercises have been done by a student who has already been tested. The class must not change as a result of this behaviour. The student *s?* must be supplied as input. An output response *r!* will be generated.

```
─AlreadyTested────────────────────────
│ ΞClass                                  (14)
│ s?: Student                             (14)
│ r!: Response                            (14)
├──────────
│ s? ∈ tested
│ r! = alreadytested
└─────────────────────────────────────
```

This behaviour is possible only when the input student is already recorded as having done the exercises, and the response is *alreadytested.*

Sometimes an attempt will be made to record that the exercises have been done by a student who is not even enrolled. The class must not change as a result of this behaviour. The student *s?* must be supplied as input. An output response *r!* will be generated.

NotEnrolled

$\Xi Class$	(14)
$s?: Student$	(14)
$r!: Response$	(14)
$s? \notin enrolled$	
$r! = notenrolled$	

This behaviour is possible only when the input student is not enrolled, and the response is *notenrolled.* This schema also specifies the behaviour for an attempt to discharge a student who is not enrolled.

2.1.12 The user interface

Users of the system have the following operations at their disposal:

$$Enrol \mathrel{\widehat=} Enrolok \vee NoRoom \vee AlreadyEnrolled \qquad (16, 20, 20)$$

If an attempt is made to enrol into a full class a student who is already enrolled, then either *noroom* or *alreadyenrolled* might be reported.

$$Test \mathrel{\widehat=} Testok \vee NotEnrolled \vee AlreadyTested \qquad (17, 21, 21)$$

$$Leave \mathrel{\widehat=} Leaveok \vee NotEnrolled \qquad (18, 21)$$

In addition the *Enquire* operation can be used.

Table 2.2 shows the inputs and outputs for each operation, and the possible values of the response.

Table 2.2 Summary of inputs, outputs and responses.

Operation	Inputs	Outputs	Responses
Enrol	*s?: Student*	*r!: Response*	*success* *noroom* *alreadyenrolled*

Operation	Inputs	Outputs	Responses
Test	*s?*: *Student*	*r!*: *Response*	*success* *notenrolled* *alreadytested*
Leave	*s?*: *Student*	*r!*: *Response*	*cert* *nocert* *notenrolled*
Enquire	*s?*: *Student*	*r!*: *Response*	*alreadyenrolled* *alreadytested* *notenrolled*

2.1.13 Summary of responses

The following values are possible:

success The *Enrol* or *Test* operation completed successfully.

notenrolled The *Leave* or *Test* operation failed because the student provided as input was not recorded as enrolled. The student provided as input to the *Enquire* operation was not enrolled.

nocert The student provided as input to the *Leave* operation had been enrolled, but had not done the exercises. The operation to discharge the student has been completed successfully.

cert The student provided as input to the *Leave* operation had been enrolled, and had done the exercises. The operation to discharge the student has been completed successfully.

alreadyenrolled The student provided as input to the *Enrol* operation is already recorded as being enrolled, and the operation has not been performed. The student provided as input to the *Enquire* operation was enrolled, but had not done the exercises.

alreadytested The student provided as input to the *Test* operation is already recorded as having done the exercises, and the operation has not been performed. The student provided as input to the *Enquire* operation had done the exercises.

noroom The *Enrol* operation failed because the class is full.

2.2 Notes on the style of the specification

2.2.1 Creating and recording models

The model for a specification is arrived at tentatively by studying such informal statements of requirement as are to hand. These requirements give hints about the kind of information that needs to be maintained. The primary function of the model is to give the user a rational explanation of the operations. The model must be as simple as possible consistent with this need. A secondary function of the model is to establish a precise technical vocabulary that can be used to discuss the interface being defined.

The model consists of some things about which we wish to speak, and some important constraints on them. In the case of the class manager's assistant, the things are the two sets *enrolled* and *tested*, and the constraints are the size limit on *enrolled* and the fact that every member of *tested* must also be a member of *enrolled*. This combination of introducing things to be spoken about and then making important statements about them is fundamental to the Z approach to writing specifications.

If the requirements had been slightly different, then the model proposed might not have been adequate. For instance, if the class manager requires a new operation to list students in the order in which they were enrolled, our model does not contain enough information to support it. This is no criticism of the model – it was drawn up for different requirements, and specifiers should have no hesitation in insisting that if the user changes the requirements, then the specifier must be allowed to change the specification of the system that is to meet them. Of course professional software specifiers must be aware of the directions that changes of requirements are likely to lead in, and might even try to anticipate future requirements, or construct specifications that will accept changes of requirement without rewriting.

Given a set of requirements there are many specifications that would serve to formalize them. For instance we could take the enrolled students and divide them into two sets, one set for those who had done the exercises and one for those who had not. This is, in fact, the approach taken in the specification of the problem in Jones (1980). The explanations of the operations would now look different, but the system being specified would have the same properties as the original. A model must of course be capable of making the effect of the operations precise, but otherwise the choice of model appears to be quite arbitrary. Since the primary purpose of a specification is to improve communication between a software user and a software supplier, a simple model that the user can understand is to be preferred to a complex model. The effectiveness of a model is often best seen in simple and convincing specifications of the operations. The subject of what constitutes a good model is considered further in Gravell (1991).

2.2.2 Specifying operations

The specification of the *Enrol* operation looks like this:

$$Enrol \mathrel{\widehat{=}} Enrolok \lor NoRoom \lor AlreadyEnrolled$$

This means that when the class manager uses the *Enrol* operation he or she will see either what is specified by *Enrolok* or what is specified by *NoRoom* or what is specified by *AlreadyEnrolled.* These schemas are defined earlier in the specification, though the order of presentation is a matter of style, not a requirement of the language. The specification of *Enrolok* involves speaking about the contents of *enrolled* and *tested* before the operation occurs, the inputs to the operation, the outputs from the operation, and the contents of *enrolled* and *tested* afterwards. In Z there are conventions about how this should be done. The notation $\Delta Class$ introduces *enrolled* and *tested* (to denote the starting values), and *enrolled'* and *tested'* (to denote the ending values). The input names end with a question mark, and the output names end with an exclamation mark. Again the principle is to introduce the six names first, and then say what has to be said about them. What has to be said in this case has two aspects. The first aspect is the precondition, a statement about the situation that must obtain for the specified behaviour to occur. It is good style to write the precondition first in the formal text and discuss it first in the informal text. For *Enrolok* the precondition is that the input student must not already be enrolled, and there must be enough room for another. The other aspect of what has to be said is the postcondition, a statement about the situation that must obtain as a result of the specified behaviour. For *Enrolok* the postcondition is that the *enrolled* set must contain all the students that were in it before and the input student besides, that the *tested* set must not change, and that the response will be *success.*

2.2.3 Robust and partial interfaces

The operations offered to the class manager are all **robust** – that is to say they can be attempted in any circumstances and will produce some result – the interface is never at a loss for a response. The operation *Enrolok* on the other hand is not robust, but **partial**, since it has a precondition that might be false. If *Enrolok* were offered as an operation in the class manager's assistant, the responsibility for seeing that the precondition was true would be the class manager's.

Attempting the operation when the precondition was not true would have unpredictable results. Indeed, the reason for specifying the *NoRoom* and *AlreadyEnrolled* schemas was to augment the partial operation *Enrolok* into the robust one required by the class manager.

The non-determinism of the *Enrol* operation requires comment. When the class is full, and the input student is already enrolled, the specification says that either *NoRoom* or *AlreadyEnrolled* will occur. This non-determinism, which is noted in the informal text of the specification, should be explored with the class manager to make sure that it is acceptable. If it is not, i.e. if one response is to be preferred to the other, then the specification should be changed. If the non-determinism is acceptable, the specification should not make a choice between the two. To document a choice where none is required would be over-specification.

2.2.4 Generic specifications

The notion of a student plays a special role in this specification. Very little is said or implied about the nature of the members of *Student* except that they are suitable to be passed across the interface as input parameters. Similarly, very little is assumed about the nature of *size*. The specification is **generic** with respect to the set *Student* and the number *size* in the sense that values need to be supplied for these two items before the specification can really be said to be specifying anything. Supplying values for the generic sets and constants we shall call **instantiation**, following the usage of several programming languages. An instantiation in which *size* has the value zero is possible, but not useful.

The specification could be instantiated using 'the set of all vehicle registration numbers' for *Student*, and applied to quite a different purpose from that envisaged when it was first drawn up. A dealer in second-hand cars could use it to control some aspects of his stock by interpreting *enrolled* as 'cars bought but not yet sold', and *tested* as 'cars inspected, repaired, and ready for sale under guarantee'.

Chapter 3
Sets and predicates

Summary: Sets – types – given sets – declarations – enumeration – equality – null sets – membership – enumerated types – subsets – power sets – syntactic equivalence – numbers – finite and infinite sets Venn diagrams – union, intersection and difference – comprehension – predicates – negation, disjunction, conjunction, implication and equivalence – existential and universal quantifiers – definite descriptions – theorems and proofs – deduction rules and axioms.

In writing specifications we shall be using the mathematical theory of sets to formalize the notions that potential users of a system can rely on to illuminate their dealings with it. We shall use sets and their members to build models and explain operations. The precise notations we shall use are of three kinds. Notations of the first kind introduce the names of the values that we wish to speak about, and they are called **declarations**. Notations of the second kind denote values of which we wish to speak, and they are called **terms**. They are built up in various ways from the names that are introduced in declarations, and they are the formalization of the informal natural language notion of noun phrase. Notations of the third kind express statements about terms, and are called **predicates**. They are formalizations of the informal natural language notion of declarative sentence. This chapter introduces the ideas of declarations, terms and predicates.

3.1 Sets and types

3.1.1 What is a set?

To the mathematician a set is a well-defined collection of values. 'Well-defined' means that given a value, it is possible to decide whether it is a member of the set. In informal descriptions of requirements, noun phrases that hint at sets are often to be found. Phrases such as these might occur in the informal requirements of systems for library management, banking, taxation or education.

- The books still on the library shelves.
- The accounts that are overdrawn for which no arrangement has been made.
- The full-time employees of IBM United Kingdom Laboratories Ltd.
- The books currently overdue from the library.
- The students who are enrolled on the class, but have not yet done the exercises.
- The borrowers who have reserved *War and Peace*.

The members of a set are distinct values, that is to say there is no notion of how many times a value occurs in a set; either it is there or it is not. The members of a set are not considered to be in any particular order.

3.1.2 Types in set theory

It should be noted that each of the above sets is a set of values of the same kind; that is to say the sets are **homogeneous**. This notion of things being of the same kind is very important in efforts to formalize a user's view of a system, since it pervades the informal notions that are used when talking about it. To formalize the notion 'of the same kind' we introduce into a Z specification certain sets called **types**. The decision about which sets are to be types is part of the specification process. It is a decision that has to be taken quite early in the process, since the well-formedness of any terms or predicates used in the specification depends on it. It is difficult to give general rules about how to recognize the types from informal requirements. In this book we shall teach type selection mostly by example.

3.1.3 Types in a library management system

In the text and exercises we shall explore some requirements for a system to support the operation of a library that lends books to borrowers. We shall refer to this system as the library management system. In discussing the requirements with the librarian we shall establish the need for certain sets to be types, and then formalize the concepts of library management in terms of these sets. Two of these types have already been introduced.

- *Book* is the type from which the books in the library are drawn. The members of *Book* represent the things that can be taken from the library shelves and, in most cases, borrowed from it. *Book* must be supposed to be big enough to contain all the books ever likely to appear on the library shelves. In the event, the members of *Book* will probably turn out to be strings of characters encoded in a magnetic stripe or bar code firmly stuck to the inside cover of the physical books, but for the purpose of a specification we abstract from this detail, and leave the set *Book* undefined.

- *Person* is a set from which the borrowers are drawn, and it will be a type of the specification. This set must be big enough to contain all the people ever likely to be borrowers from the library. We abstract away the detail that the members of *Person* will probably be strings of characters encoded in a magnetic stripe on borrowers' identification cards, and leave the set *Person* undefined.

By nominating these sets as types of the theory that we develop about the library, we acknowledge the librarian's feeling that books and borrowers are things of different kinds.

3.1.4 Given sets

One way to introduce a type into a Z specification is as a **given set**. In the class manager's assistant, the given set *Student* was introduced on p. 14 by putting its name in square brackets thus:

[*Student*]

Square brackets used in this way are called **given set brackets**. This piece of notation is a declaration introducing the name *Student*. A name will be said to **denote** the thing that it names, in this case a certain set that is to be a type. Conversely we might say that the set is the **denotation** of the name. (The reader who might think that we should use 'meaning' instead of 'denotation' should scan the references to 'sense of a name' in the index.)

Names in Z are constructed from a variety of characters. Most commonly used are the 52 alphabetic characters (upper and lower case), the ten numeric characters, and the break or underscore. Other characters are also used, often with some conventional meaning, and these will be introduced as they are required.

In the library management system, the types *Book* and *Person* should be introduced as given sets:

[*Book*, *Person*]

The names in a list of given sets are separated by commas. The use of names beginning with capital letters for given sets is a personal style of the author's, and is connected with the scheme of cross-references used in this book.

3.1.5 Declaration of variables

The set theory on which Z is based is a typed set theory, that is to say every value we speak of must be assigned a type. A name is assigned a type when it is declared. Thus if *Student* is a type we can declare a student *stud1* with the following declaration:

stud1: *Student* (14)

Note that the name being declared is followed by a colon, and then by the name of the set from which it takes its values. The name *stud1* is called a **variable**, that is to say we do not know the denotation of the name *stud1*, only that it denotes some undetermined value of type *Student*. (Readers with programming knowledge should note that the mathematical meaning of a variable being used here is not the same as the meaning of a variable in programming. In programming a variable is a store in which different values can appear from time to time. In mathematics a variable does not change its value, but its value might not be determined.)

There are variations of this notation that permit the declaration of several names of the same type on one line, and of names of different types on the same line. In the following examples we suppose that *Book* and *Person* are sets that are types.

This example

$$war\_and\_peace\_1, jane\_eyre\_5: Book; jbw: Person \qquad (29, 29)$$

declares two names to be of type *Book* and one of type *Person*. A comma separates names of the same type, and a semicolon separates the batches of declarations. Note that declaring two names to be of a given type does not guarantee that they denote different values of that type.

3.1.6 More sets for the library

We shall introduce more sets that will be of use in formalizing the requirements for the library management system, and for the moment we do so informally.

books is the set of books owned by the library. All the members of *books* are of the same type, being drawn from the set *Book*.

on_loan is the set of books that have been borrowed. All the members of *on_loan* are drawn from the set *Book*.

on_shelves is the set of books that have not been borrowed, and are still believed to be on the library shelves. All the members of *on_shelves* are drawn from the set *Book*.

reference is the set of books that may never be borrowed, but are to be used only on the library premises. All the members of *reference* are drawn from the set *Book*.

borrowers is the set of people who are entitled to borrow books from the library. All the members of *borrowers* are drawn from the set *Person*.

3.1.7 Set enumeration

A set may be defined by listing its members in some order, and this is called **set enumeration**. Suppose the following declarations have been made:

$$whittaker, c\_ox\_dict, ox\_comp\_to\_music: Book \qquad (29)$$

The set *reference* might, in a small library, have the following value:

$\{whittaker, c\_ox\_dict, ox\_comp\_to\_music\}$

The set enumeration is enclosed in **braces**, and the members are separated by commas. The use of a single space between a comma and the following item is a typographical convention of my own. The order of the items is arbitrary, but they must of course all be of the same type. Unless we know that the names denote different values, and in this case there is a hint that they do, we cannot say exactly how many values there are in a set.

A notation that denotes a set is a term in our language for formalizing requirements in a specification, i.e. a notation that denotes a value rather than one that declares a name or makes a statement. The question at once arises: what is the type of this term? We know that each member of the set is of type *Book*, but *Book* cannot be the type of the set. The answer to this question is deferred until p. 34.

A set enumeration can denote a set with just one member thus: $\{jane\_eyre\_2\}$. Such a set is called a **singleton** set. Note that this singleton set is a set of books with just one member, and is not the same as the book itself.

3.1.8 Equality of sets

Two sets of values of the same type are equal if and only if they have the same members. The usual sign for equality will be used for sets. In the library management system, *on_shelves* and *reference* are two sets whose members are of the same type, so the predicate

$$on\_shelves = reference$$

means that every book that can be borrowed has indeed been borrowed, since only the reference books are left on the shelves. We shall reject the notation

$$on\_shelves = borrowers$$

since the two sets are of different types, and say that the notation is not well-formed.

Sometimes we wish to say that two sets of values of the same type are not equal, and we use the following notation:

$$on\_shelves \neq reference$$

For sets *on_shelves* and *borrowers*, we should refrain from saying anything about whether they were equal or not, since their members are not of the same type. The notation

$$on\_shelves \neq borrowers$$

is not well-formed.

3.1.9 Null sets

We can imagine a set with no members. Such a set is called a **null set** or an **empty set**, and in formal text we use the sign Ø for it. The reader will see this sign used to formalize the statement 'no students will be enrolled' in the class manager's assistant on p. 15. The enumeration {} could be used to denote an empty set, but in this book we shall use Ø.

The notation for empty sets is an ambiguous notation, since the type of the members of the set is not indicated. If persons and books are types, the empty set of books is quite a different thing from the empty set of persons. In the library management system, the fact that no books were on loan could be formalized by writing

$$\mathit{on\_loan} = \emptyset$$

and the fact that no one was allowed to borrow books could be formalized by writing

$$\mathit{borrowers} = \emptyset$$

but we should remember that the first empty set is an empty set of books, while the second is an empty set of people. It would be foolish to attempt to draw the conclusion that in this case

$$\mathit{on\_loan} = \mathit{borrowers}$$

as this notation is not well-formed.

3.1.10 Members of a set

If *jane_eyre_1* is a **member** of the set *on_shelves*, we can write

$$\mathit{jane\_eyre\_1} \in \mathit{on\_shelves}$$

This is a statement that can be true or false, depending on whether *jane_eyre_1* is a member of the set *on_shelves*, and it is therefore not a term in our language but a predicate. Notice that the predicate contains two terms *jane_eyre_1* and *on_shelves*, and the sign ∈, which formalizes the relation 'is a member of'.

The statement 'the student has been enrolled' on p. 17 is formalized with the help of ∈.

The reader must not confuse the declaration *stud1*: *Student* with the predicate *stud1* ∈ *Student*. If *stud1* has been declared in the declaration, the predicate is true, but the function of declaration and predicate in a specification document are quite different. The declaration introduces the name *stud1*, and makes it possible to use the name in the predicate.

If *jane_eyre_1* is not a member of the set *on_shelves*, we can write

$jane\_eyre\_1 \notin on\_shelves$

but this notation will be not be used like this:

$jane\_eyre\_1 \notin borrowers$

since the type of the first term is *Book*, while the second term can only have values of type *Person* as members. Such a notation is not well-formed.

The statement 'the student ... has not yet done the exercises' on p. 17 is formalized with the help of $\notin$.

3.1.11 Enumerated types

Sometimes we wish to introduce a type with a small number of members, and give names to the members of the type. Here is an instance of a declaration to define a type called *YesNo* with exactly two values, *yes* and *no*.

$YesNo ::= yes \mid no$

The above notation is called a **data type** definition. The sign '::=' is the data type definition symbol, and the sign '|' is the **branch separator**. This data type definition is a shorthand for a number of declarations and predicates, as follows.

$[YesNo]$
$yes: YesNo$
$no: YesNo$
$yes \neq no$
$YesNo = \{yes, no\}$

YesNo is a given set, and *yes* and *no* are distinct values of it. The values *yes* and *no* are the only two values of the type.

In the class manager's assistant, a data type definition was used to specify the type *Response* on p. 14.

We shall see data type definitions used again for a more elaborate purpose on p. 84 in the next chapter.

3.1.12 Subsets

One set is said to be a **subset** of another if all the members of the one are also members of the other. In the library management system, *on_shelves* and *books* are sets of values of the same type, so we can formalize the requirement that every member of *on_shelves* is a member of *books* by writing the following predicate.

$on\_shelves \subseteq books$

This might be read '*on_shelves* is a subset of *books*'.

A set is always a subset of itself, whatever the type of its members.

$$borrowers \subseteq borrowers$$

The subset relation between sets is **transitive**, that is to say if $reference \subseteq on\_shelves$ and $on\_shelves \subseteq books$ then $reference \subseteq books$.

In the class manager's assistant, 'the students who have done the exercises must all have been enrolled' on p. 15 is formalized with the help of the subset notation.

3.1.13 Power sets

The **power set** of a set A is the set of all its subsets. We shall use the notation $\mathbb{P}A$ to denote the power set of a set A.

Suppose that A is a set with just two members x and y; we can then enumerate its power set.

$$\mathbb{P}A = \{\emptyset, \{x\}, \{y\}, \{x, y\}\}$$

The two predicates following have the same meaning:

$$A \subseteq B \qquad\qquad A \in \mathbb{P}\, B$$

The following predicates about the power set are true:

$$A \in \mathbb{P}\, A$$

$$\emptyset \in \mathbb{P}\, A$$

In the last predicate it is important to understand that $\emptyset$ denotes the empty set of values of the type to be found in A.

Now the question posed on p. 31 can be answered. The type of a set whose members are all of type *Book* is $\mathbb{P}\ Book$.

In the class manager's assistant, the power set notation was used on p. 14 to declare *enrolled* and *tested* to be of type 'set of student'. In general, if T is a set that is a type, then so is $\mathbb{P}\ T$.

In the library management system, we can now declare properly the sets we introduced earlier.

$$books, on\_shelves, reference, on\_loan: \mathbb{P}\ Book \qquad (29)$$

$$borrowers: \mathbb{P}\ Person \qquad (29)$$

3.1.14 Syntactic equivalence

It is often convenient to introduce names for terms whose values can be defined by expressions like the set enumeration above. Bearing in mind declarations made earlier in this chapter, the declaration

$$basic\_reference == \{whittaker, c\_ox\_dict, ox\_comp\_to\_music\}$$

is called a declaration by **syntactic equivalence**, and '==' is the symbol of syntactic equivalence. It establishes the name on the left-hand side as a name denoting the set on the right-hand side. It is equivalent to the declaration

$$basic\_reference\colon \mathbb{P}\ Book \qquad (29)$$

together with the predicate

$$basic\_reference = \{whittaker, c\_ox\_dict, ox\_comp\_to\_music\}$$

and can be regarded as an abbreviation for them. Note that the expression on the right-hand side must be well-formed, and any names used in it must be declared.

3.1.15 Sets of numbers

Numbers of various kinds appear in informal requirements, and thus in formal specifications. There are two sets of numbers that are particularly useful:

- **Integers**, denoted in formal text by $\mathbb{Z}$, is the set of positive or negative whole numbers including zero. $\mathbb{Z}$ is a type in any specification; it does not have to be introduced formally. Since $\mathbb{Z}$ is a set of integers, its type is $\mathbb{P}\mathbb{Z}$.
- **Natural numbers**, denoted in formal text by $\mathbb{N}$, is the set of whole numbers from zero upwards. The natural numbers are a subset of the integers, so the type of $\mathbb{N}$ is $\mathbb{P}\mathbb{Z}$.

The following notations in Table 3.1 and Table 3.2 will be used for constructing integer terms and predicates. It is assumed that a, b are declared to be of type $\mathbb{Z}$.

Parentheses can be used to show how terms are to be grouped in building extended expressions such as $((a+b)/b)^2$. The use of spaces in these expressions is a matter of individual style.

Table 3.1 Integer terms.

Name	Notation	Remarks
constants	... -2 -1 0 1 2 ...	Usual notation for numeric constants
sum	$a + b$	
difference	$a - b$	
product	$a * b$	
quotient	a / b	Integral division only, $b \neq 0$
remainder	$a // b$	$b \neq 0$
square, etc.	a^2	And other indices

Table 3.2 Integer predicates.

Name	Notation
equality	$a = b$
inequality	$a \neq b$
less than	$a < b$
greater than	$a > b$
less than or equal to	$a \leq b$
greater than or equal to	$a \geq b$

Sometimes we need to speak about a more restricted set of numbers, those numbers lying in a certain range. Such a set is called a **subrange**, and here are some examples showing the formal notation used to denote them.

$1..4$ denotes $\{1, 2, 3, 4\}$

$2..6$ denotes $\{2, 3, 4, 5, 6\}$

$1..0$ denotes $\varnothing$ (of type $\mathbb{P}\mathbb{Z}$)

Since $\mathbb{N}$ is a subset of $\mathbb{Z}$, it is not itself a type. By declaring

$size: \mathbb{N}$

we mean that the type of *size* is $\mathbb{Z}$, but any reasoning we do that uses *size* is entitled to use the predicate $size \geq 0$. The predicate is called an **implicit predicate** of the declaration. It is often convenient in declarations to use a set after the colon that is not a type, and to take advantage of the brevity introduced by not having to write the implicit predicate.

3.1.16 Finite and infinite sets

In writing and reading specifications it is sometimes necessary to distinguish finite and infinite sets. The formal definition of the distinction does not concern us in this book; however, the following examples are informally described as **finite** sets.

- *1..100*

  'The set of authors with at least one work published by Addison-Wesley'

and the following are **infinite** sets.

  $\mathbb{Z}$

  'The set of natural numbers that are prime'

  'The set of even integers'

If X denotes some finite set, then the number of elements in the set is called its **cardinality** or **size**, and is denoted by $\#X$. This notation was used in the class manager's assistant in formalizing the statements 'Not more than *size* students can be enrolled' on p. 15, and 'There must be room to add a new student' on p. 16.

3.1.17 Venn diagrams

Informal text is often made more illuminating by including diagrams in it. The reader will have seen examples in the class manager's assistant in the previous chapter. Diagrams to illustrate sets and their members are called **Venn diagrams** after their inventor, John Venn. The set $\{1, 2, 3, 4, 5\}$ can be represented by a Venn diagram as in Figure 3.1. The rectangle represents the type $\mathbb{Z}$, so any marker inside the rectangle represents an integer, though not every integer can be so represented, since $\mathbb{Z}$ is infinite. The circle represents the set named above, and the markers inside it represent the five members. The other members of $\mathbb{Z}$ are not shown, but they are all supposed to be inside the rectangle but outside the circle.

The subset relation is illustrated in Figure 3.2. The set A is supposed to contain only the three values marked in the diagram as

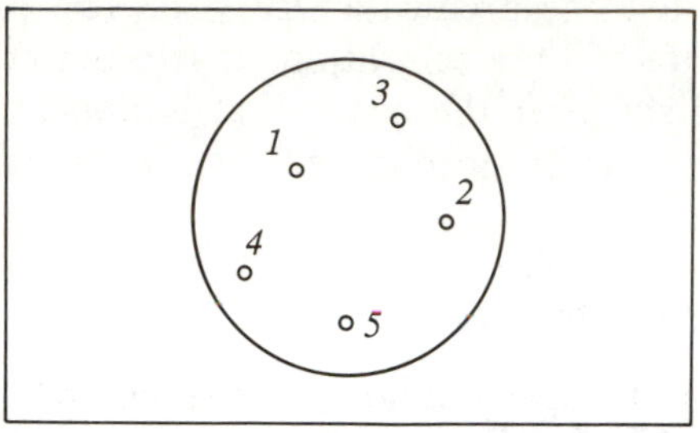

Figure 3.1 A Venn diagram of a finite set of integers.

being inside the shape labelled *A*, while the set *B* contains those and the other three.

A Venn diagram was used in the class manager's assistant on p. 15 to illustrate the relation between the sets *tested* and *enrolled*.

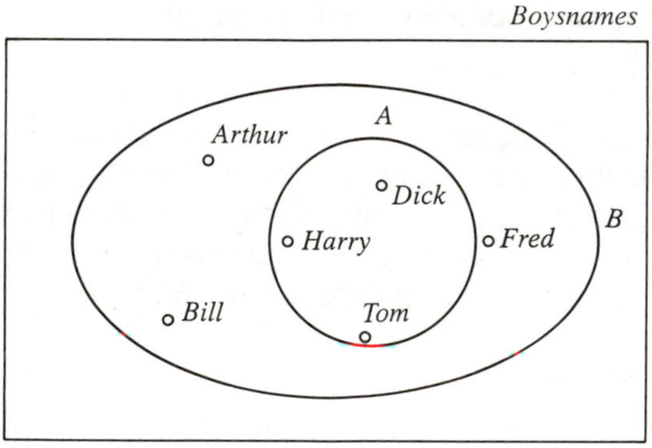

Figure 3.2 Venn diagram of the subset relation.

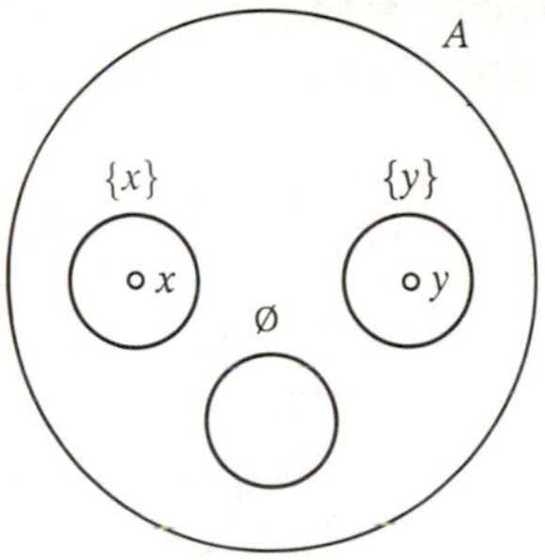

Figure 3.3 Venn diagram of a power set.

The diagram in Figure 3.3 represents the power set of a set A with exactly two members x and y. The dotted circles represent the four members of $\mathbb{P}A$, namely

the empty set,

the singleton set containing x,

the singleton set containing y, and

the whole of A.

3.1.18 Union of two sets

Given two sets A and B of the same type, we can speak of the set whose members are the members of A and B together. This new idea is called the **union** of A and B, and is denoted by the following expression.

$$A \cup B$$

The union of two sets is of the same type as the sets themselves. The predicates in Table 3.3 express important properties of the union.

Table 3.3 Some properties of set union.

Notation	Property
$A \cup A = A$	
$A \cup \varnothing = A$	$\varnothing$ is a unit for union
$A \cup B = B \cup A$	union is commutative
$A \cup (B \cup C) = (A \cup B) \cup C$	union is associative

Now we are able to formalize the idea that books belonging to the library are exactly those that are borrowed and those that are on the shelves.

$$on\_loan \cup on\_shelves = books$$

This predicate says that the names $on\_loan \cup on\_shelves$ and *books* denote the same set. The first name contains more information than the second because it has a meaning that expresses the relation of its denotation to the sets *on_loan* and *on_shelves*. This additional information or meaning will be referred to as the **sense** of the name.

3.1.19 Intersection of two sets

Given two sets A and B of the same type, we can speak of the set whose members are the members that A and B have in common. This new idea is called the **intersection** of A and B, and is denoted by the following expression.

$$A \cap B$$

The intersection of two sets is of the same type as the sets themselves. The predicates in Table 3.4 express important properties of the intersection.

Table 3.4 Some properties of set intersection.

Notation	Property
$A \cap A = A$	
$A \cap \varnothing = \varnothing$	$\varnothing$ is a zero for intersection
$A \cap B = B \cap A$	intersection is commutative
$A \cap (B \cap C) = (A \cap B) \cap C$	intersection is associative
$A \cap (B \cup C) = (A \cap B) \cup (A \cap C)$	intersection distributes over union
$A \cup (B \cap C) = (A \cup B) \cap (A \cup C)$	union distributes over intersection

Two sets are called **disjoint** if they have no members in common, so the fact that no book can be both on the shelves and borrowed can be formalized by the statement

$$on\_shelves \cap on\_loan = \varnothing$$

3.1.20 Difference of two sets

Given two sets A and B of the same type, we can speak of the set whose members are the members of A but not of B. This new idea is called the **difference** of A and B, and is denoted by the following expression.

$$A \setminus B$$

The difference of two sets is of the same type as the sets themselves. The difference of two sets was used in the class manager's assistant on p. 18 to help in formalizing the statement 'The student is removed from the enrolled set'.

The predicates in Table 3.5 express important properties of the difference.

Table 3.5 Some properties of set difference.

Notation	Property
$A \setminus A = \varnothing$	
$A \setminus \varnothing = A$	$\varnothing$ is a unit for difference

In the library management system, the books that are on the shelves but are not reference books can be denoted by

$$on\_shelves \setminus reference$$

3.1.21 Using predicates as constraints

A declaration is intended to express some restriction on the values that variables can denote by saying what type those values must be. Thus, in the class manager's assistant, in describing the notion of a class on p. 14, we used declarations

$$enrolled, tested\colon \mathbb{P}\ Student \qquad (14)$$

to say that *enrolled* and *tested* denoted sets of students, rather than students, or sets of integers, etc. It often happens that declarations are not sufficient to fix the nature of the things declared, and declarations have to be supplemented by predicates to place additional limits on the permitted values. In the class manager's assistant on p. 14, the predicates

$$\#\, enrolled \leq size$$
$$tested \subseteq enrolled$$

were used in this way. Where predicates are used to place limits on the values that names can denote, we shall call them **constraints.**

3.1.22 Set comprehension

We now introduce a powerful means of defining a set by stating a property that distinguishes its members from other values of the same type.

$$\{x: \mathbb{N} \mid x \leq 5 \bullet x^2\}$$

denotes the same set as

$$\{0, 1, 4, 9, 16, 25\}$$

Suppose **D** denotes some declarations, **P** a predicate constraining the values and **E** an expression denoting a term; then an expression of the form

$$\{\mathbf{D} \mid \mathbf{P} \bullet \mathbf{E}\}$$

is called a **set comprehension** term, and it denotes a set of values consisting of all values of the term **E** for everything declared in **D** satisfying the constraint **P**. The vertical line separating the declaration from the constraint is called a **constraint bar**. It separates the declaration from the constraint, while the **heavy dot** separates the constraint from the term. The whole is enclosed in braces.

Sometimes the term and the preceding heavy dot are omitted. In such a case the term is taken to be the thing declared. So

$$\{x: \mathbb{N} \mid x < 5\}$$

denotes $0..4$. This causes no difficulties when a single name is declared. The meaning of such an expression when several names are declared will be explained in the next chapter on p. 88.

Sometimes the constraint and the preceding constraint bar are omitted, so

$$\{x: \mathbb{N} \bullet x^2\}$$

is the set of square natural numbers.

Reading a set comprehension term out loud causes a bit of difficulty. The first example in this section might be read

> The set formed from the natural numbers *x* such that *x* is less than or equal to five consisting of the squares of the *x*s.

A better way might be to ignore the constraint bar and heavy dot in reading, and proceed in the order term – declaration – constraint, giving

The set of squares of the natural numbers that are less than or equal to five.

Notice, however, that our search for brevity has introduced a hint of ambiguity, since the English expression might be interpreted as meaning

$$\{x: \mathbb{N} \mid x^2 \leq 5 \bullet x^2\}$$

3.2 Logical connectives

In this section we look at ways of building more complex predicates from simple ones. Predicates formalize the declarative sentences of natural language. The following sentences cannot be formalized using predicates.

'Is the sun shining?'

'Peace, be still.'

The first of these is a question, the second is a command.

The sentences of a natural language can be joined by conjunctions like 'and' and 'or' to make longer sentences, and we shall now formalize the grammatical notions with **logical connectives**. Predicates can be true or false, and the truth or falsity of a predicate is called its **truth value**. True predicates have the truth value **true**, and false predicates have the truth value **false**. In what follows we shall show how to build a **compound predicate** from simple predicates of the kind introduced earlier in this chapter, using the logical connectives. In addition, we show how the truth value of the compound predicate is related to the truth values of its constituents. It will be convenient to use bold capital letters **P**, **Q**, etc. to denote predicates when we are not concerned about their structure, but only their truth value.

3.2.1 Negation

Given a predicate **P** we can construct a new predicate $\neg$**P** called the **negation** of **P**. Negation corresponds to the informal idea of 'not', which is grammatically an adverb. Table 3.6, a **truth table**, shows that the negation of a true predicate is false, while the negation of a false predicate is true.

Table 3.6 Truth table for negation.

Value of **P**	Value of $\neg$**P**
true	false
false	true

Negation is a **truth function**, so that knowing the truth value of a predicate we are able, with the aid of the table, to decide the truth value of its negation.

Table 3.7 gives formal and informal examples of predicates and their negations.

Table 3.7 Examples of negation, formal and informal.

Today is Tuesday	Today is not Tuesday
$2 + 2 = 3$	$2 + 2 \neq 3$
$x \in A$	$x \notin A$
Men were deceivers ever	At least one man was not a deceiver on at least one occasion

The first three examples are straightforward. A proper analysis of the last example must wait until the exercises to Chapter 4.

3.2.2 Disjunction

The informal notion of 'or' used between sentences is made precise in the logical notion of **disjunction**. If **P** and **Q** are two predicates, then we can construct a new predicate

$$\mathbf{P} \vee \mathbf{Q}$$

called the disjunction of **P** and **Q**. The predicates **P** and **Q** are called the **disjuncts** of this expression. The notion is made precise by Table 3.8, which defines disjunction as a truth function of its arguments.

Table 3.8 Truth table for disjunction.

Value of **P**	Value of **Q**	Value of **P** ∨ **Q**
true	true	true
true	false	true
false	true	true
false	false	false

A disjunction is considered to be true when either or both of the disjuncts is true. The expression 'inclusive disjunction' is sometimes used to describe this. Disjunction is a commutative truth function, that is to say the value of

$$\mathbf{P} \vee \mathbf{Q}$$

is always the same as the value of

$$\mathbf{Q} \vee \mathbf{P}$$

Disjunction is an associative truth function, since for given truth values of **P**, **Q** and **R**, the expression

$$\mathbf{P} \vee (\mathbf{Q} \vee \mathbf{R})$$

has the same truth value as the expression

$$(\mathbf{P} \vee \mathbf{Q}) \vee \mathbf{R}$$

Consequently we shall allow either of these expressions to be written thus:

$$\mathbf{P} \vee \mathbf{Q} \vee \mathbf{R}$$

Parentheses are used in predicates in the same way as in terms to show how the various predicates and connectives are to be associated.

We can build truth tables for more elaborate logical expressions; for instance, for

$$(\neg \mathbf{P}) \vee \mathbf{Q}$$

we can build a truth table like Table 3.9.

Table 3.9 Truth table for an extended function.

Value of **P**	Value of **Q**	Value of $\neg$**P**	Value of $(\neg \mathbf{P}) \vee \mathbf{Q}$
true	true	false	true
true	false	false	false
false	true	true	true
false	false	true	true

First we put down columns for **P** and **Q** showing every pairing of true and false, then we derive the third column for $\neg$**P** from the first, and then we use the truth table for disjunction to complete the fourth column from the contents of the second and third.

Disjunction is closely related to set union, for if A and B are two sets of values of type T, then

$$A \cup B = \{t: T \mid t \in A \vee t \in B\}$$

Indeed, we should regard the above statement as defining the notion of the union of two sets.

3.2.3 Conjunction

The informal notion of 'and' used between sentences is made precise in the logical notion of **conjunction**. If **P** and **Q** are two predicates, then we can construct a new predicate

$$\mathbf{P} \wedge \mathbf{Q}$$

called the conjunction of **P** and **Q**. The predicates **P** and **Q** are called the **conjuncts** of this expression. The notion is made precise by Table 3.10, which defines conjunction as a truth function of its arguments.

Table 3.10 Truth table for conjunction.

Value of **P**	Value of **Q**	Value of **P** ∧ **Q**
true	true	true
true	false	false
false	true	false
false	false	false

There can be no surprises here. A conjunction is true only when both its conjuncts are true. Conjunction is a commutative truth function, and associative, so the expression

$$\mathbf{P} \wedge \mathbf{Q} \wedge \mathbf{R}$$

can mean either of the following:

$$\mathbf{P} \wedge (\mathbf{Q} \wedge \mathbf{R})$$

$$(\mathbf{P} \wedge \mathbf{Q}) \wedge \mathbf{R}$$

Conjunction is closely related to set intersection, for if A and B are two sets of values of type T, then

$$A \cap B = \{t: T \mid t \in A \wedge t \in B\}$$

Indeed, we should regard this predicate as defining set intersection.

Similarly the notion of set difference is captured by

$$A \setminus B = \{t: T \mid t \in A \wedge t \notin B\}$$

and this predicate should be regarded as defining the difference of two sets.

The analogy between the set operations union and intersection and the logical operations of disjunction and conjunction is very close. The rules about distribution of union over intersection, and of intersection over union, have their analogues in logic. Thus the predicates

$$\mathbf{P} \wedge (\mathbf{Q} \vee \mathbf{R})$$

and

$$(\mathbf{P} \wedge \mathbf{Q}) \vee (\mathbf{P} \wedge \mathbf{R})$$

have the same truth table, as do the predicates

$$\mathbf{P} \vee (\mathbf{Q} \wedge \mathbf{R})$$

and

$$(\mathbf{P} \vee \mathbf{Q}) \wedge (\mathbf{P} \vee \mathbf{R})$$

3.2.4 Implication

The informal notion of 'if...then...' used to connect sentences is made precise in the logical notion of **implication**. If **P** and **Q** are two predicates, then we can build an implication by writing

$$\mathbf{P} \Rightarrow \mathbf{Q}$$

The predicate **P** is called the **antecedent** and **Q** is called the **consequent** of the implication. The notion of implication is made precise by Table 3.11, which defines implication as a truth function of its arguments.

Table 3.11 Truth table for implication.

Value of **P**	Value of **Q**	Value of **P** ⇒ **Q**
true	true	true
true	false	false
false	true	true
false	false	true

An implication is true when its antecedent is false, or when its consequent is true. This definition of implication is somewhat surprising to those who have not met it before. 'If today is Tuesday, then Dr Shrewdly-Withit is lecturing on analytic topology' is certainly true if its antecedent and consequent are both true, and certainly false if its antecedent is true and its consequent is false. We should expect any predicate to imply itself, even when it is false, but it is less intuitively clear what is to be the truth value when the antecedent is false and the consequent is true. The solution presented in the above truth table has certain merits. In the first place, it distinguishes implication from equivalence, as described in the next section, and in the second place it allows us to regard implication as a kind of summary of logical possibilities. In a sense, saying that **P** implies **Q** is an abbreviation for saying that one has a good logical argument that will allow the deduction of **Q** from **P**, with whatever other truths are necessary to assist. From a false predicate it is possible to deduce consequences that are true or consequences that are false, so we agree that if the antecedent is false, the implication will be considered true whatever the truth value of the consequent.

Implication is not commutative; that is to say **P** ⇒ **Q** has no bearing on whether **Q** ⇒ **P**. Implication is not associative, as Table 3.12 shows.

Table 3.12 Truth table for non-associativity of implication.

P	**Q**	**R**	**P ⇒ Q**	**Q ⇒ R**	**P ⇒ (Q ⇒ R)**	**(P ⇒ Q) ⇒ R**
true	true	true	true	true	true	true
true	true	false	true	false	false	false
true	false	true	false	true	true	true
true	false	false	false	true	true	true
false	true	true	true	true	true	true
false	true	false	true	false	true	false
false	false	true	true	true	true	true
false	false	false	true	true	true	false

On comparing the last two columns we see that the truth values are not the same.

Implication is, however, transitive; that is to say if **P** ⇒ **Q** and **Q** ⇒ **R** then we can be sure that **P** ⇒ **R**.

If **P** ⇒ **Q**, we shall say that **P** is **stronger** than **Q**, or that **Q** is **weaker** than **P**. Among predicates, strength is a sort of resistance to being proved, so one predicate is stronger than another if it is more difficult to prove. A predicate that is always false is stronger than any other, since it is impossible to prove, and since a false predicate can imply any other. A predicate that is always true is weaker than any other, since it is no trouble to prove and since a true predicate is implied by any other. Figure 3.4 illustrates some aspects of the strength and weakness in predicates. In the diagram the stronger predicates are above and the weaker predicates below. The arrows represent implication, and so point in the direction of decreasing strength.

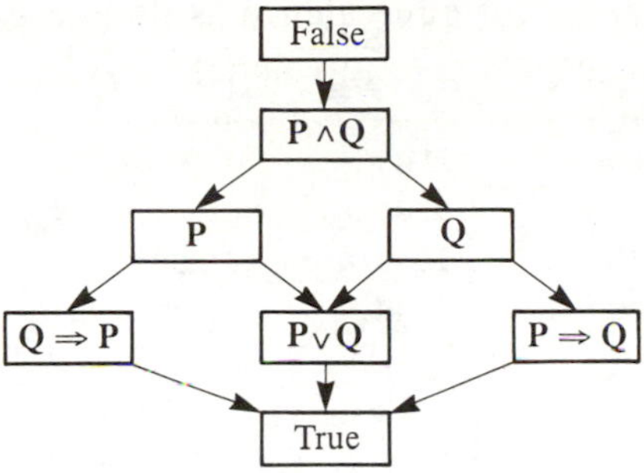

Figure 3.4 Strength and weakness in predicates.

Since implication is transitive, there should be more arrows in the diagram; each pair of boxes that are joined by a sequence of arrows should also be joined directly.

3.2.5 Equivalence

The informal notion of 'if and only if' used to connect two sentences is made precise in the logical notion of **equivalence**. Two predicates are equivalent if and only if they have the same truth value. If **P** and **Q** are two predicates, then we can construct a new predicate

$$\mathbf{P} \Leftrightarrow \mathbf{Q}$$

Table 3.13 defines equivalence as a truth function of its arguments.

Table 3.13 Truth table for equivalence.

Value of **P**	Value of **Q**	Value of **P** ⇔ **Q**
true	true	true
true	false	false
false	true	false
false	false	true

Equivalence is a commutative, associative, and transitive truth function that plays the same role for predicates as equality plays for terms.

We should note that $(\mathbf{P} \Rightarrow \mathbf{Q}) \wedge (\mathbf{Q} \Rightarrow \mathbf{P})$ has the same truth table as $\mathbf{P} \Leftrightarrow \mathbf{Q}$ (Table 3.14).

Table 3.14 Truth table for equivalence as double implication.

$\mathbf{P}$	$\mathbf{Q}$	$\mathbf{P \Rightarrow Q}$	$\mathbf{Q \Rightarrow P}$	$\mathbf{(P \Rightarrow Q) \wedge (Q \Rightarrow P)}$
true	true	true	true	true
true	false	false	true	false
false	true	true	false	false
false	false	true	true	true

3.2.6 Tautologies

Consider the truth table (Table 3.15) of the following predicate:

$$\mathbf{P \Rightarrow (Q \Rightarrow P)}$$

Table 3.15 Truth table of a tautology.

$\mathbf{P}$	$\mathbf{Q}$	$\mathbf{Q \Rightarrow P}$	$\mathbf{P \Rightarrow (Q \Rightarrow P)}$
true	true	true	true
true	false	true	true
false	true	false	true
false	false	true	true

Predicates of the form $\mathbf{P \Rightarrow (Q \Rightarrow P)}$ are true no matter what the truth values of the predicates **P** and **Q**, and such a predicate is called a **tautology**. There are many other tautologies, and several of them appear in the exercises to this chapter. In doing proofs we can say that predicates that have the form of a tautology are true without enquiring into the truth or falsehood of their constituents.

3.3 Quantifiers

Suppose that x and y are integers. To decide whether the predicate

$$x = y^2$$

is true or false we need to know the values of x and y. For instance it would be true if x were *9* and y were *−3*, but false if x were *0* and y were *1*. The variables x and y are called the **free** variables of this predicate. Other ways of saying the same thing are that x and y are free in the predicate, or that the predicate is free for x and y.

3.3.1 Existential quantifier

We consider now how we might adapt the predicate

$$x = y^2$$

to say that x is a square integer. Informally the predicate says that x is the square of y, so we need to prefix the predicate with some expression like 'for some integer y', or 'there is an integer y such that'. In formal notation we write

$$\exists y: \mathbb{Z} \bullet x = y^2$$

The sign '∃' is called the **existential quantifier**, and the new predicate formed from $x = y^2$ by applying the quantifier is called an **existential quantification**. In the notation we shall use, the existential quantifier is always followed by a declaration, and there will always be a heavy dot before the predicate that is being quantified. There might also be (though not in this instance) a constraint on the declaration, so the constraint bar might also appear. The general form is

$$\exists \mathbf{D} \mid \mathbf{P} \bullet \mathbf{Q}$$

where **D** represents declarations, **P** represents a predicate acting as the constraint and **Q** represents the predicate being quantified.

Whether the existential quantification

$$\exists y: \mathbb{Z} \bullet x = y^2$$

is true depends only on the choice of a value for x, so x is still free in the existential quantification. If we choose *4*, it is true; if we choose *73*, or -14, it is false. The variable y is called a **bound** variable of the existential quantification. The effect of quantification is to bind the variables in the declaration. The name y could in fact be replaced by almost any name, and the meaning of the existential quantification would be unchanged:

$$\exists p: \mathbb{Z} \bullet x = p^2$$

The exception is of course x. If we chose x to be the name of the bound variable, we should change the meaning of the existential quantification. In the expression

$$\exists x: \mathbb{Z} \bullet x = x^2$$

x is no longer free, and the value of the expression is just true. This kind of disruption that arises when we choose a bad name for a bound variable is called **variable capture**. The variable x, which we intended to remain free, has been captured by the existential quantifier.

We now give an example of an existential quantification in which the declaration is modified by a constraint, and there are no free variables.

$$\exists n\colon \mathbb{N} \mid n \leq 10 \bullet n^2 = 64$$

might be read informally thus:

> 'For some natural number *n*, less than or equal to ten, *n* squared is sixty-four.'

or thus

> 'There is a natural number less than or equal to ten whose square is sixty-four.'

This existential quantification is true, and to prove it we need only exhibit a natural number that satisfies the constraint and makes the predicate after the heavy dot true. One such, indeed the only one, is eight.

An existential quantification with a constraint can be recast in various ways.

$$\exists \mathbf{D} \mid \mathbf{P} \bullet \mathbf{Q}$$

is equivalent to

$$\exists \mathbf{D} \bullet (\mathbf{P} \wedge \mathbf{Q})$$

If we remember that declarations might themselves include implicit predicates, we see that the following statements are equivalent.

$$\exists n\colon \mathbb{N} \mid n \leq 10 \bullet n^2 = 64$$

$$\exists n\colon \mathbb{N} \bullet (n \leq 10 \wedge n^2 = 64)$$

$$\exists n\colon \mathbb{Z} \mid n \geq 0 \bullet (n \leq 10 \wedge n^2 = 64)$$

$$\exists n\colon \mathbb{Z} \bullet (n \geq 0 \wedge n \leq 10 \wedge n^2 = 64)$$

$$\exists n\colon \mathbb{Z} \mid n \leq 10 \bullet (n \geq 0 \wedge n^2 = 64)$$

$$\exists n\colon \mathbb{Z} \mid (n \leq 10 \wedge n \geq 0) \bullet n^2 = 64$$

$$\exists n\colon \mathbb{Z} \mid n^2 = 64 \bullet (n \leq 10 \wedge n \geq 0)$$

The distinction between the predicate and constraint is a matter of presentation rather than of logic.

Existential quantification can be regarded as generalized disjunction. When we write

$$\exists n: \mathbb{N} \mid n \leq 10 \bullet n^2 = 64$$

we can regard this as an abbreviation for

$$0^2 = 64 \vee 1^2 = 64 \vee 2^2 = 64 \vee \ldots \vee 10^2 = 64$$

and we can extend this notion even to infinite sets.

If there are several existential quantifiers at the beginning of a predicate, they can often be moved around without any effect on the truth value. Thus the two predicates

$$\exists \mathbf{D}_1 \bullet (\exists \mathbf{D}_2 \bullet \mathbf{P})$$

$$\exists \mathbf{D}_2 \bullet (\exists \mathbf{D}_1 \bullet \mathbf{P})$$

are equivalent unless either quantifier can capture variables that are free in the other. Consider for instance the following predicate.

$$\exists x: \mathbb{P}\ \mathbb{Z} \bullet (\ \exists t: x \bullet t = y\ )$$

This predicate asserts that there is a set of integers (represented by the bound variable x) that has a member (represented by the bound variable t) that is equal to y, which is the only free variable in the predicate, and which must be declared elsewhere with type $\mathbb{Z}$. If we exchange the quantifiers, the following predicate is the result.

$$\exists t: x \bullet (\ \exists x: \mathbb{P}\ \mathbb{Z} \bullet t = y\ )$$

In its first occurrence, x is free, and there must be some declaration of x that gives it a type that is a set, so that t can be a member of it. In its second occurrence, x is bound by the quantifier, though the predicate following the quantifier does not contain x as a free variable. In this predicate y is again free.

The exchange of quantifiers produces strange results in cases like these, but the rule given above forbids its application, since the quantifier $\exists t: x$ contains a free variable x that is captured by the quantifier $\exists x: \mathbb{P}\ \mathbb{Z}$.

3.3.2 Universal quantifier

We now present a related notation for formalizing the notion that everything of a certain kind has a certain property. For instance from the predicate $y^2 > x$ we could construct a new predicate

$$\forall y: \mathbb{Z} \bullet y^2 > x$$

to formalize the statement 'every integer has a square that is greater than x'.

The sign '∀' is called the **universal quantifier**, and the new predicate formed from $y^2 > x$ by applying the quantifier is called a **universal quantification**. In the notation we shall use, the universal quantifier is always followed by a declaration, and there will always be a heavy dot before the predicate that is being quantified. There might also be (though not in this instance) a constraint on the declaration, so the constraint bar might also appear thus:

$$\forall \mathbf{D} \mid \mathbf{P} \bullet \mathbf{Q}$$

In this general form, **D** represents declarations, **P** represents a predicate acting as the constraint and **Q** represents the predicate being quantified.

Whether the above universal quantification is true depends only on the choice of a value for x, so x is still free in the universal quantification. If we choose 5, it is false; if we choose -8, it is true. The variable x is free, but y has become bound by the quantifier.

We now give an example of a universal quantification in which the declaration is modified by a constraint, and there are no free variables.

$$\forall n: \mathbb{N} \mid n \leq 10 \bullet n^2 \leq 100$$

might be read informally thus:

> 'For every natural number n, less than or equal to ten, n squared is less than or equal to a hundred,'

or thus

> 'Every natural number less than or equal to ten has a square less than or equal to one hundred.'

This universal quantification is true, and to prove it we might consider a general natural number that satisfies the constraint and show that its square has the desired property.

A universal quantification with a constraint can be recast in various ways.

$$\forall \mathbf{D} \mid \mathbf{P} \bullet \mathbf{Q}$$

is equivalent to

$$\forall \mathbf{D} \bullet (\mathbf{P} \Rightarrow \mathbf{Q})$$

If we remember that declarations might themselves include implicit predicates, we see that the following statements are equivalent.

$\forall n: \mathbb{N} \mid n \leq 10 \bullet n^2 \leq 100$

$\forall n: \mathbb{N} \bullet (n \leq 10 \Rightarrow n^2 \leq 100)$

$\forall n: \mathbb{Z} \mid n \geq 0 \bullet (n \leq 10 \Rightarrow n^2 \leq 100)$

$\forall n: \mathbb{Z} \bullet ((n \geq 0 \land n \leq 10) \Rightarrow n^2 \leq 100)$

$\forall n: \mathbb{Z} \mid n \leq 10 \bullet (n \geq 0 \Rightarrow n^2 \leq 100)$

The distinction between the predicate and constraint is a matter of presentation rather than of logic.

Universal quantification can be regarded as generalized conjunction. When we write

$\forall n: \mathbb{N} \mid n \leq 10 \bullet n^2 \leq 100$

we can regard this as an abbreviation for

$0^2 \leq 100 \land 1^2 \leq 100 \land 2^2 \leq 100 \land \ldots \land 10^2 \leq 100$

and we can extend this notion even to infinite sets.

If there are several universal quantifiers at the beginning of a predicate, they can sometimes be moved around without any effect on the truth value. Thus the two predicates

$\forall \mathbf{D}_1 \bullet (\forall \mathbf{D}_2 \bullet \mathbf{P})$

and

$\forall \mathbf{D}_2 \bullet (\forall \mathbf{D}_1 \bullet \mathbf{P})$

are equivalent unless either quantifier can capture variables that are free in the other.

The universal quantifier can be used with implication to give a precise meaning to the subset relation between sets. If A and B are two sets of values of type T, then

$A \subseteq B \Leftrightarrow \forall t: T \bullet (t \in A \Rightarrow t \in B)$

and we should regard this as defining the subset relation.

Similarly the universal quantifier can be used with equivalence to give a precise meaning to the equality relation between sets, for if A and B are two sets of values of type T, then

$A = B \Leftrightarrow \forall t: T \bullet (t \in A \Leftrightarrow t \in B)$

and we should regard this as defining equality of sets.

3.3.3 Unique existential quantifier

The universal quantifier allows us to introduce a notation to formalize the informal notion of there being only one thing of a certain kind. For instance to say that there is exactly one integer greater than zero whose square is one hundred, we might write

$$\exists_1 x: \mathbb{Z} \bullet x > 0 \land x^2 = 100$$

The sign '$\exists_1$' is called the **unique existential quantifier**, and this whole predicate is called a **unique existential quantification**. The heavy dot and constraint bar might also appear. The general form is

$$\exists_1 \mathbf{D} \mid \mathbf{P} \bullet \mathbf{Q}$$

where **D** represents declarations, **P** represents a predicate acting as the constraint and **Q** represents the predicate being quantified.

The property of the unique existential quantifier is explained by the following equivalence:

$$\begin{aligned} &(\exists_1 x: T \bullet \mathbf{P}(x)) \\ &\Leftrightarrow ((\exists x: T \bullet \mathbf{P}(x)) \\ &\quad \land (\forall x_1, x_2: T \bullet ((\mathbf{P}(x_1) \land \mathbf{P}(x_2)) \Rightarrow x_1 = x_2))) \end{aligned}$$

3.3.4 Mixing quantifiers

Where a predicate begins with two quantifiers, one existential and one universal, we must take care about changing their order, as in general this is not possible. The following predicate

$$\forall x: \mathbb{Z} \bullet (\exists y: \mathbb{Z} \bullet y > x)$$

says that given any integer we can always find one bigger than it, and it is true. On the other hand

$$\exists y: \mathbb{Z} \bullet (\forall x: \mathbb{Z} \bullet y > x)$$

says that we can find an integer that is bigger than all the integers, and it is false. In general the best we can say in such circumstances is as follows:

$$(\exists \mathbf{D}_1 \bullet (\forall \mathbf{D}_2 \bullet \mathbf{P})) \Rightarrow (\forall \mathbf{D}_2 \bullet (\exists \mathbf{D}_1 \bullet \mathbf{P}))$$

unless either quantifier can capture variables that are free in the other.

3.3.5 Truth functions and quantifiers

There are some simple rules about negating quantified statements that are presented now.

The negation of 'Everything of a certain kind has a certain property' is 'At least one thing of that kind does not have that property', and this is illustrated in Table 3.16.

Table 3.16 Negating a universal quantification.

$\forall n \colon \mathbb{N} \mid n > 5 \bullet n^2 > 100$	$\exists n \colon \mathbb{N} \mid n > 5 \bullet n^2 \leq 100$
Every natural number greater than 5 has a square that is greater than 100.	Some natural number greater than five has a square that is not greater than 100.

More generally

$$(\neg \forall \mathbf{D} \mid \mathbf{P} \bullet \mathbf{Q}) \Leftrightarrow (\exists \mathbf{D} \mid \mathbf{P} \bullet (\neg \mathbf{Q}))$$

Similarly the negation of 'At least one thing of a certain kind has a certain property' is 'Everything of that kind does not have that property', and this is illustrated in Table 3.17.

Table 3.17 Negating an existential quantification.

$\exists n \colon \mathbb{N} \mid n > 5 \bullet n^2 = 100$	$\forall n \colon \mathbb{N} \mid n > 5 \bullet n^2 \neq 100$
There is a natural number greater than 5 whose square is 100.	Every natural number greater than 5 has a square that is not 100.

More generally,

$$(\neg \exists \mathbf{D} \mid \mathbf{P} \bullet \mathbf{Q}) \Leftrightarrow (\forall \mathbf{D} \mid \mathbf{P} \bullet (\neg \mathbf{Q}))$$

The existential quantifier distributes over disjunction, that is to say

$$(\exists \mathbf{D} \mid \mathbf{P} \bullet (\mathbf{Q} \vee \mathbf{R})) \Leftrightarrow ((\exists \mathbf{D} \mid \mathbf{P} \bullet \mathbf{Q}) \vee (\exists \mathbf{D} \mid \mathbf{P} \bullet \mathbf{R}))$$

Unfortunately the same is not true for conjunction, for instance

$$(\exists x \colon \mathbb{N} \bullet x = 3) \wedge (\exists x \colon \mathbb{N} \bullet x = 4)$$

is true, while

$$\exists x \colon \mathbb{N} \bullet (x = 3 \wedge x = 4)$$

is not. The best we can do here is to say

$$(\exists \mathbf{D} \mid \mathbf{P} \bullet (\mathbf{Q} \land \mathbf{R})) \Rightarrow ((\exists \mathbf{D} \mid \mathbf{P} \bullet \mathbf{Q}) \land (\exists \mathbf{D} \mid \mathbf{P} \bullet \mathbf{R}))$$

but this is not much use if we want to prove the antecedent.

The rules for the universal quantifier with disjunction and conjunction are similar. For conjunction we have

$$(\forall \mathbf{D} \mid \mathbf{P} \bullet (\mathbf{Q} \land \mathbf{R})) \Leftrightarrow ((\forall \mathbf{D} \mid \mathbf{P} \bullet \mathbf{Q}) \land (\forall \mathbf{D} \mid \mathbf{P} \bullet \mathbf{R}))$$

while for disjunction we have

$$((\forall \mathbf{D} \mid \mathbf{P} \bullet \mathbf{Q}) \lor (\forall \mathbf{D} \mid \mathbf{P} \bullet \mathbf{R})) \Rightarrow (\forall \mathbf{D} \mid \mathbf{P} \bullet (\mathbf{Q} \lor \mathbf{R}))$$

3.3.6 Definite descriptions

The notion of 'the thing of a certain kind that has a certain property' is closely related to the notions formalized by quantifiers, as the form of the informal expression shows. However, the quoted phrase is not a sentence like a quantified predicate, but a noun phrase, so it will be formalized not by a predicate but by a term. We first write the notation to formalize a simple example, 'the integer greater than zero whose square is one hundred'.

$$\mu x : \mathbb{Z} \mid (x > 0 \land x^2 = 100)$$

This notation is called a **definite description**. The sign 'μ' (mu) is the definite description symbol. Note that the variable x is bound in this expression.

In the following general form of a definite description, **D** denotes declarations, **P** a predicate constraining the values and **E** is an expression denoting a term. The constraint bar and heavy dot perform their usual roles as separators.

$$\mu \mathbf{D} \mid \mathbf{P} \bullet \mathbf{E}$$

denotes the unique value **E** obtained from the variables of **D** when they are constrained by **P**. Either the constraint **P** (and the constraint bar) or the expression **E** (and the heavy dot) may be omitted. When **E** is omitted, the expression denotes whatever is declared in **D**, as in the examples above. This causes no difficulties when the declaration declares a single name. The meaning of such an expression when the declaration declares several names will be explained in the next chapter.

The definite description must denote a unique value, as the following implication explains.

$$((\exists x: T \mid \mathbf{P} \bullet x = y) \wedge (\forall x: T \mid \mathbf{P} \bullet x = y))$$
$$\Rightarrow y = (\mu x: T \mid \mathbf{P} \bullet x)$$

Thus

$$\mu x: \mathbb{Z} \mid x^2 = 100$$

does not denote, since there are two possible denotations, namely *10* and *−10*. The above definite description is an instance of an **undefined term**, and we shall say more about undefined terms later. An informal instance of such a definite description is to be found in the following sentence:

'The present king of France is bald.'

This contains a name 'the present king of France' that, at the time of writing, has no denotation. This name has however a perfectly clear sense, and it is only by understanding the sense that we can be sure that it has no denotation.

3.4 Theorems and proofs

Predicates are used in specifications to make statements about the system being specified. Many of these statements arise from the informal requirements, while others are observations of properties of the system that stem from the requirements, but were not explicit in them. It is often desirable to document these properties and prove that they are a consequence of the requirements. In later chapters we shall state theorems that express the notion that designs are correct refinements of specifications, and we shall look at examples of proofs of such theorems. This section introduces the notation for stating theorems, and discusses some common techniques for presenting proofs.

3.4.1 A notation for theorems

We begin with a simple example of a **theorem**.

$$[x: \mathbb{N} \mid x > 5] \vdash x^2 > 25$$

This theorem says that if x is a natural number greater than 5, we can conclude that its square is greater than 25. The sign '$\vdash$' is called **turnstile**, and it separates the **hypothesis** on the left from the **conclusion** on the right. The hypothesis – declarations and predicates – is enclosed in square brackets as shown. (In a later chapter we shall see the same notation applied to building schemas.) The conclusion is a predicate.

The same theorem could have been expressed as follows:

$$[x: \mathbb{N}] \vdash x > 5 \Rightarrow x^2 > 25$$

and a good way of proving an implication is to assume the antecedent and derive the consequent from it in logical steps. This principle is called the **deduction theorem.**

If the conclusion of a theorem contains free variables, these must be declared in the hypothesis. If the conclusion contains no free variables, the hypothesis is unnecessary, as follows.

$$\vdash \forall x: \mathbb{N} \mid x > 5 \bullet x^2 > 25$$

3.4.2 Some examples of proof

Suppose the sets A and B are sets of values of type X.

$$[A, B: \mathbb{P}\, X \mid A \subseteq B \wedge B \subseteq A] \vdash A = B$$

This theorem says that if we assume that every member of A is a member of B, and every member of B is a member of A, then we must inescapably conclude that A and B are the same set. The proof could be documented as follows:

(1)	$\forall x: X \bullet (x \in A \Rightarrow x \in B)$	Since $A \subseteq B$ is in the hypothesis
(2)	$\forall x: X \bullet (x \in B \Rightarrow x \in A)$	Since $B \subseteq A$ is in the hypothesis
(3)	$\forall x: X \bullet ((x \in A \Rightarrow x \in B) \wedge (x \in B \Rightarrow x \in A))$	From (1) and (2) by the conjunction rule for the universal quantifier
(4)	$\forall x: X \bullet (x \in A \Leftrightarrow x \in B)$	From (3) by truth tables for $\Leftrightarrow$ and $\Rightarrow$
(5)	$A = B$	From (4) by definition of set equality

We prove the next theorem

$$[A, B: \mathbb{P}\, X \mid A \subseteq B \wedge A \neq B] \vdash \exists x: X \bullet (x \in B \wedge x \notin A)$$

by a method of great antiquity called ***reductio ad absurdum***. This theorem says that if every member of A is a member of B, but A and B are not the same set, then there is at least one member of B that is not in A. The first step is to assume that the conclusion is false, and then to deduce something that contradicts the hypothesis, as follows:

(1)	$\forall x: X \bullet (x \notin B \vee x \in A)$	By negating the conclusion, using the negation rule for the existential quantifier
(2)	$\forall x: X \bullet (x \in B \Rightarrow x \in A)$	From (1) by truth tables for $\vee$ and $\Rightarrow$
(3)	$B \subseteq A$	From (2) by the definition of the subset relation
(4)	$A \subseteq B$	From the hypothesis
(5)	$A = B$	From (3) and (4) by the previous theorem
(6)	$A \neq B$	From the hypothesis, contradicting (5)

Another method of proof that we shall exploit later is proof by **mathematical induction**, using the following example. If A is a finite set, that is for some n: $\mathbb{N}$ we have $\#A=n$, then A has 2^n subsets.

$$[A: \mathbb{P}\ X] \vdash \# A = n \Rightarrow \# (\mathbb{P}\ A) = 2^n$$

The proof is organized as follows:

- First we prove that the theorem is true when $n = 0$. This case is called the **basis** of the induction.
- Next we suppose the theorem true for some value k. This assumption is called the **induction hypothesis**. From this we prove that it must be true for the next value $k+1$. This case is called the **induction step**.
- We conclude that the theorem must be true for all values of n.

The basis is $\# A = 0$, that is that A is an empty set. But A has exactly one subset, namely the empty set, so $\#\mathbb{P}A = 1$, and this is 2^0.

The induction step assumes that the theorem is true for a certain value k. Suppose B is a set of size $k+1$, then there must be a set A of size k, and a value x not a member of A such that

$$B = A \cup \{x\}$$

We now list the subsets of B. First we note that every subset of A must be a subset of B:

$$\varnothing, \ldots, A$$

We know that there are 2^k of these by the induction hypothesis. The remaining subsets of B must all contain x, and they are the sets got by adding x to each of the sets in the preceding list:

$$\{x\}, \ldots, B$$

There are 2^k of these as well. Hence

$$\# B = 2^k + 2^k = 2^{k+1}$$

as we were required to prove.

3.4.3 Deduction as a formal process

The proofs given so far have been presented in an intuitive fashion. We have relied in part on the reader's knowledge of the subject matter (set theory and arithmetic) and on informal procedures for deducing one statement from others. This informal approach to deduction can be made more precise as follows.

A proof is a sequence of theorems that establish that the conclusion of the theorem being proved can be deduced from its hypothesis. Each theorem in a proof must either be a statement of some fundamental property of its subject matter (sets, relations, numbers), or must follow from previous theorems in the sequence by some **deduction rule**. The basic deduction rule, which has been used many times in the above examples, is called ***modus ponens***. We present it as follows:

$$\frac{\mathbf{H} \vdash \mathbf{P} \qquad \mathbf{H} \vdash \mathbf{P} \Rightarrow \mathbf{Q}}{\mathbf{H} \vdash \mathbf{Q}}$$

H is a hypothesis, and **P** and **Q** are predicates. Each theorem above the line is called a **premiss** of the rule, and the theorem below the line is called the **conclusion** of the rule. A rule may have several premisses, but only one conclusion. Provided that the premisses already appear in the proof, the conclusion may be added to it and used in its turn as a premiss.

The deduction theorem introduced above can be expressed as a rule in this form, but we need to see the structure of the hypothesis in order to express it:

$$\frac{[\mathbf{D} \mid \mathbf{P}] \vdash \mathbf{Q}}{[\mathbf{D}] \vdash \mathbf{P} \Rightarrow \mathbf{Q}}$$

The converse of the deduction theorem is also a deduction rule:

$$\frac{[\mathbf{D}] \vdash \mathbf{P} \Rightarrow \mathbf{Q}}{[\mathbf{D} \mid \mathbf{P}] \vdash \mathbf{Q}}$$

The rule of *reductio ad absurdum* is expressed as follows:

$$\frac{[\mathbf{D} \mid \mathbf{P}] \vdash (\neg \mathbf{Q}) \Rightarrow (\neg \mathbf{P})}{[\mathbf{D} \mid \mathbf{P}] \vdash \mathbf{Q}}$$

The rule of mathematical induction is expressed as follows:

$$\frac{\mathbf{H} \vdash \mathbf{P}(\mathit{0}) \quad \mathbf{H} \vdash (\ \forall k \colon \mathbb{N} \bullet (\ \mathbf{P}(k) \Rightarrow \mathbf{P}(k+\mathit{1})\ )\ )}{\mathbf{H} \vdash \forall n \colon \mathbb{N} \bullet \mathbf{P}(n)}$$

Other rules can be derived from *modus ponens* with the aid of tautologies. For instance

$$\mathbf{P} \Rightarrow (\ \mathbf{P} \vee \mathbf{Q}\ )$$

is a tautology, so we can derive a rule called **or-introduction**.

$$\frac{\mathbf{H} \vdash \mathbf{P}}{\mathbf{H} \vdash \mathbf{P} \vee \mathbf{Q}}$$

provided that all the free variables of **Q** are declared in **H**.

This rule short-circuits the following deductive steps:

(1)	$\mathbf{H} \vdash \mathbf{P}$	Premiss
(2)	$\mathbf{H} \vdash \mathbf{P} \Rightarrow (\mathbf{P} \vee \mathbf{Q})$	Tautology
(3)	$\mathbf{H} \vdash \mathbf{P} \vee \mathbf{Q}$	From (1) and (2) by *modus ponens*

The following rule (**and-elimination**)

$$\frac{\mathbf{H} \vdash \mathbf{P} \wedge \mathbf{Q}}{\mathbf{H} \vdash \mathbf{P}}$$

relies on the tautology

$$(\mathbf{P} \wedge \mathbf{Q}) \Rightarrow \mathbf{P}$$

If two predicates have the same truth table, and either is a premiss, the other can be deduced as a conclusion. Thus the following two predicates have the same truth table,

$$\mathbf{P} \wedge (\mathbf{Q} \vee \mathbf{R})$$

$$(\mathbf{P} \wedge \mathbf{Q}) \vee (\mathbf{P} \wedge \mathbf{R})$$

so we can derive two deduction rules, of which the first is as follows:

$$\frac{\mathbf{H} \vdash \mathbf{P} \wedge (\mathbf{Q} \vee \mathbf{R})}{\mathbf{H} \vdash (\mathbf{P} \wedge \mathbf{Q}) \vee (\mathbf{P} \wedge \mathbf{R})}$$

The pairs of equivalent predicates in Table B.2 can be the basis of deduction rules.

The rule of **proof by cases** is often useful.

$$\frac{\mathbf{H} \vdash \mathbf{P}_1 \vee \ldots \vee \mathbf{P}_n \quad \mathbf{H} \vdash \mathbf{P}_1 \Rightarrow \mathbf{Q} \quad \ldots \quad \mathbf{H} \vdash \mathbf{P}_n \Rightarrow \mathbf{Q}}{\mathbf{H} \vdash \mathbf{Q}}$$

The predicates $\mathbf{P}_1 \ldots \mathbf{P}_n$ distinguish the cases to be proved.

Deduction rules for quantifiers were hinted at when quantifiers were introduced earlier in this chapter. For the universal quantifier the following deduction rule, called **universal quantifier introduction**, applies provided that x is not free in the constraint **P**.

$$\frac{[\mathbf{D};\ x\colon \mathbf{T} \mid \mathbf{P}] \vdash \mathbf{Q}}{[\mathbf{D} \mid \mathbf{P}] \vdash \forall x\colon \mathbf{T} \bullet \mathbf{Q}}$$

The rule for **universal quantifier elimination** is of the following form:

$$\frac{[\mathbf{D} \mid \mathbf{P}] \vdash \forall x\colon \mathbf{T} \bullet \mathbf{Q}}{[\mathbf{D};\ x\colon \mathbf{T} \mid \mathbf{P}] \vdash \mathbf{Q}}$$

provided that x is not declared in **D**, and that it is not free in **P**.

For the existential quantifier, if we know that **P** is true for some specific value of its free variable x of type **T**, then we can use the **existential quantifier introduction** rule.

$$\frac{\mathbf{H} \vdash \mathbf{P}(\mathbf{E})}{\mathbf{H} \vdash \exists x\colon \mathbf{T} \bullet \mathbf{P}(x)}$$

Proving theorems whose conclusion is an existential quantification often involves constructing something that satisfies the predicate being quantified. Thus

$$\vdash \exists x\colon \mathbb{Z} \bullet (x > 0 \wedge x^2 = 9)$$

is proved by offering the number *3* and showing that

$$3 > 0 \land 3^2 = 9$$

Sometimes an existential quantification includes an explicit value for the bound variable, and the proof reduces to showing that the explicit value has the other properties in the predicate. Thus to prove

$$\vdash \exists x\colon \mathbb{Z} \bullet (\, x = 3 \land x^2 = 9)$$

it is necessary only to observe that

$$\vdash 3^2 = 9$$

In fact

$$\vdash (\, \exists x\colon \mathbb{Z} \bullet (\, x = 3 \land x^2 = 9)\,) \Leftrightarrow 3^2 = 9$$

This simplification of an existential quantification is called the **one-point rule**. In general it can be stated as the following equivalence:

$$(\exists x\colon \mathbf{T} \bullet (x = \mathbf{E} \land \mathbf{P}(x))) \Leftrightarrow (\mathbf{P}(\mathbf{E}) \land \mathbf{E} \in \mathbf{T})$$

where x is a variable, **T** is a set expression, **E** is an expression of appropriate type, **P**(x) is a predicate in which x is not bound (it will usually be free), and **P**(**E**) is the result of replacing x by **E** in each of its free occurrences in **P**(x).

A more general rule is the deduction rule for **existential quantifier elimination**:

$$\frac{\mathbf{H} \vdash \exists \mathbf{D} \bullet \mathbf{P} \qquad \mathbf{H} \vdash \forall \mathbf{D} \bullet (\mathbf{P} \Rightarrow \mathbf{Q})}{\mathbf{H} \vdash \mathbf{Q}}$$

provided that the free variables of **Q** are not declared in **D**.

3.4.4 Using axioms and tautologies

The introduction of fundamental properties of the subject matter into a proof is done by means of **axioms**. An axiom is a deduction rule that has no premisses. An axiom to introduce the notion of set comprehension might be as follows:

$$\frac{}{\mathbf{H} \vdash x \in \{\mathbf{D} \mid \mathbf{P} \bullet \mathbf{E}\} \Leftrightarrow (\, \exists \mathbf{D} \mid \mathbf{P} \bullet x = \mathbf{E}\,)}$$

provided that **H** declares x to be of the same type as **E**.

All other basic ideas of set theory and arithmetic can be introduced into proofs by axioms.

There is one other deduction rule that has no premisses the we shall use to help in constructing proofs. If the predicate **P** is a tautology, then **H** $\vdash$ **P** is a theorem, provided that all the free variables of **P** are declared in **H**. This rule is called **tautology introduction**.

Exercises

(3.1) What is the type of the given set *Student* in the class manager's assistant?

(3.2) Given the declarations

$$x, y, z: \mathbb{Z}; a: Author; b: Book \qquad (72, 29)$$

$$on\_shelves: \mathbb{P}\ Book; novelists: \mathbb{P}\ Author \qquad (29, 72)$$

say what the type is of each of the following terms.

(a) x

(b) $x + y$

(c) $\{x, y\}$

(d) $\{\{x\}, \{y\}\}$

(e) $\{on\_shelves\}$

(f) $on\_shelves \cup \{b\}$

(3.3) Given the following declarations

$$x, y, z: \mathbb{Z}; a: Author; b: Book \qquad (72, 29)$$

$$on\_shelves: \mathbb{P}\ Book; novelists: \mathbb{P}\ Author \qquad (29, 72)$$

say whether the following notations are well-formed, and for each that is well-formed, say whether it is a term or a predicate.

(a) $x > y$

(b) $x \in on\_shelves$

(c) $a \in on\_shelves$

(d) $a \in novelists$

(e) $on\_shelves \subseteq novelists$

(f) $on\_shelves \subseteq Book$

(g) $\{a\}$

(h) $\{a, b\}$

(i) $\{on\_shelves\}$

(j) $\{on\_shelves, novelists\}$

(3.4) In what circumstances will $A \setminus B = B \setminus A$?

(3.5) Construct truth tables for the following predicates:

(a) $\neg(\neg \mathbf{P})$

(b) $(\neg \mathbf{P}) \vee (\neg \mathbf{Q})$

(c) $\mathbf{P} \wedge (\neg \mathbf{P})$

(d) $\mathbf{P} \wedge (\neg \mathbf{Q})$

(e) $((\mathbf{P} \Rightarrow \mathbf{Q}) \wedge (\mathbf{Q} \Rightarrow \mathbf{R}))$

(3.6) Show that the following predicates are tautologies:

(a) $\mathbf{P} \vee (\neg \mathbf{P})$

(b) $\mathbf{P} \Rightarrow (\mathbf{P} \vee \mathbf{Q})$

(c) $(\mathbf{P} \wedge \mathbf{Q}) \Rightarrow \mathbf{P}$

(d) $\mathbf{P} \Rightarrow (\mathbf{Q} \Rightarrow (\mathbf{P} \wedge \mathbf{Q}))$

(e) $(\mathbf{P} \wedge (\mathbf{P} \Rightarrow \mathbf{Q})) \Rightarrow \mathbf{Q}$

(f) $((\neg \mathbf{P}) \wedge (\mathbf{P} \vee \mathbf{Q})) \Rightarrow \mathbf{Q}$

(g) $((\mathbf{P} \Rightarrow \mathbf{Q}) \wedge (\mathbf{Q} \Rightarrow \mathbf{R})) \Rightarrow (\mathbf{P} \Rightarrow \mathbf{R})$

(h) $((\neg \mathbf{P}) \vee \mathbf{Q}) \Leftrightarrow (\mathbf{P} \Rightarrow \mathbf{Q})$

(3.7) Show that $\neg(\mathbf{P} \wedge \mathbf{Q})$ has the same truth table as $(\neg \mathbf{P}) \vee (\neg \mathbf{Q})$. (This is one of De Morgan's laws.)

(3.8) Show that $\neg(\mathbf{P} \vee \mathbf{Q})$ has the same truth table as $(\neg \mathbf{P}) \wedge (\neg \mathbf{Q})$. (This is De Morgan's other law.)

(3.9) Show that $\mathbf{P} \Rightarrow \mathbf{Q}$ and $(\neg \mathbf{Q}) \Rightarrow (\neg \mathbf{P})$ have the same truth table. (This is the law of **contraposition**.)

(3.10) Show that $\mathbf{P} \Rightarrow (\mathbf{Q} \Rightarrow \mathbf{R})$ and $(\mathbf{P} \Rightarrow \mathbf{Q}) \Rightarrow (\mathbf{P} \Rightarrow \mathbf{R})$ have the same truth table.

(3.11) Construct a truth table for the following logical expression,

$$\mathbf{P} \diamondsuit \mathbf{Q}$$

which is true only when at least one of the predicates **P** and **Q** is false.

Use truth tables to prove the following equivalences.

(a) $\neg\ \mathbf{P} \Leftrightarrow (\mathbf{P} \Diamond \mathbf{P})$

(b) $(\mathbf{P} \wedge \mathbf{Q}) \Leftrightarrow ((\mathbf{P} \Diamond \mathbf{Q}) \Diamond (\mathbf{P} \Diamond \mathbf{Q}))$

(c) $(\mathbf{P} \vee \mathbf{Q}) \Leftrightarrow ((\mathbf{P} \Diamond \mathbf{P}) \Diamond (\mathbf{Q} \Diamond \mathbf{Q}))$

(d) $(\mathbf{P} \Rightarrow \mathbf{Q}) \Leftrightarrow ((\mathbf{Q} \Diamond \mathbf{Q}) \Diamond \mathbf{P})$

(3.12) Construct a truth table for bi-negation,

$$\mathbf{P} \blacklozenge \mathbf{Q}$$

which is true only when the predicates **P** and **Q** are both false.

Use truth tables to prove the following equivalences.

(a) $\neg\ \mathbf{P} \Leftrightarrow (\mathbf{P} \blacklozenge \mathbf{P})$

(b) $(\mathbf{P} \wedge \mathbf{Q}) \Leftrightarrow ((\mathbf{P} \blacklozenge \mathbf{P}) \blacklozenge (\mathbf{Q} \blacklozenge \mathbf{Q}))$

(c) $(\mathbf{P} \vee \mathbf{Q}) \Leftrightarrow ((\mathbf{P} \blacklozenge \mathbf{Q}) \blacklozenge (\mathbf{P} \blacklozenge \mathbf{Q}))$

(d) $(\mathbf{P} \Rightarrow \mathbf{Q}) \Leftrightarrow ((\mathbf{P} \blacklozenge \mathbf{Q}) \blacklozenge \mathbf{Q}) \blacklozenge ((\mathbf{P} \blacklozenge \mathbf{Q}) \blacklozenge \mathbf{Q})$

In the exercises that follow we shall formalize some of the ideas in the management of bank accounts. This banking system will be used in the exercises to later chapters as well. In the banking system, a customer's account is identified by an account number.

(3.13) Write a declaration to introduce *AcctNo* as a given set for account numbers.

(3.14) Write a single declaration to introduce the following sets:

active is the set of account numbers that are in use. (The other account numbers might be yet to be allocated, or might be the numbers of accounts that have been closed.)

overdrawn is the set of account numbers of the accounts that are overdrawn.

depositors is the set of account numbers of deposit accounts, i.e. accounts that receive interest.

current is the set of account numbers of current accounts, i.e. accounts that receive no interest.

(3.15) Write predicates to formalize the following statements:

(a) Only active accounts can be overdrawn.

(b) Only current accounts can be overdrawn.

(c) The active accounts are the deposit accounts and the current accounts taken together.

(d) No account can be both a deposit account and a current account.

(e) No deposit account can be overdrawn.

(3.16) Draw some Venn diagrams to illustrate the relations between the various sets introduced in formalizing the banking system.

(3.17) Prove the following theorems.

(a) $[A, B: \mathbb{P}\ X \mid A = B] \vdash A \subseteq B$

(b) $[A, B: \mathbb{P}\ X \mid A = B] \vdash A \setminus B = \varnothing$

(c) $[A, B, C: \mathbb{P}\ X] \vdash A \cap (B \setminus C) = (A \cap B) \setminus C$

(d) $[A: \mathbb{P}\ X] \vdash \varnothing \setminus A = \varnothing$

(3.18) Where was the notion of a bound variable introduced, but not so called, before the section on the existential quantifier?

(3.19) Formulate and prove a tautology to justify the following deduction rule, a simplified version of proof by cases in which there are only two cases.

$$\frac{\mathbf{H} \vdash (\mathbf{P} \wedge \mathbf{Q}) \Rightarrow \mathbf{R} \qquad \mathbf{H} \vdash ((\neg \mathbf{P}) \wedge \mathbf{Q}) \Rightarrow \mathbf{R}}{\mathbf{H} \vdash \mathbf{Q} \Rightarrow \mathbf{R}}$$

(3.20) Write axioms for set equality, set union, set intersection, set difference and the subset notation.

Chapter 4
Relations and functions

Summary: Ordered pairs – Cartesian product – binary relation – domain, range and inverse – comprehension and enumeration – composition – domain and range restriction and subtraction – functions – lambda abstraction – application – total functions and injections – data type definitions – overriding – tuples – prefix, infix and postfix notations – sequences – axiomatic descriptions – generic definitions.

4.1 Relations

In the previous chapter we saw that the mathematical notion of a set of values of the same type could be used to formalize many commonly occurring ideas in software specification. Making sets homogeneous has the disadvantage that it is not possible to bring together values of different types, a defect which we now remedy.

4.1.1 Ordered pairs

Examining informal requirements for software systems only slightly more complicated than the class manager's assistant shows that close associations between values of different types are required. In the library management system introduced in the previous chapter, it does not take much research into the requirements to discover that a close association between values of type *Book* and values of type *Person* is required to keep track of who has borrowed what. We now introduce a new kind of term called an **ordered pair**. If *Book* and *Person* are types, and if

cider_with_rosie: *Book*; *jean_simmons*: *Person* (29, 29)

we can create an ordered pair whose first member is *cider_with_rosie* and whose second member is *jean_simmons*. The notation for this term is as follows.

$cider\_with\_rosie \mapsto jean\_simmons$

The arrow is called a **maplet**, and it emphasizes the asymmetric nature of an ordered pair.

4.1.2 Cartesian product of two sets

The type of an ordered pair cannot be the type of either of its members. We need a way of constructing a new set from *Book* and *Person* to be the type of all ordered pairs whose first members are books and whose second members are persons. It is called the **Cartesian product** of *Book* and *Person*, and is written thus:

$Book \times Person$ (29, 29)

The order of the two sets in this expression is significant, so $Person \times Book$ is by no means the same thing. It is the set of all ordered pairs whose first members are persons and whose second members are books.

The notion of Cartesian product can be applied to any two sets, and the types of those sets need not be different. For instance, the set of all ordered pairs of integers is $\mathbb{Z} \times \mathbb{Z}$.

A set of ordered pairs is called a **relation**. Of course, all the ordered pairs in a set must be of the same type; that is, their first members must all be of one type, and their second members must all be of one type, though the two types might be different. A few examples follow.

4.1.3 A bibliographical example

Part of the library management system is to be a bibliography that records the association between authors and the books they have written. We need to introduce two new types.

- *Author* is the set of authors who might ever figure in the bibliography. Although authors are people, we do not draw our authors from *Person*, but declare a separate type for them. (*Author* has already appeared in the exercises in the previous chapter, but this time we want *Author* to be a type in the library system.)

  $[Author]$

- *Title* is the type from which titles are taken. A distinction has to be drawn between the type *Book*, whose values represent the copies of works on the shelves, and the type *Title*, whose values represent the works of which the individual copies are the physical manifestations.

  $[Title]$

A relation on given sets *Author* and *Title* is a set of ordered pairs whose first members are in *Author* and whose second members are in *Title*. An instance of such a relation is illustrated in Figure 4.1. The small circles represent particular authors and titles. The sets *Author* and *Title*, being given sets, probably contain many more members than those shown in the diagram. Two of the authors have written several titles, and collaborated on one of the titles.

If such a relation is to be maintained as part of the library management system, we need to name it, declare it, and develop notations for using the name for making sensible statements about it. Since the illustrated relation is just a set of ordered pairs we could declare it thus:

$$wrote : \mathbb{P}\,(Author \times Title) \qquad (72, 72)$$

In Z specifications this notation is rarely to be found, and the usual abbreviation is

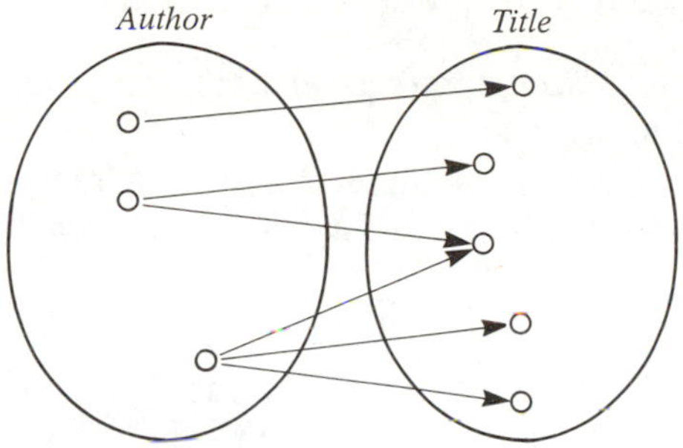

Figure 4.1 A relation.

wrote: *Author* ↔ *Title* (72, 72)

The second notation means exactly the same as the first. The sign '↔' is called the relation symbol.

If *charlotte_bronte* is of type *Author*, and is known to denote Charlotte Brontë, and if *jane_eyre* is of type *Title*, and is known to denote the book *Jane Eyre*, then either of the following statements

charlotte_bronte ↦ *jane_eyre* ∈ *wrote*

charlotte_bronte wrote jane_eyre

means that the bibliography *wrote* records the fact that Charlotte Brontë was the author of *Jane Eyre*.

4.1.4 Terminology of relations

Some general terminology of relations must now be introduced. Suppose X and Y are two sets, then the set $X \leftrightarrow Y$ of all relations from X to Y is defined to be $\mathbb{P}\ (X \times Y)$. The definition

$$X \leftrightarrow Y == \mathbb{P}\ (X \times Y)$$

is a **generic** definition, i. e. one that summarizes a whole family of definitions. Each member of the family is obtained by choosing particular values for the sets X and Y. The sets X and Y are the **generic parameters** of the definition. For any such relation, X will be called the **from-set**, and Y will be called the **to-set**.

The **domain** of a relation is the set of first members of the pairs in the relation. Suppose

R: $X \leftrightarrow Y$

then ***dom*** R is the set

$$\{x: X \mid (\exists y: Y \bullet x \mapsto y \in R)\}$$

Thus in Figure 4.1, ***dom*** *wrote* is exactly the three authors at the starting ends of the arrows.

The **range** of a relation is the set of second members of the pairs in the relation. With the same declaration of *R*, ***ran*** *R* is the set

$$\{y: Y \mid (\exists x: X \bullet x \mapsto y \in R)\}$$

Thus in Figure 4.1, ***ran*** *wrote* is exactly the five titles at the finishing ends of the arrows.

The **inverse** of a relation is the set of ordered pairs obtained by reversing each pair in the relation. For the same *R* as before, R^{-1} is the relation

$$\{x: X; y: Y \mid x\ R\ y \bullet y \mapsto x\}$$

The inverse of the instance of *wrote* represented in Figure 4.1 could be represented by reversing all the arrows.

Because relations are sets (of ordered pairs), they can be empty, and can be used in constructions involving union, intersection and difference. One relation can be a subset of another.

4.1.5 A genealogical example

The genealogy of historical personages can be pursued, or at least recorded, with computer assistance, and the binary relation is the ideal model for a repository of genealogical information. Suppose *Person* is a type, and suppose that *V*, *A*, *C*, *L*, *Vy*, *E*, *Aa*, *D*, *W*, *G* and *N* are distinct members of it. The state of our knowledge about their relationships might be modelled by

$$is\_a\_parent\_of: Person \leftrightarrow Person \qquad (29, 29)$$

and Figure 4.2 represents a possible value of *is_a_parent_of*. Note that in this example the from-set and the to-set are the same. That *V*

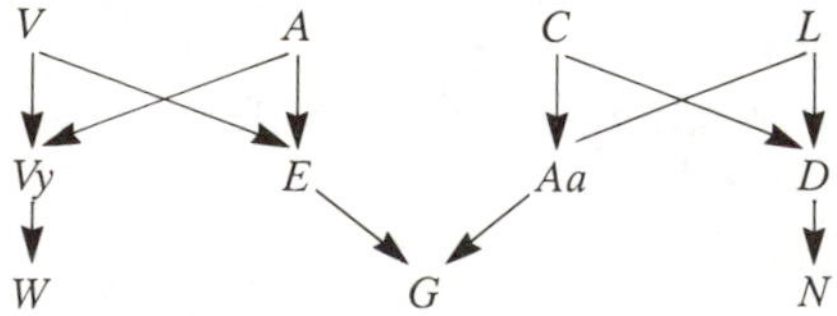

Figure 4.2 A genealogical table.

is a parent of E is illustrated in the diagram by the arrow from V to E, and expressed formally by the notation

$$V\ is\_a\_parent\_of\ E$$

4.1.6 Relations defined by comprehension or by enumeration

A relation with a fixed denotation can often be defined by a set comprehension notation. For instance, the less-than relation on integers can be defined by the following set comprehension.

$$less\_than == \{x, y: \mathbb{Z} \mid (\exists p: \mathbb{Z} \mid p > 0 \bullet x + p = y) \bullet x \mapsto y\}$$

By looking at the term in the set comprehension we see that the type of *less_than* is $\mathbb{P}(\mathbb{Z} \times \mathbb{Z})$, or $\mathbb{Z} \leftrightarrow \mathbb{Z}$. Well-known properties of integers can be used to show that the domain and range of *less_than* are the whole of $\mathbb{Z}$.

A small relation can be defined by enumeration. If *heart*, *diamond*, *spade*, *club* and *notrump* are the five distinct members of the type *Biddable_suit*, then a relation familiar to contract bridge players will be

$$\begin{aligned} is\_stronger\_than == \{&notrump \mapsto spade,\ notrump \mapsto heart,\\ &notrump \mapsto diamond,\ notrump \mapsto club,\\ &spade \mapsto heart,\ spade \mapsto diamond,\\ &spade \mapsto club,\ heart \mapsto diamond,\\ &heart \mapsto club,\ diamond \mapsto club\} \end{aligned}$$

4.1.7 Composition of relations

If the from-set of one relation is of the same type as the to-set of another, it is possible to create a new relation from the two by **composition**. Figure 4.3 illustrates this notion.

Suppose that *Author*, *Title*, and *Publisher* are types, then Table 4.1 shows the types of the relations illustrated in the figure.

Table 4.1 Types in relation composition.

Relation	Type
wrote	$\mathbb{P}\ (Author \times Title)$
issued_by	$\mathbb{P}\ (Title \times Publisher)$
wrote ; *issued_by*	$\mathbb{P}\ (Author \times Publisher)$

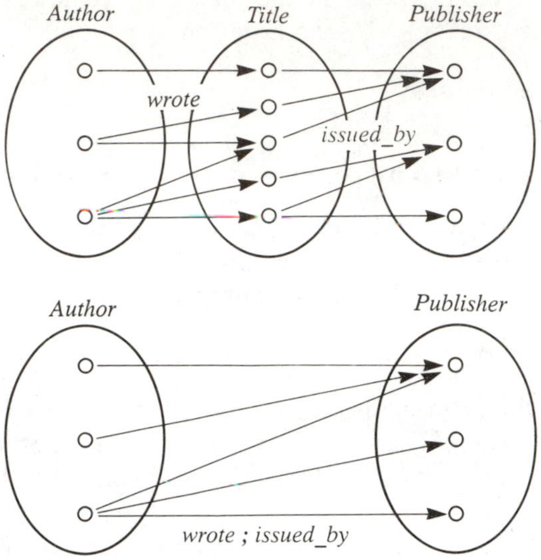

Figure 4.3 Composition of relations.

The fat semicolon ‘;’ is the symbol for the composition of two relations.

If R and S are two relations declared as follows:

$$R: X \leftrightarrow Y; S: Y \leftrightarrow Z$$

then their composition $R \mathbin{;} S$ is defined by the following set comprehension.

$$\{x: X; z: Z \mid (\exists y: Y \bullet (x \mathrel{R} y \wedge y \mathrel{S} z)) \bullet x \mapsto z\}$$

4.1.8 Domain and range restriction and subtraction

Suppose that the bibliography relating authors to titles is too big for the purpose we have in mind, but we wish to speak of only a part of that bibliography. For instance we might wish to speak about the part of the bibliography that concerns female authors, or we may wish to restrict our attention to that part of the bibliography that deals with novels. We now introduce four notations that are very useful for restricting relations to particular subsets.

First we look at **domain restriction**, a technique for drawing attention to those pairs in a relation whose first members are members of some other set of interest. To confine the relation *wrote* illustrated in Figure 4.4 to those pairs whose first members are in the set *female*, a set of authors, we write

$female \lhd wrote$

This notation denotes the set of ordered pairs in *wrote* whose first members are in *female*. It is an abbreviation for either of the following expressions:

$$\{a\colon female;\ t\colon Title \mid a\ wrote\ t \bullet a \mapsto t\} \qquad (72)$$

$$(female \times Title) \cap wrote \qquad (72)$$

Next we look at **domain subtraction**, a technique for drawing attention to those pairs in a relation whose first members are NOT members of some other set of interest. To confine the relation *wrote* illustrated in Figure 4.4 to those pairs whose first members are not in the set *female*, we write

$female \ntriangleleft wrote$

This notation denotes the set of ordered pairs in *wrote* whose first members are not in *female*. It is an abbreviation for either of the following expressions:

$$\{a\colon Author;\ t\colon Title \mid a \notin female \wedge a\ wrote\ t \bullet a \mapsto t\} \qquad (72, 72)$$

$$wrote \setminus (female \times Title) \qquad (72)$$

The other two notations place emphasis on the range of the relation as deciding which pairs are to be considered. We look at **range restriction**, a technique for drawing attention to those pairs in a relation whose second members are members of some other set of interest. To confine the relation *wrote* illustrated in Figure 4.5 to

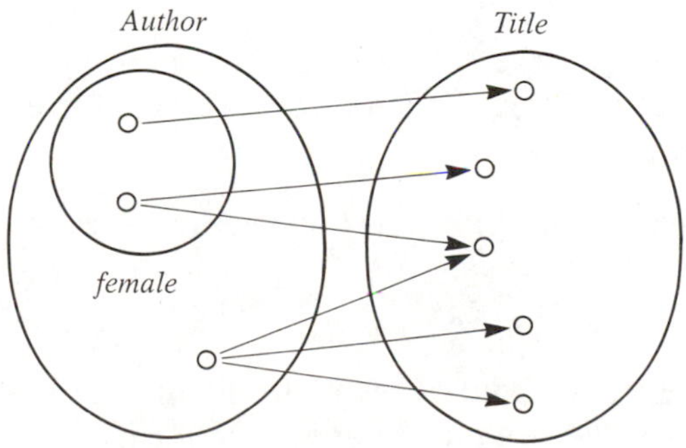

Figure 4.4 Domain restriction and domain subtraction.

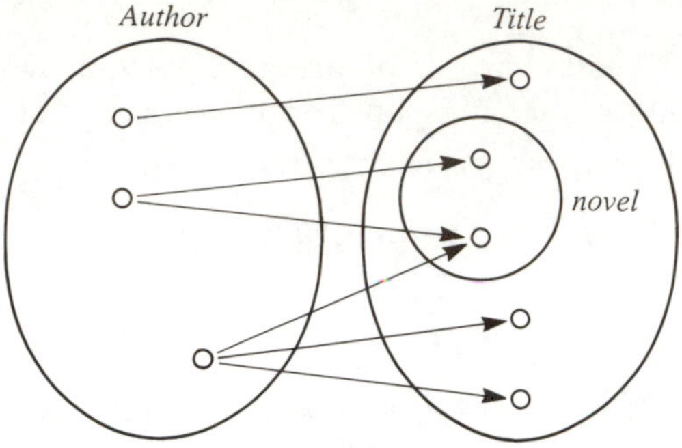

Figure 4.5 Range restriction and range subtraction.

those pairs whose second members are in the set *novel*, a set of titles, we write

$$wrote \rhd novel$$

This notation denotes the set of ordered pairs in *wrote* whose second members are in *novel*. It is an abbreviation for either of the following expressions:

$$\{a: Author; t: novel \mid a\ wrote\ t \bullet a \mapsto t\} \qquad (72)$$

$$(Author \times novel) \cap wrote \qquad (72)$$

Next we look at **range subtraction**, a technique for drawing attention to those pairs in a relation whose second members are NOT members of some other set of interest. To confine the relation *wrote* illustrated in Figure 4.5 to those pairs whose second members are not in the set *novel*, we write

$$wrote \Rightarrow novel$$

This notation denotes the set of ordered pairs in *wrote* whose second members are not in *novel*. It is an abbreviation for either of the following expressions:

$$\{a: Author; t: Title \mid t \notin novel \wedge a\ wrote\ t \bullet a \mapsto t\} \qquad (72, 72)$$

$$wrote \setminus (Author \times novel) \qquad (72)$$

There are some rules about types of terms that can be used in these constructions that we summarize now. The forms

$$X \lhd R, \quad X \ntriangleleft R, \quad R \rhd Y, \quad R \ntriangleright Y$$

are well-formed provided that there are types $\mathbf{T}_1$, $\mathbf{T}_2$, not necessarily different, such that

The type of X is $\mathbb{P}\mathbf{T}_1$

The type of Y is $\mathbb{P}\mathbf{T}_2$

The type of R is $\mathbb{P}(\mathbf{T}_1 \times \mathbf{T}_2)$

In each case the type of the expression is the type of R.

The following properties might be of usc in proving properties of these constructions.

$$\mathit{dom}\ (X \lhd R) \subseteq X$$

$$\mathit{ran}\ (X ⩤ R) \subseteq \mathit{ran}\ R$$

$$\mathit{dom}\ (R ⩥ Y) \subseteq \mathit{dom}\ R$$

$$\mathit{ran}\ (R \rhd Y) \subseteq Y$$

4.1.9 Summary of types so far

The type rules so far established are as follows:

(1) A given set is a type. (Sets introduced by data definition are included in this category.)

(2) The set $\mathbb{Z}$ of integers is a type.

(3) If $\mathbf{T}$ is a type, then so is $\mathbb{P}\mathbf{T}$.

(4) If $\mathbf{T}_1$ and $\mathbf{T}_2$ are types, then so is $\mathbf{T}_1 \times \mathbf{T}_2$.

There are other ways of constructing types that we shall explore in later chapters.

4.2 Functions

4.2.1 What is a function?

A **function** between two sets X and Y is a relation between those sets that has a special property, namely that each member of the from-set is related to at most one member of the to-set. In pictorial terms this means that at most one arrow has its origin in each member of the from-set.

In the upper diagram in Figure 4.6, the illustrated relation does not have the function property, but in the lower diagram it does. The

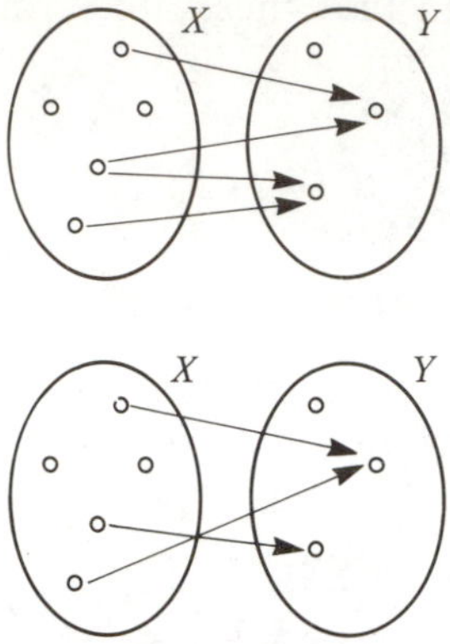

Figure 4.6 The function property illustrated.

term **partial function** is sometimes used to describe what is here called a function.

Functions are extremely common in models of requirements for building software products. If the library has a rule that a book can be borrowed by only one person at a time, then we should use a function from books to persons to model that part of the state of the library. If this function is called *lent_to*, then we should declare it as follows:

$$lent\_to: Book \rightarrowtail\!\!\!\!\!\!+\ Person \qquad (29, 29)$$

In this declaration the expression *Book* ⇸ *Person* denotes the set of all functions from the set *Book* to the set *Person*. The sign '⇸' is the function arrow. The type of *lent_to* is $\mathbb{P}(Book \times Person)$. The predicate

$$Book \nrightarrow Person \subseteq Book \leftrightarrow Person \qquad (29, 29, 29, 29)$$

formalizes the fact that every function from *Book* to *Person* is also a relation from *Book* to *Person*. A formal expression of the function property is given next as a predicate that says that the set of functions is just all those relations that have the property.

$$\begin{aligned} Book \nrightarrow Person = \{r: Book \leftrightarrow Person \qquad & (29, 29, 29, 29) \\ \mid (\forall b: Book;\ p_1, p_2: Person \qquad & (29, 29) \\ \bullet ((b\ r\ p_1 \wedge b\ r\ p_2) \Rightarrow p_1 = p_2))\} & \end{aligned}$$

The notions of domain, range, domain subtraction, range subtraction, domain restriction, range restriction, inverse and composition apply to functions because they are relations. Note, however, that the inverse of a function might not be a function. Similarly, because functions are sets we can use them in constructions involving union, intersection and difference, though the union of two functions might not be a function.

4.2.2 Function definition by enumeration

A function can be defined by enumeration as follows. If *joe_c*, *sue_s* and *les_a* are distinct values of the set *Person*, and books are represented by natural numbers, then we might find the following to be the value of *lent_to* at a certain time:

$$\{29 \mapsto joe\_c,\ 567 \mapsto sue\_s,\ 49 \mapsto joe\_c,\ 1022 \mapsto les\_a\}$$

However the following relation would not be a possible value of *lent_to*:

$$\{29 \mapsto joe\_c,\ 567 \mapsto sue\_s,\ 49 \mapsto joe\_c\ \ 567 \mapsto les\_a\}$$

since the book *567* is recorded as being lent to two different borrowers.

4.2.3 Function definition by set comprehension

Since a function is just a set of ordered pairs it could be defined by a set comprehension term. The following definition

$$isqrt == \{n: \mathbb{Z} \mid n \geq 0 \bullet n^2 \mapsto n\}$$

establishes *isqrt* as the name of a limited square root function for integers. Its domain is the set of all the integers that have integral square roots, and each such integer is paired with its positive square root. What is the type of the term *isqrt*? Since it is a set of ordered pairs of integers, its type must be $\mathbb{P}(\mathbb{Z}\times\mathbb{Z})$.

4.2.4 Function definition by lambda abstraction

Another method of defining a function consists in using declarations and constraints to fix the domain, and giving an expression for a typical range element. Thus a function to relate a natural number to the sum of the natural numbers up to and including that number would be defined as follows:

$$triangle == \lambda n: \mathbb{N} \bullet n*(n+1)/2$$

The definition begins with the sign 'λ' (lambda) that gives this method of definition its name – **lambda abstraction**. The declaration, without an explicit constraint in this case, defines the domain to be the set of natural numbers, and the heavy dot separates the declaration from the range element expression. The above syntactic equivalence is an abbreviation for the following declaration and predicate:

$triangle: \mathbb{Z} \rightarrow\!\!\!\!\!\rightarrow \mathbb{Z}$

$triangle = \{n: \mathbb{N} \bullet n \mapsto n*(n+1)/2\}$

The general form of a lambda abstraction is as follows:

$\lambda \mathbf{D} \mid \mathbf{P} \bullet \mathbf{E}$

where **D** represents declarations, **P** is a predicate constraining the values declared in **D** and **E** is an expression giving the value of the function in terms of the values declared in **D**. As in similar notations, the constraint bar separates the declaration from the constraint.

4.2.5 Function application

We now come to an important notation for functions, called **function application**. Given the declaration of *lent_to* on p. 80 above, suppose that *b*: *Book* is in the domain of *lent_to*. Then we apply *lent_to* to *b*, and write

lent_to b

to denote the person to whom the book *b* has been lent.

In this expression the value *b* is called the **argument** of the function application, and *lent_to b* is the **value** of the function for argument *b*. For the function *isqrt* declared on p. 81 we have

$isqrt\ 9 = 3$

If we had not named the function, we could just as well have written

$\{n: \mathbb{Z} \mid n \geq 0 \bullet n^2 \mapsto n\}\ 9 = 3$

Similarly, we could write

$(\lambda n: \mathbb{N} \bullet n*(n+1)/2)\ 3 = 6$

for the function *triangle* defined on p. 81.

The function application notation is equivalent to a definite description.

lent_to b

is the same as

$\mu p: Person \mid (b \mapsto p) \in lent\_to$

that is 'the person who is the second member of the pair in *lent_to* whose first member is *b*'. We noted on p. 59 that a definite description can give rise to an undefined term, and we can see that if *b* is not in the domain of *lent_to*, that is if *b* is not on loan, but on the shelves, the definite description is undefined. There are various ways of dealing with this difficulty and of giving a value, true or false, to a predicate like

$$b \notin \mathbf{dom}\ lent\_to \lor lent\_to\ b = p$$

even though when the first disjunct is true, the second contains an undefined term. The merits of the different approaches are, at the time of writing, the subject of a healthy dispute, and the reader should consult Woodcock (1991) for more details. The approach taken here is as follows. A function application notation is always taken to be of the type of the to-set, so

$$lent\_to\ b$$

is definitely a person. All applications of *lent_to* to books outside its domain denote the same person, but we do not know which person it is. In general, every type contains a value that will be the value of the undefined term of that type, but we never know which value it is, unless the type contains only one value. Returning to the predicate

$$b \notin \mathbf{dom}\ lent\_to \lor lent\_to\ b = p$$

we can say that when *b* is in the domain of *lent_to*, the first disjunct will be false, and the second disjunct will be true if *p* is the borrower and false if not. However, when *b* is not in the domain of *lent_to*, the first conjunct is true, but the value of the second disjunct might be true or might be false, depending on whether *p* happens to be the person chosen to be the undefined term in *Person*. Whichever it is, true or false, the whole predicate is true because the first disjunct is true.

4.2.6 Total functions

A function whose domain is the whole of its from-set is called a **total function**. The set of total functions from *X* to *Y* is defined by the following generic syntactic equivalence.

$$X \rightarrow Y == \{f : X \nrightarrow Y \mid \mathbf{dom}\ f = X\}$$

The sign '→' is the total function arrow.

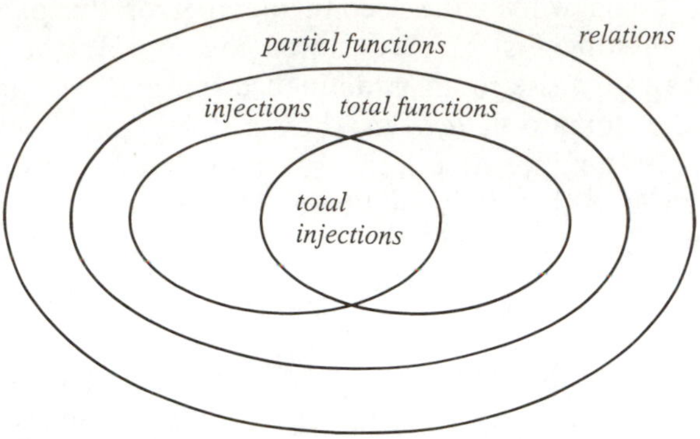

Figure 4.7 Relations and functions.

4.2.7 Injections

A function in which the second members of the pairs are unique is called an **injection**. The following definition defines the set of all injections from *X* to *Y*.

$$X \pinj Y == \{F\colon X \pfun Y \mid f^{-1} \in Y \pfun X\}$$

This definition says that injections are functions whose inverses are also functions. The sign '$\pinj$' is the injection arrow. The terms **partial injection** and **1 − 1 function** are sometimes used for what is here called an injection.

If the domain of an injection is the whole of the from-set, we shall call the injection a **total injection**. The following definition defines the set of total injections from *X* to *Y*, and introduces the total injection arrow.

$$X \inj Y == \{f\colon X \pinj Y \mid \mathbf{dom}\, f = X\}$$

The Venn diagram in Figure 4.7 illustrates some of the relationships discussed in this chapter.

4.2.8 Data type definition

Suppose that in investigating the requirements for the library management system we had formed the opinion that the librarian made a firm distinction between fiction books and non-fiction books, and we responded to this by making two given sets thus:

$$[Fiction, Non\_fiction]$$

How shall we construct a type *Book* that covers both kinds? Set union is not possible, because *Fiction* and *Non_fiction* are different types. The following definition, an extension of the data type definition introduced in Chapter 3, constructs a new type *Book* from *Fiction* and *Non_fiction*.

$$Book ::= fict \langle\!\langle Fiction \rangle\!\rangle \mid nfict \langle\!\langle Non\_fiction \rangle\!\rangle \qquad (84, 84)$$

This definition introduces three names: the new type *Book*, and two **constructor functions** *fict* and *nfict*. The purpose of the constructor functions is to convert values of the contributing types *Fiction* and *Non_fiction* to values of the new type *Book*. The signs '≪' and '≫' are called **disjoint union brackets**. The above data type definition is equivalent to the declarations and predicates in Table 4.2 and illustrated in Figure 4.8.

Table 4.2 A data type definition explained.

(1)	$[Book]$ *Book* is introduced as a given set.
(2)	$fict: Fiction \rightarrowtail Book$ *fict* converts every member of *Fiction* (because *fict* is total) to a member of *Book*, distinct members of *Fiction* being related to distinct members of *Book* (because *fict* is an injection).
(3)	$nfict: Non\text{-}fiction \rightarrowtail Book$ *nfict* converts every member of *Non_fiction* (because *nfict* is total) to a member of *Book*, distinct members of *Non_fiction* being related to distinct members of *Book* (because *nfict* is an injection).
(4)	$\mathbf{ran}\ fict \cap \mathbf{ran}\ nfict = \varnothing$ If a book is a fiction book, i.e. is obtained by applying *fict* to a value of type *Fiction*, it cannot also be a non-fiction book, i.e. obtained by applying *nfict* to a value of type *Non_fiction*.
(5)	$Book = \mathbf{ran}\ fict \cup \mathbf{ran}\ nfict$ Every book is either a fiction book or a non-fiction book.

Given a value *b* of type *Book*, then the predicate

$$b \in \mathbf{ran}\ fict$$

is true exactly when the book is a fiction book.

Given the following declarations

$$f: Fiction;\ lent\_to: Book \rightarrow\!\!\!\!\!\!+ \ Person \qquad (84, 29, 29)$$

the person who has borrowed *f* is given by the following expression:

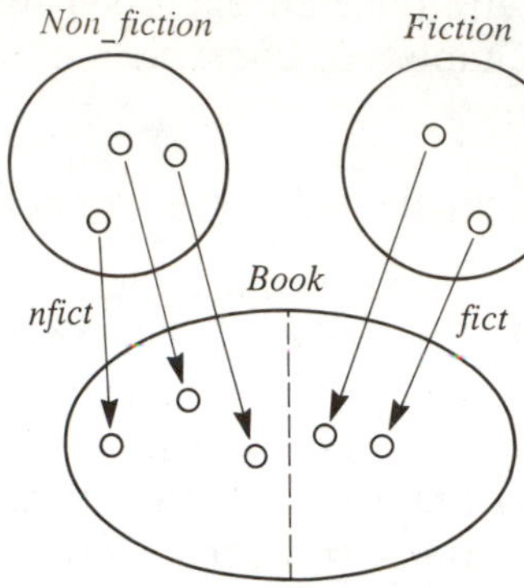

Figure 4.8 A data type definition illustrated.

$$lent\_to\ (fict\ f)$$

Note that f has to be subjected to *fict* before it becomes of the correct type to be an argument to *lent_to*, and that the book *fict f* must be in the domain of *lent_to* for this expression to denote a person.

The form of data type definition with constructor functions can be combined with the one introduced earlier. If the library catalogue was to be regarded as a special book, neither fiction nor non-fiction, we might have defined *Book* as follows:

$$Book ::= catalogue \mid fict \langle\!\langle Fiction \rangle\!\rangle \qquad (84)$$
$$\mid nfict \langle\!\langle Non\_fiction \rangle\!\rangle \qquad (84)$$

Table 4.3 Amended explanation of data type definition.

(5) $Book = \mathbf{ran}\ fict \cup \mathbf{ran}\ nfict \cup \{catalogue\}$

Every book is either a fiction book or a non-fiction book, or is the catalogue.

(6) $catalogue : Book$

The catalogue is a book.

(7) $catalogue \notin \mathbf{ran}\ fict$

The catalogue is not fiction.

(8) $catalogue \notin \mathbf{ran}\ nfict$

The catalogue is not non-fiction.

We now have a new declaration, two new predicates, and a replacement for (5) in Table 4.2 as shown in Table 4.3.

4.2.9 Overriding

The following method of constructing new functions from old is of frequent application in specifications. Suppose that the present value of the *lent_to* function in the library is given by the following set enumeration, where the names denote values of the appropriate types.

$$old == \{29 \mapsto joe\_c,\ 567 \mapsto sue\_s,\ 49 \mapsto joe\_c,\ 1022 \mapsto les\_a\}$$

Suppose that certain amendments are to be incorporated, and the following enumeration defines these.

$$new == \{29 \mapsto jim\_s,\ 95 \mapsto joe\_c\}$$

means that book *29* has been transferred to *jim_s*, and that book *95*, previously on the shelves, has been lent to *joe_c*. We wish to construct a new set of pairs that will include all the new pairs and such of the old ones as did not conflict with the new, i.e. such as did not have the same first member as a new pair. The notation for this is

$$old \oplus new$$

the sign '⊕' being the sign for **overriding**. The result is the following set of ordered pairs.

$$\{29 \mapsto jim\_s,\ 95 \mapsto joe\_c,\ 567 \mapsto sue\_s,\ 49 \mapsto joe\_c,\ 1022 \mapsto les\_a\}$$

In general for any functions *f* and *g* of the same type,

$$f \oplus g = g \cup ((\mathbf{dom}\ g) \lhd f)$$

and this expression should be considered as defining the meaning of overriding. If *f* and *g* are functions of different types, then the notation is not well-formed.

4.2.10 Tuples and functions of several arguments

The notion of an ordered pair can be extended to longer ordered collections – ordered triples, ordered quartets etc. These ordered collections of values are called **tuples**, an ordered collection of *n* values being called an *n*-tuple. The type of a tuple is given by a continued Cartesian product. Thus a tuple consisting of a value of type *Book*, a value of type *Person*, and a value of type *Title* would be of type

$$Book \times Person \times Title \qquad (29, 29, 72)$$

A tuple is usually displayed as a list of values in parentheses, the values being separated by commas. Thus an ordered pair, being a tuple of the smallest kind, might appear either as $a \mapsto b$, or as (a, b).

A function that takes three integers as arguments and gives as its value the sum of the squares of the first two minus the square of the last could be declared as follows:

$$qpyth: (\mathbb{Z} \times \mathbb{Z} \times \mathbb{Z}) \rightarrow \mathbb{Z}$$

and its type is

$$\mathbb{P}\ ((\mathbb{Z} \times \mathbb{Z} \times \mathbb{Z}) \times \mathbb{Z})$$

This function could be defined by lambda abstraction as follows:

$$qpyth == \lambda x, y, z: \mathbb{Z} \bullet x^2 + y^2 - z^2$$

The meanings of certain cases of some notations introduced earlier can now be explained. The set comprehension term

$$\{x, y, z: \mathbb{Z} \mid x > y \wedge y > z\}$$

denotes a set of ordered triples of integers that are in descending order of magnitude. Any set comprehension that declares several variables, and has no expression to define a term, defines a set of tuples of the types of the variables in the order in which they were declared.

Similarly the definite description

$$\mu x, y: \mathbb{Z} \mid x = y^2 \;\wedge x = 2 * y$$

denotes the ordered pair of integers $4 \mapsto 2$. Any definite description that declares several variables, and has no expression to define a term, defines a tuple of the types of the variables in the order in which they were declared.

4.2.11 Prefix, infix and postfix notations

The less-than relation among integers is an example of an **infix notation**. This means that although both the following notations say that -3 is less than 2, the first is more usual.

$$-3 < 2$$

$$(-3 \mapsto 2) \in \;<$$

Indeed, we explained that the name of any relation can be treated in this way as an infix notation.

Many functions are treated as **prefix notations**; that is to say the function symbol is placed before its arguments in a function application notation. However there are well-known functions of two arguments where the function sign is commonly treated as an infix notation. The three notations following all express the same truth, but the first is the most familiar.

$$2 + 2 = 4$$

$$+\ (2, 2) = 4$$

$$((2 \mapsto 2) \mapsto 4) \in +$$

In the first case, '+' is being used as an infix notation.

Very occasionally a **postfix notation**, where the function symbol follows the arguments, is used. One of the instances of this we have seen in this book is the use of the index notation for the square function on p. 36.

4.3 Sequences

4.3.1 What is a sequence?

The mathematical notation so far developed has used sets and relations to formalize intuitive notions, but the informal notion of order is limited to being able to distinguish the first and second members of an ordered pair, or the members of a tuple of a given length. Consider the situation of a librarian whose library allows books that are out on loan to be reserved by disappointed borrowers. If the library's rule is that waiting borrowers are to have the book in the order in which they applied for it, then to formalize this idea we need the notion of a **sequence**, an ordered collection of values of the same kind (in this case, borrowers). A sequence can be of arbitrary length, but we shall have no need to introduce infinite sequences. Our notion of a sequence can be derived from the notion of a partial function as follows. A sequence of values of type X is a partial function from natural numbers $\mathbb{N}$ to X whose domain is just $1..n$, where n is the length of the sequence. Formally we can define the set of all sequences of values of type X as follows:

$$\textbf{\textit{seq}}\ X == \{f: \mathbb{N} \rightarrow\!\!\!\!\!+ X \mid (\exists n: \mathbb{N} \bullet \textbf{\textit{dom}}\ f = 1..n)\}$$

Since $\textbf{\textit{seq}}\ X$ is a set of functions, the type of $\textbf{\textit{seq}}\ X$ must be $\mathbb{P}\ (\mathbb{P}\ (\mathbb{Z} \times X)$, and the type of any sequence of values of type X is $\mathbb{P}\ (\mathbb{Z} \times X)$.

Suppose b, e and r are distinct members of a type *Roman_alphabet*; then the following notations both denote the sequence of letters b, e, e, r, in that order.

$$\{1 \mapsto b, 2 \mapsto e, 3 \mapsto e, 4 \mapsto r\}$$

$$\langle b, e, e, r \rangle$$

The first notation emphasizes the fact that a sequence is a function, a set of ordered pairs. The second is a more compact enumeration of the same sequence. The signs '$\langle$' and '$\rangle$' are **sequence brackets**, and the values are separated by commas. If we let s denote the above sequence, then the following statements are well-formed and true:

$$\textbf{dom}\ s = 1..4$$

$$\textbf{ran}\ s = \{b, e, r\}$$

$$\# s = 4$$

$$s\ 3 = e$$

There is nothing in our definition of $\textbf{seq}\ X$ to prohibit empty sequences. We can denote an empty sequence by $\langle\rangle$. Note that this notation is ambiguous, since it will be used to denote empty sequences of different types.

4.3.2 Sequence notation

Provided a sequence s is not empty we can make the following true statements, introducing some useful notations.

$$\textbf{head}\ s = s\ 1$$

$$\textbf{tail}\ s = \{i: 1..\#s-1 \bullet i \mapsto s(i+1)\}$$

$$\textbf{last}\ s = s\ \#s$$

$$\textbf{front}\ s = \{\#s\} \mathbin{⩤} s$$

$$\textbf{rev}\ s = \{i: 1..\#s \bullet (\#s-i+1) \mapsto (s\ i)\}$$

For example:

$$\textbf{\textit{head}}\ \langle b, e, e, r\rangle = b$$

$$\textbf{\textit{tail}}\ \langle b, e, e, r\rangle = \langle e, e, r\rangle$$

$$\textbf{\textit{last}}\ \langle b, e, e, r\rangle = r$$

$$\textbf{\textit{front}}\ \langle b, e, e, r\rangle = \langle b, e, e\rangle$$

$$\textbf{\textit{rev}}\ \langle b, e, e, r\rangle = \langle r, e, e, b\rangle$$

A notation that allows us to name the result of attaching one sequence to the end of another to form a new sequence is called **concatenation**. If s and t are sequences of values of the same type, then their concatenation is

$$s \mathbin{\hat{}} t = s \cup \{i\colon 1..\#t \bullet (i + \#s) \mapsto (t\ i)\}$$

Sometimes it is convenient to say that a sequence has no repetitions. The set of non-repetitive sequences of values of type X is given by either of the following expressions:

$$\{s\colon \textbf{\textit{seq}}\ X \mid \#\, s = \#\ \textbf{\textit{ran}}\ s\}$$

$$\{s\colon \textbf{\textit{seq}}\ X \mid s^{-1} \in X \twoheadrightarrow \mathbb{N}\}$$

We shall not introduce a special notation for non-repetitive sequences, but we shall add one of the above predicates as a constraint when we declare a sequence and intend it to have no repetitions.

4.4 Extending the Z basic library

The notations introduced so far are all part of the Z **basic library**, that is to say they are built in to the Z language. Z allows the writer of documents to extend the mathematical language in various ways, and we shall explore some of them in this section.

4.4.1 Axiomatic descriptions

New functions, relations etc. on values of existing types can be introduced by an **axiomatic description** as follows.

$$
\begin{array}{|l}
max: \mathbb{Z} \times \mathbb{Z} \rightarrow \mathbb{Z} \\
\hline
\forall m, n: \mathbb{Z} \bullet \\
((m \geq n \land max(m, n) = m) \\
\lor (n \geq m \land max(m, n) = n))
\end{array}
$$

The first part of this description declares the new name *max* to be the name of a total function that takes a pair of integers for its arguments and has an integer for its value. The second part of the description is the predicate that fixes the value of *max* for any two integers as arguments. The function might have defined by a syntactic equivalence:

$$
\begin{aligned}
max == \{m, n, p: \mathbb{Z} \mid p \geq m \land p \geq n \land (p = m \lor p = n) \\
\bullet (m \mapsto n) \mapsto p\}
\end{aligned}
$$

An axiomatic description need not fix the value of the thing declared. In fact, in the class manager's assistant, the declaration

$$
\begin{array}{|l}
size: \mathbb{N}
\end{array}
$$

was an axiomatic description that might have been presented thus:

$$
\begin{array}{|l}
size: \mathbb{Z} \\
\hline
size \geq 0
\end{array}
$$

If we wish to show in a declaration that a function symbol is to be used as an infix notation, we use underscores as **place holders** in the definition, as follows:

$$
\begin{array}{|l}
\_ \sim \_: \mathbb{N} \times \mathbb{N} \rightarrow \mathbb{N} \\
\hline
\forall x, y: \mathbb{N} \bullet x \sim y = x^2 + y^2
\end{array}
$$

This declaration introduces '$\sim$' as an infix notation for a total function that for any pair of natural numbers as arguments has a value that is the sum of the squares of the numbers.

4.4.2 Generic definitions

The definition

$$X \rightarrow Y == \{f: X \nrightarrow Y \mid \mathbf{dom}\, f = X\}$$

is a syntactic equivalence that is generic with respect to the sets X and Y. These generic parameters appear explicitly on the left-hand side of the definition. Another instance of a syntactic equivalence with generic parameters is the following:

$$smallset[X] == \{xs: \mathbb{P}X \mid \# xs \leq 1\}$$

This definition introduces *smallset* as a name for all the sets of things of a certain kind that are empty or singletons. The 'certain kind' is represented by X, and to use *smallset* in a specification we would have to supply some set value for X. For instance if we use $\mathbb{N}$ for X we would write

$$smallset[\mathbb{N}]$$

and this would represent the set

$$\{\varnothing, \{0\}, \{1\}, \dots\}$$

which contains the empty set of natural numbers, and all the singleton sets of natural numbers. The supplied set might be quite small, so

$$smallset[\{0, 1\}] = \{\varnothing, \{0\}, \{1\}\}$$

Sometimes a more elaborate scheme of generic definition is required. For instance, the notion of function overriding cannot conveniently be defined with a syntactic equivalence, since the notion of $f \oplus g$ is generic not with respect to f and g, but rather with respect to the from-set and to-set of these functions.

The following example shows how function overriding might be introduced if it were not in the Z basic library.

```
=[X, Y]==========================================
| _ ⊕ _: ((X ⇸ Y) × (X ⇸ Y)) → (X ⇸ Y)
|-----------------
| ∀f, g: X ⇸ Y • f ⊕ g = g ∪ ((dom g) ⩤ f)
---------------------------------------------------
```

The definition begins by naming the generic parameters in square brackets. The declaration shows that the symbol being defined is to be used as an infix notation. The function '$\oplus$' is a total function that takes any two functions of the same type as its arguments, and has a function of the same type as its value. The predicate defines the value of $f \oplus g$ for any two functions f and g of type $\mathbb{P}(X \times Y)$.

We next have an example of a generic definition that introduces a function of use in handling sequences. The need for this function arises as follows. Suppose we wish to remove certain elements from a sequence s of elements of type X, and the elements to be removed are those whose positions are the numbers in a certain set *nset* of natural numbers. The expression

$$\{nset\} \ntriangleleft s$$

looks at first sight as if it would do to denote the new sequence, but unfortunately it is not a sequence, since its domain is not *1..n* for some natural number n – it might have holes in it. We need some means of condensing a sequence with holes into a proper sequence, and the following function will do it.

$$
\begin{array}{l}
[X] \\
\hline
squash: (\mathbb{N} \nrightarrow X) \nrightarrow \mathbf{seq}\ X \\
\hline
(\ \forall f: \mathbb{N} \nrightarrow X \\
\mid (\ \exists n: \mathbb{N} \bullet (\ \forall m: \mathbf{dom}\ f \bullet n > m\ )\ ) \\
\bullet (\ (\ f = \varnothing \wedge squash\ f = \langle\rangle\ ) \\
\quad \vee (\ \exists least: \mathbf{dom}\ f \\
\quad\quad \mid (\ \forall m: \mathbf{dom}\ f \bullet least \leq m\ ) \\
\quad\quad \bullet\ squash\ f = \langle f\ least \rangle \ \hat{}\ squash\ (\{least\} \ntriangleleft f))\ )\ )
\end{array}
$$

Notice that the function *squash* is not total, and the universal quantification below the line has a constraint that limits the domain to those functions that are finite. The definition says that the squash of a sequence-with-holes is the same as the concatenation of the sequence of the first member of the sequence-with-holes with the squash of the rest. Thus this is a **recursive** definition, that is to say the definition of *squash* relies in one of its cases on an expression in which *squash* appears. Readers can convince themselves of the validity of this definition technique in particular cases with simple examples. An investigation of which recursive definitions are sound is beyond the scope of this book. Spivey (1989) has more information under 'finitary constructions'.

Lastly, we make precise the notion that a family of sets **partition** a larger set, i.e. that their union is the larger set, and no two sets of the family have a member in common. In the following generic definition, the relation *partitions* is defined. The family of sets is indexed, that is to say the members of the family are identified by being associated with the members of another set. The notion of an indexed family of sets is made precise in the declaration of *partitions* by saying that the sets in the family are the second members of pairs in a function.

$$
\begin{array}{l}
[X, Y] \\
\hline
\_\ partitions\ \_: (X \pfun \mathbb{P}\ Y) \leftrightarrow \mathbb{P}\ Y \\
\hline
\forall f: X \pfun \mathbb{P}\ Y;\ ys: \mathbb{P}\ Y \\
\bullet\ (\ f\ partitions\ ys \Leftrightarrow \\
\qquad (\ ys = \{y: Y \mid \exists x: X \bullet y \in f\ x\} \\
\qquad \wedge\ (\forall x_1, x_2: \mathbf{dom}\ f \mid x_1 \neq x_2 \bullet (f\ x_1) \cap (f\ x_2) = \varnothing)\ )\ )
\end{array}
$$

As an instance of partitioning consider the library management system, where each borrower has a set (possibly empty) of books on loan. The collection of such sets is an indexed family of sets, the borrowers serving as the index. This family of sets partitions the set *on-loan*.

The reader might notice that many of the notions introduced informally in Chapters 3 and 4 might have been defined using generic and axiomatic descriptions in terms of a few basic notions like set membership, ordered pair, natural number etc. This approach to defining the mathematical notation is used in Spivey (1989). Strictly speaking, a generic definition like the definition of overriding above introduces not just one new symbol '$\oplus$', but a whole family of symbols, different members of the family having different values for the generic parameters. If

$$f, g: Book \pfun Person \qquad (29, 29)$$

then the overriding of f by g should be expressed by some such notation as

$$f \oplus[Book, Person]\ g \qquad (29, 29)$$

to make precise which of the many members of the override symbol family is meant. However, the context, in the shape of the types of f and g, is sufficient to establish which override symbol we mean, so we permit **overloading** of the override symbol, allowing it to serve for any member of the family. Without overloading, the notation would become very cumbersome: overloaded symbols so far introduced include '$\cup$', '$\cap$' and '$\subseteq$', and there are many others.

Exercises

(4.1) List the domain and range of the relation *is_a_parent_of* illustrated in Figure 4.2 on p. 74.

(4.2) Let the set *Phenomenon* of phenomena be given, and let the binary relation *cause_of* be defined on it, so $(p_1 \mapsto p_2)$ is an ordered pair in the relation *cause_of* if phenomenon p_1 is the cause of phenomenon p_2. Write down a predicate to express the theorem of Saint Thomas Aquinas that there exists a unique phenomenon g that is a cause of other phenomena but has itself no cause.

(4.3) List the relation *is_a_parent_of* from Figure 4.2 on p. 74 when domain restricted to the set $S\_of\_E == \{V, E, G\}$.

(4.4) List the relation *is_a_parent_of* from Figure 4.2 on p. 74 when range subtracted by the set $S\_of\_E == \{V, E, G\}$.

(4.5) Suppose *Man* and *Occasion* are types for men and occasions, and suppose that $D{:}Man \leftrightarrow Occasion$ is a relation between men and occasions recording the occasions on which the men were deceivers. Formalize the statement 'Men were deceivers ever':

(a) as an equality between sets

(b) and as a universal quantification.

(c) Write down also the negation of the universal quantification, expressing it as an existential quantification.

(Compare your last answer with the informal expression on p. 44.)

(4.6) Suppose *NiceGirl* is the set of all nice girls, *Sailor* is the set of all sailors, and *loves* is a relation between nice girls and sailors such that *n loves s* means that nice girl *n* loves sailor *s*. Make precise the sentence 'All the nice girls love a sailor' to expose at least two distinct meanings of this ambiguous utterance.

(4.7) Write down an expression for the set of library books on loan to person *p*. What does your expression denote if *p* is not a member of *borrowers*? Write down a predicate to formalize the requirement that no one shall be allowed to have more than eight books on loan.

In the banking system, part of which was introduced in the exercises to Chapter 3, the balance in each account is recorded by a partial function

$$balance: AcctNo \rightarrow\!\!\!\!\!\!+ \mathbb{Z} \qquad (271)$$

where integers are used to record sums of money.

(4.8) If *acno*: *AcctNo* is in the domain of *balance*, say what the type is of each of the following terms.

(a) $acno \mapsto 1000$

(b) *balance acno*

(c) **dom** *balance*

(d) **ran** *balance*

(e) $depositors \lhd balance$

(f) $balance \rhd \mathbb{N}$

(4.9) Write down a predicate to formalize the statement 'the active accounts are those for which there are balances'.

(4.10) Write down a predicate to formalize the statement 'overdrawn accounts are those accounts that have negative balances'.

(4.11) Write down an expression for the set of account numbers of deposit accounts with balances exceeding 100000.

(4.12) The bank keeps details of its customers, and *Customer* is the given set of customer details.

[*Customer*]

$$details: AcctNo \rightarrow\!\!\!\!\!\!+ Customer \qquad (271, 97)$$

is the relation that gives the customer details for a given account number. Formalize the rule that the active accounts and those for which there are customer details are the same.

(4.13) If *c*: *Customer* is a particular customer, write down an expression for the account numbers associated with *c*.

(4.14) In formalizing the operations of a building society, the following types are introduced representing different kinds of account.

[*Mortgage*, *Deposit*, *HighInterest*]

In addition there is a special account, attracting no interest, which is used to rectify cash shortages or surpluses at the end of a day's business. Write a data type definition of a new type *Account* that includes the special account and the three other types. Invent your own name for special account and the constructor functions.

(4.15) Recall the definitions of non-repeating sequences, and use mathematical induction to prove that

$$\vdash \forall s: \mathbf{seq}\ X \bullet (\ s^{-1} \in X \rightarrowtail \mathbb{N} \Rightarrow \#\, s = \#\, \mathbf{ran}\ s\ )$$

(4.16) Write an axiomatic description of a function

$$sum\_of: (AcctNo \rightarrowtail \mathbb{Z}) \rightarrow \mathbb{Z} \qquad (271)$$

that gives the sum of all the balances in any function relating account numbers to integers.

(4.17) Using the function *sum_of* defined in the previous question, write down an expression for the total of all the balances of accounts of customer *c*.

(4.18) A function *min* takes two integers as arguments and has the smaller of them for its value.

(a) Write an axiomatic description of this function.

(b) Write also a syntactic equivalence that would declare the same function.

(4.19) Write an axiomatic description of a function *mins* that takes a non-empty set of natural numbers for its argument, and has the smallest natural number in the set for its value. (You may use the function *min* of the previous question if it seems appropriate.)

(4.20) Define *duni* (distributed union), a function that takes as its argument a set of sets of the same type and has as its value the union of all the sets. Define also *dint* (distributed intersection) in a similar way.

(4.21) Define the notion that one sequence is a permutation of another.

(4.22) Write a definition of distributed concatenation, a function that takes a sequence of sequences as its argument, and has as its value their concatenation. For instance if the argument is

$$\langle\langle 1, 5, 9\rangle, \langle 2, 8\rangle, \langle 3, 5, 1\rangle\rangle$$

the value is

$$\langle 1, 5, 9, 2, 8, 3, 5, 1\rangle$$

(4.23) Define the set of all palindromes of values of a given type. (A sequence is a palindrome if it is the same backwards as forwards.)

(4.24) Write a generic definition of the **relational image** notation, using the following example as a guide.

A function $f: X \nrightarrow Y$ is given, and A is a set of values of type X. The relational image of A under f is the set of values of type Y that are related by f to any value in A. The notation for this set is

$$f (\!| A |\!)$$

and the signs '$(\!|$' and '$|\!)$' are the relational image brackets.

Chapter 5
Schemas and specifications

Summary: Scope of names – schemas – declaration part – predicate part – signature and property – abstract states – abstract operations – decoration and inclusion – notation conventions – initialization – schema conjunction – precondition calculation – schema implication – schema equivalence – schema quantifiers – schema types and bindings – hiding – schema names in mathematical expressions – promotion – schema piping – renaming – schema composition – hints for writers – inspecting and validating specifications.

In this chapter we study the library system further, showing how to construct a Z specification from informally stated requirements. The class manager's assistant is used to illustrate techniques for building larger specifications from small ones.

5.1 The nature of a schema

5.1.1 Scope of names in a Z specification

So far we have used declarations of various kinds to introduce names, and have constructed expressions to denote new terms, and predicates to express properties of the values of the names declared. All this has been done in a relatively unstructured way; now we propose to use schemas to impose structure on the declarations and predicates.

First we must observe that there will be in any Z specification a number of names that are not confined inside schemas:

- names of given sets
- names introduced by syntactic equivalence
- names introduced by axiomatic description
- names introduced by generic definition
- names of data types
- names of schemas

These declarations are called **global declarations**. Names introduced in global declarations are called **global variables**.

5.1.2 What is a schema?

A **schema** is a piece of mathematical text that specifies some aspect of the software system we are discussing. A schema contains a **declaration part**, and a **predicate part**. The declaration part declares some variables – these are **local declarations** – and the predicate part expresses some requirements about the values of the variables.

The name of a schema will be used elsewhere in the document to refer to the mathematical text. The writing of specifications often involves reusing the same notion many times, and the use of names for notions improves the readability of specification documents, and reduces the errors that arise when one specification is copied in other contexts. In the class manager's assistant, the notion of a class was such a notion that was needed several times in the specification. It was defined once, and then reused by name to help in the specification of the initial value, and of the effects of the various operations in the class manager's interface. In this book schema names will always begin with a capital letter, and so will be cross-referenced in accordance with the convention described on p. 13.

A schema may be written in a vertical or a horizontal format. The former is preferred if there are more than a very few declarations and predicates. First we illustrate the vertical form. If *Userid* and *Password* are given sets, the following schema might be part of a specification of an operating system component that keeps track of the passwords of users, and which of them are logged on.

```
┌─ Time_sharing ──────────────────────────
│ password: Userid ⇸ Password
│ logged_on: ℙ Userid
├──────────
│ logged_on ⊆ dom password
└─────────────────────────────────────────
```

The variables *password* and *logged_on* in the declaration part are called the **components** of the schema *Time_sharing*.

The following schema has only one component, and it is convenient to present its definition in horizontal form.

$$Res \mathrel{\widehat{=}} [w\colon Title \nrightarrow \mathbf{seq}\ Person \mid \forall sp\colon \mathbf{ran}\ w \bullet sp \neq \langle\rangle] \qquad (72, 29)$$

The sign '$\widehat{=}$' is used for schema definition in the horizontal form. The signs '[' and ']' are **schema brackets**.

If *Res* were written in vertical form it would be as follows.

```
┌─ Res ───────────────────────────────────
│ w: Title ⇸ seq Person                          (72, 29)
├──────────
│ ∀sp: ran w • sp ≠ ⟨⟩
└─────────────────────────────────────────
```

The schema definition is in fact a declaration. It declares the schema name, and associates it with a type characterized by the names and types introduced in the declaration part. We shall say more about the type of a schema later. A schema is a term in the language of Z.

Some rules about what might be written in the declaration and predicate parts are presented next.

5.1.3 The declaration part

The declaration part introduces some names and establishes their types. To establish the types of the names we can use any names of sets that are globally declared. These sets can be used in any of the constructions that yield set values, such as

- power set
- union, intersection etc.
- Cartesian product

- relation, function etc.
- domain, range etc.

Thus the declaration part of *Reservations* is valid provided that the names *Title* and *Person* are names of sets introduced into the specification by global declarations. No significance is attached to the order of the declarations in the declaration part.

The following schema draws together several ideas from the library management system.

```
┌─Library──────────────────────────────────────
│ on_loan, on_shelves, books: ℙ Book                  (29)
│ borrowers: ℙ Person                                 (29)
│ lent_to: Book ⇸ Person                          (29, 29)
├──────────
│ ...
└──────────────────────────────────────────────
```

In this declaration part the names *on_loan*, *on_shelves*, *books*, and *borrowers* are declared to be set values, but they are not known in the declaration part of this schema, and cannot be used there. The notions that

(1) the books that are associated with borrowers in *lent_to* are exactly the books in *on-loan*, and

(2) the persons associated with books in *lent_to* must all be members of *borrowers*,

cannot be formalized by declaring

lent_to: *on_loan* → *borrowers*,

but must be formalized in the predicate part, as explained below.

5.1.4 The predicate part

The predicate part of a schema defines conditions that constrain the values declared in the declaration part. The names used in the construction of predicates must be either

- globally declared, or
- declared in the declaration part of this schema.

In the *Library* schema, the predicate part was omitted. It is in the predicate part that we should write predicates that express the sort of constraints that were discussed in previous chapters. In presenting the schema we should provide enough informal text to set the scene and to explain the constraints in terms that the librarian can understand and agree with.

$$
\begin{array}{|l}
\multicolumn{1}{l}{\_Library\_\_\_\_\_\_\_\_\_\_\_\_\_\_\_\_\_\_\_\_} \\
on\_loan, on\_shelves, books: \mathbb{P}\ Book \qquad (29) \\
borrowers: \mathbb{P}\ Person \qquad (29) \\
lent\_to: Book \nrightarrow Person \qquad (29, 29) \\
\hline
on\_loan = \mathbf{dom}\ lent\_to \\
\mathbf{ran}\ lent\_to \subseteq borrowers \\
on\_loan \cup on\_shelves = books \\
on\_loan \cap on\_shelves = \varnothing \\
\hline
\end{array}
$$

In writing several predicates on separate lines it is to be understood that conjunction is meant, since we want these four requirements to be met. The following informal explanation of the predicates should be provided:

- The books on loan are exactly those for which we have a record of a borrower.
- Books can only be recorded as having been lent to known borrowers.
- Every book belonging to the library is either on loan or on the shelves.
- No book can be recorded as being on loan and on the shelves.

Some readers might observe that the size of this schema could be reduced by omitting *on_loan*, since this is just the domain of *lent_to*. Also the component *on_shelves* could be omitted, since it is just the books not in the domain of *lent_to*. This simplification is possible, but it is not essential. We are not so much interested in the most compact expression of the model as in the model the librarian finds most friendly. Redundancy among the components of the state schema can help to establish the important notions of the system we are specifying, and can help to convince the librarian that we have understood his or her requirements. Redundancy does, however, mean that we have more in the predicate part of the schema.

The relationship between the given sets and the components of the schema is illustrated in Figure 5.1.

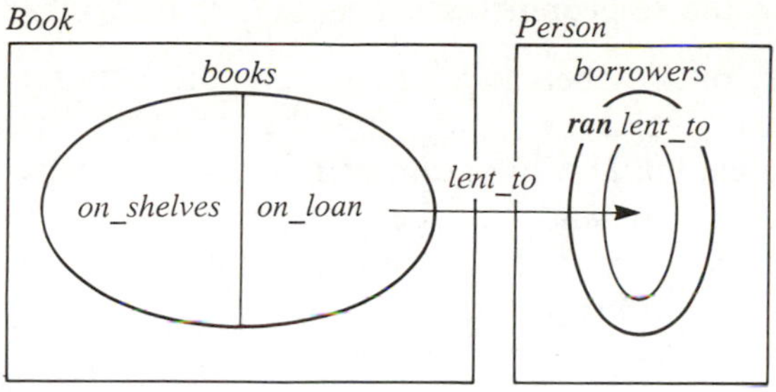

Figure 5.1 Sets and relations for the library.

5.1.5 Implicit predicates

Although the declaration of *lent_to* above uses the notation $Book \rightarrowtail\!\!\!\!\!+ Person$ in the place we might expect to find the type, the actual type of *lent_to* is $\mathbb{P}(Book \times Person)$. The function property of this relation is not expressed in a predicate that is written in the predicate part, but the declaration forces that predicate to be there, though it is implicit rather than explicit. When using the predicate part of *Library* to reason about the library system, we must remember to include in our reasoning the predicate

$$(\forall b\text{: } Book;\ p_1, p_2\text{: } Person \bullet ((lent\_to\ b = p_1 \wedge lent\_to\ b = p_2) \Rightarrow p_1 = p_2)) \qquad (29, 29)$$

or its abbreviation

$$lent\_to \in Book \nrightarrow Person \qquad (29, 29)$$

The *Class* schema on p. 14 has the following implicit predicates:

$$enrolled \in \mathbb{P}\ Student \qquad (14)$$

$$tested \in \mathbb{P}\ Student \qquad (14)$$

and the whole specification has an implicit predicate

$$size \geq 0$$

5.1.6 Signatures and properties

The **signature** of a schema is an association between the names declared in the declaration part and the types of the values that those names denote. The signature of a schema is closely related to the declaration part, since the declaration part tells us the names explicitly, and the types can be deduced from the declarations. Thus the signature of *Library* is the following association between names and types.

$$on\_loan: \mathbb{P}\ Book \qquad (29)$$
$$on\_shelves: \mathbb{P}\ Book \qquad (29)$$
$$books: \mathbb{P}\ Book \qquad (29)$$
$$borrowers: \mathbb{P}\ Person \qquad (29)$$
$$lent\_to: \mathbb{P}\ (Book \times Person) \qquad (29, 29)$$

The **property** of a schema is a predicate that is obtained from the predicate part of a schema together with the predicates implicit in the declaration part. The property of *Library* is thus the following predicate.

$$
\begin{array}{ll}
(\ on\_loan \in \mathbb{P}\ Book & (29) \\
\land\ on\_shelves \in \mathbb{P}\ Book & (29) \\
\land\ books \in \mathbb{P}\ Book & (29) \\
\land\ borrowers \in \mathbb{P}\ Person & (29) \\
\land\ lent\_to \in Book \mathrel{+\!\!\!\rightarrow} Person & (29, 29) \\
\land\ on\_loan = \mathbf{dom}\ lent\_to & \\
\land\ \mathbf{ran}\ lent\_to \subseteq borrowers & \\
\land\ on\_loan \cup on\_shelves = books & \\
\land\ on\_loan \cap on\_shelves = \varnothing\ ) &
\end{array}
$$

Although in writing down a schema we display a declaration part and a predicate part, the essential characteristics of a schema are its signature and its property.

5.2 States and operations

5.2.1 Schemas describe data states

A schema can be used to describe the **abstract state** of an abstract data type when the state machine model is used. The signature and the property together describe the **data space**. The property is sometimes called the **data invariant**. The data space is the set of all possible **data states** for the abstract data type. If we consider the *Library* schema as defining an abstract state, then each row in Table 5.1

describes a possible state, and therefore each row describes a member of the data space of *Library*. (We shall assume that *jel* and *kl* are distinct values of type *Book*, and *js* and *mm* are distinct values of type *Person*.)

Table 5.1 Data states of an abstract data type.

	on_loan	*on_shelves*	*books*	*borrowers*	*lent_to*
(1)	$\varnothing$	$\varnothing$	$\varnothing$	$\varnothing$	$\varnothing$
(2)	$\varnothing$	$\{jel\}$	$\{jel\}$	$\varnothing$	$\varnothing$
(3)	$\{jel\}$	$\{kl\}$	$\{jel, kl\}$	$\{js, mm\}$	$\{jel \mapsto mm\}$

To verify this we need to check for each row of the table that

- the values given are of the type established in the signature of *Library*, and
- the values satisfy the property.

5.2.2 Informal requirements for the library – phase 1

The library management system that has formed the basis of some of the examples of the use of Z is to be delivered in phases. The informal requirements for the first phase are to allow the librarian:

- to add books to the library;
- to add borrowers to the library;
- to remove books from the library, i.e. to dispose of them so that they are no longer available for borrowing;
- to remove borrowers from the library, i.e. revoke a person's permission to borrow books;
- to record that a book has been lent to a borrower; and
- to record that a book has been returned.

Books will be identified by bar codes fixed to the inside cover. No two books will have the same bar code, though old codes might be reused when a book is disposed of. There will be bar code readers at the borrowing and returning counters. Borrowers will be identified by numbers encoded on a magnetic stripe on a borrower's card. There will be a magnetic stripe reader at the borrowing counter. The informal requirements include the following tabular description of the operations.

Table 5.2 Informal description of library operations for phase 1.

Inputs	**Processing**	**Outputs**
Add a book		
book	If the book is already in the library, then the response is 'Book already in library'. If this is a new book, the book is added to the library, and the response is 'Book added'.	response
Add a borrower		
person	If the person is already a borrower, then the response is 'This person is already a borrower'. If the person is not already a borrower, then the response is 'Borrower added'.	response
Delete a book		
book	If the book is not owned by the library, then the response is 'Not a library book'. If the book is owned by the library, but is marked as on loan, then the response is 'Return this book first'. Otherwise the book is removed from the records, and the response is 'Book deleted'.	response
Delete a borrower		
person	If the person is not a borrower, then the response is 'This person is not a borrower'. If the person is a borrower, but has books on loan, the response is 'This borrower has books on loan'. Otherwise the person is removed from the borrowers, and the response is 'Borrower deleted'.	response
Lend a book		
book, person	If the person is not a borrower, then the response is 'This person is not a borrower'. If the book is not one owned by the library, then the response is 'Not a library book'. If the book is believed to be on loan already, the response is 'Return this book first'. Otherwise the book is recorded as being lent to the person borrowing it, and the response is 'Book lent to borrower'.	response

Inputs	Processing	Outputs
Return a book		
book	If the book is not one owned by the library, then the response is 'Not a library book'. If the book is owned by the library, but is recorded as being on the shelves, then the response is 'Not on loan'. Otherwise the book is recorded as being on the shelves, the record of its being lent is removed, and the response is 'Book is now returned'.	response

The informal description leaves a good many questions unanswered, and these should be investigated with the person providing the requirements. For what follows, the reader must suppose that the research has been well done, and that the questions have been answered in the way described.

5.2.3 Schemas describe operations

We shall use the *Library* schema defined above as the state on which to formalize the requirements for the operations. An operation on an abstract state will be called an **abstract operation.**

To deal with adding a book to the library we need to give names for the input (the book to be added), the output (the response to be produced) and the values of the components of *Library* before and after the operation. We shall build a schema in which these names appear in the declaration part, and we shall specify the required relationship between the values in the predicate part. The following conventions about names must be introduced now.

- Undashed names like *on_shelves* are used to denote the values of the components of the state before the operation, the **starting state.**
- Dashed names like *on_shelves'* are used to denote the values of the same components of the state after the operation, the **ending state.**
- Names like *s?* with a ? at the end are used to denote the values of inputs to the operation.
- Names like *r!* with a ! at the end are used to denote the values of outputs from the operation.

Now we present a specification of one aspect of the operation to add a book to the library. The schema *Add_book_to_library_ok* looks rather big at first sight, but we shall show later in this chapter how its bulk can be reduced without sacrificing any essential material.

The first six lines in the declaration part introduce names for the values of the state components before and after the operation. The next two lines document the requirement for one input, the book, and one output, the response. (No definition is given of the type *LMSResponse*. Defining the type is part of one of the exercises at the end of this chapter.)

Add_book_to_library_ok

$$\begin{array}{ll}
on_loan, on_shelves, books: \mathbb{P}\ Book & (29) \\
borrowers: \mathbb{P}\ Person & (29) \\
lent_to: Book \pfun Person & (29, 29) \\
on_loan', on_shelves', books': \mathbb{P}\ Book & (29) \\
borrowers': \mathbb{P}\ Person & (29) \\
lent_to': Book \pfun Person & (29, 29) \\
b?: Book & (29) \\
r!: LMSResponse &
\end{array}$$

$$\begin{array}{l}
on_loan = \mathbf{dom}\ lent_to \\
\mathbf{ran}\ lent_to \subseteq borrowers \\
on_loan \cup on_shelves = books \\
on_loan \cap on_shelves = \emptyset \\
on_loan' = \mathbf{dom}\ lent_to' \\
\mathbf{ran}\ lent_to' \subseteq borrowers' \\
on_loan' \cup on_shelves' = books' \\
on_loan' \cap on_shelves' = \emptyset \\
b? \notin books \\
on_loan' = on_loan \\
on_shelves' = on_shelves \cup \{b?\} \\
borrowers' = borrowers \\
lent_to' = lent_to \\
r! = book_added
\end{array}$$

The first eight predicates are just the data invariant on the starting state and on the ending state. The remaining predicates are interpreted as follows.

- $b? \notin books$ – In this schema we are describing only that aspect of the behaviour that is observed when the book being added is genuinely new, and not already owned by the library.
- $on\_loan' = on\_loan$ – It is a requirement that the set of books that are on loan shall not change.
- $on\_shelves' = on\_shelves \cup \{b?\}$ – The new book is added to the set of books that are on the shelves.
- $borrowers' = borrowers$ – There is no change to the borrowers.
- $lent\_to' = lent\_to$ – There is no change in the relation between the books on loan and the people who have borrowed them.
- $r! = book\_added$ – The response is 'Book added', though we have invented a formal name for the message that will be displayed to the operator.

The first of these predicates concerns only the input value and the starting state. It is called a **precondition** of the schema. It says something about the situation that must obtain before the operation can behave in this way.

The remaining predicates concern input, output and ending state. These are called **postconditions** of the schema. They say something about the the situation that must obtain after the operation has behaved in this way.

Nothing is said about the value of *books'*. Is this a mistake in the specification? The requirement is clearly

$$books' = books \cup \{b?\}$$

but this is not documented. In fact we can prove this from predicates that are documented. We state a theorem:

$$Add\_book\_to\_library\_ok \vdash books' = books \cup \{b?\} \qquad (110)$$

This theorem illustrates the use of a schema name as hypothesis. It states that taking the signature and property of *Add_book_to_library_ok* as hypothesis, we can prove the conclusion about *books'*. We might document the proof as follows:

(1)	$books' = on\_shelves' \cup on\_loan'$	From *Add_book_to_library_ok*
(2)	$on\_shelves' = on\_shelves \cup \{b?\}$	From *Add_book_to_library_ok*
(3)	$on\_loan' = on\_loan$	From *Add_book_to_library_ok*

(4)	*books*' = (*on_shelves* ∪ {*b?*}) ∪ *on_loan*	From (1), (2) and (3)
(5)	*books*' = *on_loan* ∪ (*on_shelves* ∪ {*b?*})	From (4), using commutative property of set union
(6)	*books*' = (*on_loan* ∪ *on_shelves*) ∪ {*b?*}	From (5), using associativity of set union
(7)	*books* = *on_shelves* ∪ *on_loan*	From *Add_book_to_library_ok*
(8)	*books* = *on_loan* ∪ *on_shelves*	From (7) using commutative property of set union
(9)	*books*' = *books* ∪ {*b?*}	From (6) and (8)

The predicate about *books*' is redundant, but there is no harm in adding it to the appropriate schemas.

The above proof has been done in small steps that have involved

- copying predicates from the hypothesis,
- replacing names by expressions that are equal to them according to earlier predicates, and
- using simple properties of set notation from an earlier chapter.

A briefer presentation might have glossed over the set notation properties, and reduced to items (1)–(4), (7) and (9) in the above table. In copying predicates from the hypothesis, we have been selective about which predicates we used. Several predicates in the hypothesis have not been used at all. Which ones to use have been arrived at largely by inspiration. It is possible to write them all down and then delete the ones that do not get used in the argument.

The operation *Add_book_to_library_ok* is partial, that is to say it is only possible when $b? \notin books$. If we were to offer this as the operation to add a book, it would be the operator's responsibility to make sure that the book was not already owned by the library. However, the librarian requires a more friendly operation than this. The behaviour in other circumstances of the operation to add a book will be specified in other schemas, and then combined with this one.

5.3 Aids to presentation

The schema *Add_book_to_library_ok* is very cluttered with information that is important to know, but not to see. We now look at some conventions that can reduce the amount we see, and draw attention to the main points of the behaviour being described.

5.3.1 Schema decoration

The first convention is called **schema decoration**. It provides a systematic way of introducing the dashed names of the components of a schema together with the data invariant on them. Under this convention, *Library'* is the name of a schema that has for its declaration part the declaration part of *Library* with a dash on the end of all the names declared.

$$on\_loan', on\_shelves', books' : \mathbb{P}\ Book \qquad (29)$$
$$borrowers' : \mathbb{P}\ Person \qquad (29)$$
$$lent\_to' : Book \nrightarrow Person \qquad (29, 29)$$

Note that the decoration is applied only to the names being declared in the declaration part. The global names (*Book*, *Person*) are unaffected. The predicate part of *Library'* is the predicate part of *Library* with dashes on the names from the declaration part.

$$on\_loan' = \mathbf{dom}\ lent\_to'$$
$$\mathbf{ran}\ lent\_to' \subseteq borrowers'$$
$$on\_loan' \cup on\_shelves' = books'$$
$$on\_loan' \cap on\_shelves' = \emptyset$$

Signs other than '' can be used as decorators of schema names with similar effect:

- exclamation *!*
- query *?*
- subscript digits $_0 \ldots _9$

5.3.2 Schema inclusion

The schema *Add_book_to_library_ok* could have been simplified by reusing the schemas *Library* and *Library'* in the following manner.

Add_book_to_library_ok

$Library$ (104)
$Library'$ (104)
$b?: Book$ (29)
$r!: LMSResponse$

$b? \notin books$
$on\_loan' = on\_loan$
$on\_shelves' = on\_shelves \cup \{b?\}$
$borrowers' = borrowers$
$lent\_to' = lent\_to$
$r! = book\_added$

This technique of reusing the name of one schema in the declaration part of another is called **schema inclusion**. When a schema is included in the declaration part of another, it brings all its declarations into the declaration part of the new schema. Its effect on the predicate part of the new schema will be described later. Consider the following two schemas.

Books_in_library

$books, on\_shelves, lent: \mathbb{P}\ Book$ (29)

$lent \subseteq books$

Books_lent

$lent: \mathbb{P}\ Book$ (29)
$lent\_to: Book \twoheadrightarrow Person$ (29, 29)

$lent = \mathbf{dom}\ lent\_to$

We can form a schema including *Books_in_library* and *Books_lent*. The declaration of *lent* will appear once only in the declaration part of the new schema. Suppose, however, we had

Titles_lent

$lent: \mathbb{P}\ Title$ (29)
$lent\_to: Title \leftrightarrow Person$ (72, 29)

$lent = \mathbf{dom}\ lent\_to$

Then a new schema including *Books_in_library* and *Titles_lent* is not possible, since the declarations of *lent* conflict. In attempting schema inclusions we must observe the rule that multiple declarations of the same name must establish the same type for it. This is not to say the declarations must be identical. For instance

$x: \mathbb{N} \quad x: \mathbb{Z}$

are compatible – they both establish $\mathbb{Z}$ as the type of x. Similarly

$s: \mathbf{seq}\ \mathbb{N} \quad s: \mathbb{Z} \nrightarrow \mathbb{Z}$

are compatible – they both establish $\mathbb{P}\ (\mathbb{Z} \times \mathbb{Z})$ as the type of s.

Now we look at the effect of inclusion on the predicate part of the new schema. The predicates of the included schemas (including the implicit predicates) are simply added to the list in the conjunction. The existence of implicit predicates should not be forgotten. Thus the inclusion of

$x: \mathbb{N} \quad x: \mathbb{Z}$

is equivalent to $x: \mathbb{N}$, since the first declaration brings the implicit predicate $x \geq 0$. Similarly the inclusion of

$s: \mathbf{seq}\ \mathbb{N} \quad s: \mathbb{Z} \nrightarrow \mathbb{Z}$

is equivalent to $s: \mathbf{seq}\ \mathbb{N}$, since the first declaration brings in all the predicates that limit s to being a sequence of natural numbers:

$s \in \mathbb{P}\ (\mathbb{Z} \times \mathbb{Z})$

$\exists n: \mathbb{N} \bullet \mathbf{dom}\ s = 1..n$

$\forall r: \mathbf{ran}\ s \bullet r \geq 0$

5.3.3 The Delta convention

Another simplification is achieved by abbreviating the inclusion of *Library* and *Library*' to the single name *ΔLibrary*. This notation is called the **Delta convention**. Note that the sign 'Δ' is part of the name of the schema, and not an operator on *Library*. This is the form in which the specification of *Add_book_to_library_ok* should appear in a Z document:

$$
\begin{array}{|l}
\hline
\textit{Add\_book\_to\_library\_ok} \\
\Delta Library \qquad (104) \\
b?: Book \qquad (29) \\
r!: LMSResponse \\
\hline
b? \notin books \\
on\_loan' = on\_loan \\
on\_shelves' = on\_shelves \cup \{b?\} \\
borrowers' = borrowers \\
lent\_to' = lent\_to \\
r! = book\_added \\
\hline
\end{array}
$$

The reader should review the operations specified in Chapter 2, in particular those on pp. 16 – 18.

5.3.4 Initialization

The value of the library when the library management system is first switched on is called the **abstract initial state**, and it is an important part of the specification. This is specified like an operation that has no before state (i. e. the current state is of no significance in describing the effect of the operation). We define a new schema incorporating the dashed version of *Library* to specify this value.

$$
\begin{array}{|l}
\hline
\textit{Init\_library} \\
Library' \qquad (104) \\
\hline
books' = \varnothing \\
borrowers' = \varnothing \\
\hline
\end{array}
$$

Note that the predicate part of this schema gives values for only two of the five components of the state. Including the *Library*' schema brings in all the predicates of that schema, including the implicit ones, so the values of the other state components can be deduced from the values given explicitly. We have an obligation to show that an abstract initial state exists, as the following theorem asserts.

$$\vdash \exists Library' \bullet Init\_library \qquad (104, 116)$$

This theorem has no hypothesis, and its conclusion is the predicate

$$
\begin{array}{ll}
(\exists on\_loan', on\_shelves', books\colon \mathbb{P}\ Book; & (29) \\
\quad lent\_to'\colon Book \nrightarrow Person; borrowers'\colon \mathbb{P} Person & (29, 29, 29) \\
\mid (on\_loan' = \mathbf{dom}\ lent\_to' & \\
\land\ \mathbf{ran}\ lent\_to' \subseteq borrowers' & \\
\land\ on\_loan' \cup on\_shelves' = books & \\
\land\ on\_loan' \cap on\_shelves' = \varnothing) & \\
\bullet (books' = \varnothing \land borrowers' = \varnothing)) &
\end{array}
$$

which has no free variables. As it is an existential quantification, we need to supply values for *on_loan'*, *on_shelves'*, *books'*, *lent_to'* and *borrowers'* to make the constraint and quantified predicate true. Since *books'* and *borrowers'* are given explicit values we can use the one-point rule. Recalling the observation on p. 52 about the existential quantifier with constraint, we can reduce the conclusion to the following predicate:

$$
\begin{array}{ll}
(\exists on\_loan', on\_shelves'\colon \mathbb{P}\ Book; & (29) \\
\quad lent\_to'\colon Book \nrightarrow Person & (29, 29) \\
\bullet (on\_loan' = \mathbf{dom}\ lent\_to' & \\
\land\ \mathbf{ran}\ lent\_to' \subseteq \varnothing & \\
\land\ on\_loan' \cup on\_shelves' = \varnothing & \\
\land\ on\_loan' \cap on\_shelves' = \varnothing)) &
\end{array}
$$

We now show that this predicate will be true if *on_loan'* and *on_shelves'* are empty sets of books, and *lent_to'* is an empty relation.

(1)	$on\_loan' = \varnothing$	Since $on\_loan' \cup on\_shelves'$ is empty
(2)	$on\_shelves' = \varnothing$	Since $on\_loan' \cup on\_shelves'$ is empty
(3)	$lent\_to' = \varnothing$	Since $\mathbf{ran}\ lent\_to'$ is empty
(4)	$on\_loan' = \mathbf{dom}\ lent\_to'$	From (1) and (3)
(5)	$\mathbf{ran}\ lent\_to' \subseteq \varnothing$	From (3)
(6)	$on\_loan' \cup on\_shelves' = \varnothing$	From (1) and (2)
(8)	$on\_loan' \cap on\_shelves' = \varnothing$	from (1) and (2)

In presenting a specification, the initial value should be specified immediately after the state schema. The existence of an abstract initial state confirms the consistency of the abstract state schema.

5.3.5 The Xi convention

We consider now how to specify what is to happen when an attempt is made to add a book that is already in the library. The schema $\Delta Library$ will provide the variables we need, but the predicate part is to say that the values before are to be the same as the values afterwards. The **Xi convention** gives us a shorthand for such a schema. The declaration part of $\Xi Library$ is the same as the declaration part of $\Delta Library$, but the predicate has, in addition to the predicates of $\Delta Library$, the following:

$$on\_loan' = on\_loan$$
$$borrowers' = borrowers$$
$$on\_shelves' = on\_shelves$$
$$lent\_to' = lent\_to$$

Now we can specify the required behaviour:

Book_already_in_library

$\Xi Library$	(104)
$b?: Book$	(29)
$r!: LMSResponse$	
$b? \in books$	
$r! = book\_already\_in\_library$	

The Xi convention was used in the class manager's assistant on p. 19 in the *Enquire* schema, and subsequently in describing the error responses.

5.4 Schema calculus

5.4.1 Schema disjunction

In order to specify the operation to add a book to the library, we must combine the schemas *Add_book_to_library_ok* and *Book_already_in_library* in such a way that an implementation will be constrained to exhibit the appropriate behaviour – change of state and response – in appropriate circumstances. We will be satisfied if the predicate part of at least one of the schemas is satisfied, so the required construction is similar to disjunction of predicates, and is called **schema disjunction**. We define

$$Add\_book\_to\_library \mathrel{\widehat=}$$
$$Add\_book\_to\_library\_ok \lor Book\_already\_in\_library \quad (116, 118)$$

The sign '$\widehat{=}$' is for schema definition. The sign '$\vee$' is for schema disjunction. The above piece of text is a declaration of the name *Add_book_to_library* to be a schema. The declaration part of a schema disjunction is obtained by merging the declaration parts of the contributing schemas in the manner explained for schema inclusion. (In this case the two schemas have the same declaration part.) The predicate part is obtained by forming the disjunction of the predicate parts of the two schemas. (Remember that each predicate part is usually a conjunction of several predicates, some of which are implicit). Schema disjunction is therefore associative and commutative, like the disjunction of predicates. I forbear from writing out *Add_books_to_library* in full, but draw attention in the following sketch to the main features of the property of the schema.

$$
\begin{array}{l}
(\; (\; b? \notin books \\
\quad \ldots \\
\quad \wedge \; on\_shelves' = on\_shelves \cup \{b?\} \\
\quad \ldots \\
\quad \wedge \; r! = book\_added \\
\quad) \\
\vee \\
\quad (\; b? \in books \\
\quad \ldots \\
\quad \wedge \; on\_shelves' = on\_shelves \\
\quad \ldots \\
\quad \wedge \; r! = book\_already\_in\_library \\
\quad) \\
)
\end{array}
$$

It is the business of an implementation of adding a book to make this predicate true. If the book is new, then the second disjunct (a conjunction beginning $b?{\in}books$) cannot be made true, since $b?{\notin}books$, so the implementation must make the first disjunct true, i.e. it must exhibit the behaviour specified by *Add_book_to_library*. If the book is not new, then the first disjunct (a conjunction beginning $b?{\notin}books$) cannot be made true, since $b?{\in}books$, so the implementation must make the second disjunct true, i.e. it must exhibit the behaviour specified by *Book_already_in_library*. Thus schema disjunction provides exactly the construction we need to specify the operation of adding a book to the library.

Schema disjunction was used in the class manager's assistant on p. 21 in creating the operations from partial operations.

The reader should now see how the rest of the requirements for phase 1 might be formalized in a Z specification, and is invited to write more of the specification in the exercises. Notice that the behaviour that responds 'Not a library book' need only be specified once in a schema, and it can then be reused in several operations.

5.4.2 Informal requirements for the library – phase 2

In the second phase of the library management system we are to support the notion of titles, and provide facilities for finding out what title is associated with a particular book. The titles of books will be represented by character strings of a certain maximum length, but in the specification we will use the given set *Title* introduced in Chapter 4 on p. 72. There are some new requirements for the operations; the existing operations are modified, and a new operation is introduced. Table 5.3 describes the operation to add a book, since the interface now has an extra input parameter. The other operations need modifying to some extent, since the notion of a library in phase 2 is different from the notion of a library in phase 1. The operation to enquire about a book is entirely new.

Table 5.3 Informal description of library operations for phase 2.

Inputs	**Processing**	**Outputs**
Add a book		
book, title	If the book is already in the library, then the response is 'Book already in library'. If this is a new book, the book is added to the library, and the response is 'Book added'.	response
Enquire about a book		
book	If the book is not a library book, the response is 'Not a library book'. If the book is a library book, but not on loan, then the title is displayed, and the response is 'Not on loan'. If the book is a library book, and on loan, then the title and borrower are displayed, and the response is 'On loan'.	title, borrower, response

In specifying the new requirements we reuse as much as possible of the specification of phase 1. We extend the state to cover the relation between books and their titles. We do not rewrite the state schema, but write a new one to describe the new parts of the state.

- *books* is the set of books for which we have title information. It is given the same name as a component of *Library* because we want it to be the same thing when we combine the schemas in a manner to be explained shortly.
- *titles* is the set of titles of which at least one copy exists in the library.
- *title_of* is the relation between books and their titles. It is a partial function, since each book in the library is an instance of exactly one title.

```
┌─ Titles_of_books ──────────────────────────
│ books: ℙ Book                                   (29)
│ titles: ℙ Title                                 (72)
│ title_of: Book ⇸ Title                          (29, 72)
├──────────
│ books = dom title_of
│ titles = ran title_of
└────────────────────────────────────────────
```

Every book in the library has a title associated with it. The set *titles* is just the set of titles of every book in the library.

5.4.3 Schema conjunction

To build the new state for phase two of the library management system, we shall use the schemas *Library* and *Titles_of_books* in an operation of the schema calculus called **schema conjunction**, which is very similar to schema inclusion, but uses a different notation. We define the new state as follows.

$$Library\_phase2 \mathrel{\hat{=}} Library \land Titles\_of\_books \qquad (104, 121)$$

This piece of text declares *Library_phase2* to be a schema whose declaration part is obtained by merging the declarations of the schemas on the right-hand side, as explained for schema inclusion. The predicate part is the conjunction of the predicate parts of the schemas on the right, including the implicit predicates. Schema conjunction is associative and commutative, like the conjunction of predicates. Schema conjunction is frequently used in the construction of states from smaller pieces.

In order to revise the operations, but make as much use as possible of the behaviour already defined, we consider how the defined operations affect only the new state. We shall then use schema conjunction to add the new behaviour to the old.

The effect of adding a book to the library is specified first. We need the book as before, and a new input, the title of the book being added.

```
─Add_book_to_titles_ok──────────────────
│ ΔTitles_of_books                          (121)
│ b?: Book                                  (29)
│ t?: Title                                 (72)
├───────────
│ b? ∉ books
│ title_of' = title_of ∪ {b? ↦ t?}
└───────────────────────────────────────
```

The book must be new. The book and title are associated in *title_of*.

Now we define

$$Add\_book\_phase2\_ok \mathrel{\widehat{=}} Add\_book\_to\_library\_ok \land Add\_book\_to\_titles\_ok \quad (116, 122)$$

The exception behaviour needs to be amended in a similar manner:

$$Book\_already\_in\_phase2 \mathrel{\widehat{=}} Book\_already\_in\_library \land \Xi Titles\_of\_books \quad (118, 121)$$

and now we can specify adding books to phase_2:

$$Add\_book\_to\_phase2 \mathrel{\widehat{=}} Book\_already\_in\_phase2 \lor Add\_book\_phase2\_ok \quad (122, 122)$$

5.4.4 Calculating preconditions

When writing schemas to specify operations we document the case we are describing by writing a precondition in the predicate part of the schema. In *Add_book_to_library_ok* we had $b? \notin books$, and in *Book_already_in_library* we had $b? \in books$. Characterizing cases of an operation in this way can be difficult, and we need a way of knowing whether we have covered all the cases.

Consider the behaviour specified in *Enrolok* in the class manager's assistant on p. 16, and suppose we had omitted the predicate on there being room in the class for at least one more student.

- Is this schema specifying a different behaviour from *Enrolok*?
- What happens if the class is full?

Enrolok_amended

$\Delta Class$	(14)
$s?: Student$	(14)
$r!: Response$	(14)

$s? \notin enrolled$
$enrolled' = enrolled \cup \{s?\}$
$r! = success$

In fact, *Enrolok_amended* specifies the same behaviour as *Enrolok*, and the schema has $\#enrolled < size$ as a precondition, even though it is not explicit. We can calculate the precondition of any schema that specifies an operation in the following way.

The question to be answered is

> For what combinations of inputs and starting states can we find outputs and ending states that satisfy the predicates of *Enrolok_amended*?

There is a hint in the need to establish existence of outputs and ending states that the existential quantifier is going to be involved. The recipe for calculating the precondition is as follows: take the given schema, remove the outputs and ending state (dashed variables) from the declaration part, and bind them in the predicate part with an existential quantifier. The notation

pre *Enrolok_amended*

will be used to denote the schema derived from *Enrolok_amended* in the above manner. It will often be convenient to use the same notation to denote the predicate that is the property of the schema. The context will always make it clear whether the notation denotes a schema or a predicate. The sign ***pre*** is the **precondition operator** for schemas. We begin with a simple example of an operation on a state with a single component x.

Downone

$x, x': \mathbb{N}$

$x' < x$

The value of x is reduced. The schema ***pre*** *Downone* is

$$[x: \mathbb{N} \mid x > 0]$$

that is to say *Downone* has an implicit precondition that x must be greater than zero, something we could have surmised. The construction is to take the predicate part of *Downone*, not forgetting the implicit predicates arising from the declaration part, and bind x' as follows.

$$\exists x': \mathbb{Z} \bullet (x' \geq 0 \land x \geq 0 \land x' < x)$$

Provided $x > 0$ we can find such an x', namely $x-1$, but if $x = 0$ there is no such x'.

We now calculate ***pre*** *Enrolok_amended.* The predicate part is

$$\begin{aligned} &(\exists enrolled', tested': \mathbb{P}\ Student;\ r!: Response \bullet && (14, 14) \\ &\quad (tested \subseteq enrolled \\ &\quad \land \# enrolled \leq size \\ &\quad \land tested' \subseteq enrolled' \\ &\quad \land \# enrolled' \leq size \\ &\quad \land s? \notin enrolled \\ &\quad \land enrolled' = enrolled \cup \{s?\} \\ &\quad \land tested' = tested \\ &\quad \land r! = success)) \end{aligned}$$

We use the one-point rule to eliminate the quantifier, taking the explicit expressions for *enrolled'*, *tested'* and *r!* and substituting these expressions in the other occurrences of the variables. Thus the predicate part is equivalent to the following:

$$\begin{aligned} &(tested \subseteq enrolled \\ &\land \# enrolled \leq size \\ &\land tested \subseteq enrolled \cup \{s?\} \\ &\land \# (enrolled \cup \{s?\}) \leq size \\ &\land s? \notin enrolled) \end{aligned}$$

The first two conjuncts are just the invariants of a class, and the third is deducible from them. The last two tell us that

$$\# enrolled + 1 \leq size$$

and hence

$$\# enrolled < size$$

So the interesting conclusions about the precondition are that

$$\# enrolled < size \land s? \notin enrolled$$

We see that *Enrolok_amended* has in fact the same precondition as *Enrolok*.

When a partial operation has been specified, we should check its precondition by calculation to see if there are any interesting circumstances that have been forgotten. It is always a good idea to make interesting implicit preconditions explicit in the predicate part of a schema.

When a number of partial operations have been specified in a Z document, it is helpful to the reader to write up their preconditions in a table, such as Table 2.1 on p. 19. This gives the reader confidence that the regular cases of the operations have been dealt with, and justifies the specification of the error cases that follow.

The precondition calculation can also reveal inconsistency in the specification of an operation, for if the specification contains a contradiction, the precondition will be false, showing that for no combination of inputs and starting state can we find outputs and an ending state that satisfy the specification. Hence there is a proof obligation on the specification of each abstract operation to show that it is implementable. For *Enrol* the obligation is expressed in the following theorem:

$$\vdash \exists Class; Class'; s?: Student; r!: Response \qquad (14, 14, 14, 14)$$
$$\bullet\ Enrol \qquad (21)$$

There are some rules about preconditions that help in calculations. The most valuable is

$$(\mathbf{pre}\ (A \lor B)) \Leftrightarrow ((\mathbf{pre}\ A) \lor (\mathbf{pre}\ B))$$

This is analogous to the rule on p. 57 for existential quantification and disjunction.

For the operation *Enrol* in the class manager's assistant, we note that it is the disjunction of three schemas with the preconditions shown in Table 5.4.

Table 5.4 Preconditions for proof of consistency of an abstract operation.

Enrolok	$s? \notin enrolled \land \# enrolled < size$
Noroom	$\# enrolled = size$
AlreadyEnrolled	$s? \in enrolled$

Hence ***pre*** *Enrol* has for its predicate part

$$(s? \notin enrolled \land \# enrolled < size)$$
$$\lor \# enrolled = size \lor s? \in enrolled$$

Using the laws of distribution of disjunction over conjunction gives

$$(s? \notin enrolled \lor \# enrolled = size \lor s? \in enrolled)$$
$$\land$$
$$(\# enrolled < size \lor \# enrolled = size \lor s? \in enrolled)$$

The predicate $(s? \notin enrolled \lor s? \in enrolled)$ is an instance of the tautology $\mathbf{P} \lor (\neg \mathbf{P})$, and so is true. The predicate $\# enrolled < size \lor \# enrolled = size$ is true because of the predicate part of *Class*. Hence each conjunct must have the value true. An operation like *Enrol* whose precondition is true for any values of inputs and starting state is called a **total operation.**

5.4.5 The class manager's assistant revisited

Now the reader should go back to Chapter 2, and read the specification of the class manager's assistant, paying attention this time to the formal text, and its relation to the informal text.

5.4.6 Schemas and logical connectives

Earlier in this chapter we saw how two schemas could be combined to give a new schema by conjunction and disjunction. The method was essentially to create a new signature by merging the signatures of the participating schemas, and to create a new property by using conjunction or disjunction on the properties of the participating schemas. In the above examples we did not need to stress the distinctions between declaration part and signature, predicate part and property, since it was enough to add a reminder about implicit predicates. We now examine **schema negation** in which these distinctions become more significant.

The negation of a schema like

```
┌─S──────────────────────
│ x: ℕ
│ y: ℤ
├──────────
│ x = y²
└────────────────────────
```

has the same signature as *S* and a property that is the negation of the property of S. The signature of S, being an association between declared names and their types, is as follows:

$x: \mathbb{Z}$
$y: \mathbb{Z}$

and its property is $x = y^2$. (That x is greater than or equal to zero could be deduced from this.) The negation of S, written $\neg S$, is therefore the following schema.

$$[x, y: \mathbb{Z} \mid y^2 \neq x]$$

The meaning of **schema implication** can be similarly defined in terms of the signatures and predicates of the participating schemas. Suppose S is as above, and T is as follows.

T
$x: \mathbb{Z}$
$x < 0$

The implication $S \Rightarrow T$ is the following schema:

$$[x, y: \mathbb{Z} \mid y^2 = x \Rightarrow x < 0]$$

The predicate part could be rewritten as follows:

$$y^2 \neq x \vee x < 0$$

and further simplified to

$$y^2 \neq x$$

The notion of **schema equivalence** is similarly defined. The notation is $S \Leftrightarrow T$.

5.4.7 Schema quantification

The universal and existential quantifiers can be used to build new schemas from old in a manner now to be described. Suppose that X and Y are defined as follows:

X
$x: \mathbb{N}$
$x > 10$

$$\begin{array}{|l} \multicolumn{1}{l}{Y} \\ \hline x, y: \mathbb{Z} \\ \hline x > y \\ \hline \end{array}$$

The expression

$$\exists X \bullet Y$$

is well-formed provided that the signature of X is compatible with the signature of Y; that is any names in common are associated with the same type. The expression denotes a schema whose signature is the signature of Y with all the names of the signature of X removed. The property of the new schema is the property of Y with an existential quantifier binding the variables of X constrained by the property of X. Thus in this instance the signature is

$$y: \mathbb{Z}$$

and the property is

$$\exists x: \mathbb{Z} \mid x > 10 \bullet x > y$$

The expression

$$\forall X \bullet Y$$

is similarly defined. Its signature is the same as for the existential quantification, but its property is

$$\forall x: \mathbb{Z} \mid x > 10 \bullet x > y$$

5.4.8 Theorems involving schemas

The notation for theorems introduced on p. 59 had declarations and constraints in its hypothesis part and predicates in its conclusion. Since a schema is constructed of declarations and constraints, it is natural to allow a schema or a schema expression to be the hypothesis of a theorem, as we did on p. 111. Sometimes it is convenient to use a schema expression as the conclusion of a theorem, as we did on p. 116. In such a case the conclusion to be drawn is the property of the schema expression, that is its predicate part and any predicates implicit in its declarations.

5.5 Schema types

The declaration

$$
\begin{array}{|l}
\hline
\textit{Class} \\
\textit{enrolled, tested}: \mathbb{P}\ \textit{Student} \\
\hline
\textit{tested} \subseteq \textit{enrolled} \\
\#\textit{enrolled} \leq \textit{size} \\
\hline
\end{array}
\qquad (14)
$$

introduces the name *Class* as a type for classes. Since a class is a pair of sets of students we might suppose that the type of a class is

$$(\mathbb{P}\ \textit{Student}) \times (\mathbb{P}\ \textit{Student}) \qquad (14, 14)$$

but this cannot be the case, since there is nothing in the declaration part of *Class* to fix the order of the two sets, and the use of the names *enrolled* and *tested* plays an essential role in defining the operations.

A **schema type** is an association or **binding** between names and types. Two schema types are considered the same if they differ only in the order in which the associations are presented in the type expression. In determining the type of a schema or schema expression it is the names and types in the declaration part that are important. The predicate part is irrelevant to establishing the type.

The schema

$$
\begin{array}{|l}
\hline
\textit{Sdwe} \\
\textit{enrolled, tested}: \mathbb{P}\ \textit{Student} \\
\hline
\textit{tested} \cap \textit{enrolled} = \varnothing \\
\#\,(\textit{tested} \cup \textit{enrolled}) \leq \textit{size} \\
\hline
\end{array}
\qquad (14)
$$

defines the same type as *Class*, even though the predicate parts are different.

The schema

$$
\begin{array}{|l}
\hline
\textit{NewClass} \\
\textit{enrolled, passed}: \mathbb{P}\ \textit{Student} \\
\hline
\textit{passed} \subseteq \textit{enrolled} \\
\#\textit{enrolled} \leq \textit{size} \\
\hline
\end{array}
\qquad (14)
$$

defines a different type, since the names in the declaration part are different.

5.5.1 Using schema types in declarations

Since *Class* is a type, we can use it in declarations. Suppose the class manager wishes to manage two classes, one called 'Z for Beginners', and the other called 'Z Advanced'. We might offer a two-class system, and begin by writing a state schema as follows.

TwoClasses

z_for_beginners: *Class*	(14)
z_advanced: *Class*	(14)

There is no constraint we need add to those that are implicit in the declarations.

In describing operations on this state we need to refer to the students enrolled on 'Z for Beginners' etc. We use the **dot notation** to do this.

z_for_beginners.enrolled

is the *enrolled* component of 'Z for Beginners', and we can use similar notation for the other components.

How can we reuse the operations developed for the class manager's assistant to explain operations of the two-class system? First we look at Δ*TwoClasses*. Its declaration part is

z_for_beginners, *z_for_beginners'*: *Class*	(14)
z_advanced, *z_advanced'*: *Class*	(14)

Suppose we want to enrol a student on 'Z for Beginners'. *Enrolok* has components *enrolled*, *enrolled'*, *tested*, and *tested'*, and these must be associated with the appropriate components of *z_for_beginners* and *z_for_beginners'* as follows:

ZfbEnrolok

Δ*TwoClasses*	(130)
Enrolok	(16)

z_advanced' = *z_advanced*
z_for_beginners.enrolled = *enrolled*
z_for_beginners.tested = *tested*
z_for_beginners'.enrolled = *enrolled'*
z_for_beginners'.tested = *tested'*

The first predicate says that 'Z Advanced' is not changed by enrolling a student on 'Z for Beginners'. The remaining predicates assert that the components of *z_for_beginners* are changed under the conditions and in the manner described in *Enrolok*. (Remember that all the predicates of *Enrolok* are included in the predicate part of *ZfbEnrolok*.)

These five predicates are required in every operation on 'Z for Beginners', so we should make a schema of them. Δ*Class* is included to introduce *enrolled, tested, enrolled'* and *tested'*.

```
┌─ ZfbOperation ──────────────────────
│ ΔTwoClasses                                  (130)
│ ΔClass                                        (14)
├──────────
│ z_advanced' = z_advanced
│ z_for_beginners.enrolled = enrolled
│ z_for_beginners.tested = tested
│ z_for_beginners'.enrolled = enrolled'
│ z_for_beginners'.tested = tested'
└─────────────────────────────────────
```

The schema *ZfbEnrolok* should be introduced not as above, but as follows:

$$ZfbEnrolok \mathrel{\widehat{=}} ZfbOperation \land Enrolok \qquad (131, 16)$$

5.5.2 Cleaning up the predicates – theta

The association of the components of *z_for_beginners* and *z_for_beginners'* with the components of *Class* and *Class'* required four predicates, and if *Class* had more components the required association would become even more long-winded. We introduce a notation to abbreviate the making of associations, called the **theta notation.**

θ*Class* is a term of type *Class*, and its components have values as follows.

- θ*Class.enrolled* has the value *enrolled*
- θ*Class.tested* has the value *tested*

θ*Class'* is a term of type *Class*, not *Class'*, and its components have values as follows.

- θ*Class'.enrolled* has the value *enrolled'*
- θ*Class'.tested* has the value *tested'*

If other signs are being used as decorations, they are treated in the same way as ''''.

Now we rewrite *ZfbOperation* using the theta notation.

```
┌─ ZfbOperation ──────────────────────────
│ ΔTwoClasses                                   (130)
│ ΔClass                                        (14)
├─────────────
│ z_advanced' = z_advanced
│ z_for_beginners = θClass                      (14)
│ z_for_beginners' = θClass'                    (14)
└─────────────────────────────────────────
```

Notice that this form will deal with a *Class* schema of any number of components.

We can now complete the description of the operation to enrol a student on 'Z for Beginners':

$$ZfbAlreadyEnrolled \mathrel{\widehat{=}} ZfbOperation \land AlreadyEnrolled \qquad (132, 20)$$

$$ZfbNoRoom \mathrel{\widehat{=}} ZfbOperation \land NoRoom \qquad (132, 20)$$

Now we build the operation to enrol a student from these parts:

$$ZfbEnrolBuilt \mathrel{\widehat{=}} ZfbEnrolok \lor ZfbNoRoom \qquad (131, 132)$$
$$\lor\ ZfbAlreadyEnrolled \qquad (132)$$

Table 5.5 is an analysis of the declaration part of *ZfbEnrolBuilt* with some remarks about the origin of the components.

Table 5.5 Analysis of the declaration part of *ZfbEnrolBuilt*

Name	**Origins**	**Remarks**
z_for_beginners *z_advanced* *z_for_beginners'* *z_advanced'*	*ZfbOperation*	Required to define the interface
enrolled *enrolled'* *tested* *tested'*	*Enrolok* *AlreadyEnrolled* *NoRoom*	Not required to define the interface
s?	*Enrolok* *AlreadyEnrolled*	Required to define the interface

Name	Origins	Remarks
r!	*Enrolok* *AlreadyEnrolled* *NoRoom*	Required to define the interface

The remarks point out that some of the components are not part of the external interface, which should be presented as an operation on *TwoClasses* with an input *s?* and an output *r!*. The components of Δ*Class* were introduced to make it possible to reuse previously defined behaviour, and are not part of the external interface, merely part of the explanation.

5.5.3 Cleaning up the declarations — hiding

To tidy up the interface to the two-class system we need to suppress the appearance of *enrolled*, *enrolled'* etc., but not their effect. The mechanism to do this is called **hiding**, and the notation for it is illustrated in the definition that follows.

$$ZfbEnrol \mathrel{\widehat{=}} ZfbEnrolBuilt \setminus (enrolled, enrolled', tested, tested') \qquad (132)$$

The sign '\' is the hiding symbol, and it is followed by the **hiding list**, the list of names to be hidden. The list is enclosed in parentheses, and the names in it are separated by commas. The effect of hiding is to remove the listed variables from the signature of the schema, and bind them in the property with an existential quantifier. The hidden variables take their types from the signature of *ZfbEnrolBuilt*. The hiding technique was used in calculating the precondition of a schema.

The definition of *ZfbEnrol* could have been done using an existential quantifier.

$$ZfbEnrol \mathrel{\widehat{=}} \exists \Delta Class \bullet ZfbEnrolBuilt \qquad (14, 132)$$

Note that in this definition it is the signature of Δ*Class* that fixes the types of the variables being hidden and also specifies the constraints that they satisfy. However, in this case the result is the same, since Δ*Class* is part of *ZfbEnrolBuilt*.

5.5.4 Using schema names in mathematical expressions

Because schemas contain declarations and predicates, schema names can be used in many of the constructions introduced in Chapters 2 and 3. We shall look at each of these constructions in turn, show how schema names can be used in place of the declaration-constraint notation, and explain any peculiarities that arise from the use of a schema name. The schema *Class* is by now familiar, so it will be the basis of the examples.

In set comprehension we can form the expression

$$\{Class\} \qquad (14)$$

and we interpret this to mean

$$\{Class \bullet \theta Class\} \qquad (14, 14)$$

or

$$\{enrolled, tested: \mathbb{P}\ Student \qquad (14)$$
$$\mid tested \subseteq enrolled \land \#\ enrolled \leq size$$
$$\bullet\ \theta Class\} \qquad (14)$$

which is the set of all possible classes. Its type is therefore $\mathbb{P}$ *Class*.

(Note that this is not the same as

$$\{enrolled, tested: \mathbb{P}\ Student \qquad (14)$$
$$\mid tested \subseteq enrolled \land \#\ enrolled \leq size\}$$

which according to conventions established earlier denotes a set of ordered pairs of sets of students subject to the constraints, and is of type $\mathbb{P}\ ((\mathbb{P}\ Student) \times (\mathbb{P}\ Student))$.)

The use of schema names in quantifiers, and in the hypotheses of theorems has already been illustrated in this chapter. A schema name can be used as if it were a predicate. The predicate it represents is its property. All the names used in the property must be declared in the context in which the schema name is used.

The definite description

$$\mu Class \mid enrolled = \varnothing \qquad (14)$$

denotes a term of type *Class*, and could have been written as

$$\mu Class \mid enrolled = \varnothing \bullet \theta Class \qquad (14, 14)$$

This definite description denotes the class in which no students are enrolled. The definite description

$$\mu Class \mid tested = \varnothing \bullet \theta Class \qquad (14, 14)$$

denotes an undefined term (unless *size* is zero), since there is not one unique class in which no students have done the exercises.

(Note that definite description

$$\mu Class \mid enrolled = \varnothing \qquad (14)$$

is not at all the same thing as

$$\mu enrolled, tested: \mathbb{P}\ Student \qquad (14)$$
$$\mid tested \subseteq enrolled \wedge \#\ enrolled \leq size \wedge enrolled = \varnothing$$

which according to conventions established earlier denotes an ordered pair of sets of students subject to the constraints, both empty.)

A schema name can also be used in a lambda abstraction, so the definition

$$class\_size == \lambda Class \bullet \#\ enrolled \qquad (14)$$

defines a function that takes a class as its argument, and has for its value the number of students enrolled on the class. It is equivalent to the following axiomatic description.

$$class\_size: Class \rightarrow \mathbb{Z} \qquad (14)$$
$$\forall c: Class \bullet class\_size\ c = \#\ c.enrolled \qquad (14)$$

(Note that the lambda abstraction

$$\lambda Class \bullet \#\ enrolled \qquad (14)$$

is not the same thing as

$$(\ \lambda enrolled, tested: \mathbb{P}\ Student \qquad (14)$$
$$\mid tested \subseteq enrolled \wedge \#\ enrolled \leq size$$
$$\bullet\ \#\ enrolled\ )$$

which denotes a function whose argument is an ordered pair of sets of students subject to the constraints, and whose value is the size of the first set.)

5.6 Promotion

We now consider how to specify another, more elaborate, system based on the notion of a class. This system, which we shall call the class management system, allows a certain number of classes to be controlled, each class being identified by a name. This kind of reuse of smaller notions is very common in software systems, whether application systems or operating systems, and we shall call it **promotion**. We shall promote the operations of the class manager's assistant into an environment in which there are many classes.

We introduce an integer for the number of classes to be supported, and a given set for the names of the classes.

$$maxclasses: \mathbb{N}$$

$$[ClassName]$$

Now we define our state, which contains a single component *classmap*, the relation between class names and the classes they denote:

$$\begin{array}{|l}
\hline \textit{ClassSystem} \\
\hline classmap: ClassName \twoheadrightarrow Class \qquad (136, 14) \\
\hline \# classmap \leq maxclasses \\
\hline
\end{array}$$

There will not be more than *maxclasses* classes to be controlled.

The abstract initial state for the class system is specified next.

$$InitClassSystem \mathrel{\widehat{=}} [ClassSystem' \mid classmap' = \varnothing] \qquad (136)$$

This definition establishes the existence of the abstract initial state, and hence the consistency of the abstract state.

5.6.1 Class management operations

The operations of the class manager's assistant can be promoted to the class management system in a way to be described shortly. First we specify two operations of the class management system that have no counterpart in the class manager's assistant, one to create a new class, and one to delete an existing class. The type *CSResponse* of responses in the class system is not defined here. Its value will depend on choices made by the reader in doing some of the exercises.

To create a new class, the operator must supply a class name. To specify that the newly created class is to be in the initial state for a class, we include *ClassInit*, which was defined on p. 15.

MakeClassok

$\Delta ClassSystem$ (136)
$ClassInit$ (15)
$cname?: ClassName$ (136)
$csr!: CSResponse$

$cname? \notin \mathbf{dom}\ classmap$
$classmap' = classmap \cup \{cname? \mapsto \theta Class'\}$ (14)
$csr! = classadded$

The name must be a new name. It is associated with a class that has no students enrolled. The response is *classadded.*

To delete a class the operator must supply the name of the class to be deleted.

DropClassok

$\Delta ClassSystem$ (136)
$cname?: ClassName$ (136)
$csr!: CSResponse$

$cname? \in \mathbf{dom}\ classmap$
$(classmap\ cname?).enrolled = \emptyset$
$classmap' = \{cname?\} \lhd classmap$
$csr! = classdeleted$

The name must be the name of an existing class. The class must have no students enrolled. The class is removed, and the response is *classdeleted.*

The reader is invited to write other schemas to make these operations robust – see the exercises at the end of the chapter.

5.6.2 Promoting the basic operations

The promotion of all the operations of the class manager's assistant can be achieved with a single schema.

- *ΔClassSystem* prepares for specifying an operation of the class management system
- *ΔClass* prepares for reusing the operations of the class manager's assistant
- *cname?* is a new input to the operations
- *csr!* is a new output from the operations

$$
\begin{array}{|ll}
\multicolumn{2}{l}{\_\mathit{ClassToSystem}\_\_\_\_\_\_\_\_\_\_\_\_} \\
\Delta \mathit{ClassSystem} & (136) \\
\Delta \mathit{Class} & (14) \\
\mathit{cname?}: \mathit{ClassName} & (136) \\
\mathit{csr!}: \mathit{CSResponse} & \\
\hline
\mathit{cname?} \in \mathbf{dom}\ \mathit{classmap} & \\
\mathit{classmap}\ \mathit{cname?} = \theta \mathit{Class} & (14) \\
\mathit{classmap}' = \mathit{classmap} \oplus \{\mathit{cname?} \mapsto \theta \mathit{Class}'\} & (14) \\
\mathit{csr!} = \mathit{classfound} & \\
\hline
\end{array}
$$

The first predicate asserts that this behaviour can occur only if the input name is the name of a class. The next predicate explains that the class manager's assistant operation (enrol, test etc.) will take for its starting state the class referred to by the input name. The third predicate explains that the class system changes only in the named class, and its new value is the ending state of the class manager's assistant operation. The last predicate says that there will be a response of *classfound*. (Each class manager's assistant operation produces in addition a response of a different type.)

We need one other schema to cover the case when the input class name is not found.

$$
\begin{array}{|ll}
\multicolumn{2}{l}{\_\mathit{UnknownClass}\_\_\_\_\_\_\_\_\_\_\_\_} \\
\Xi \mathit{ClassSystem} & (136) \\
\mathit{cname?}: \mathit{ClassName} & (136) \\
\mathit{csr!}: \mathit{CSResponse} & \\
\hline
\mathit{cname?} \notin \mathbf{dom}\ \mathit{classmap} & \\
\mathit{csr!} = \mathit{unknownclass} & \\
\hline
\end{array}
$$

When the input name is not the name of a class, the response is *unknownclass*.

Now we can promote the class manager's assistant operations:

$$
\begin{array}{ll}
\mathit{CSEnrol} \mathrel{\widehat=} (\ (\ \mathit{Enrol} \land \mathit{ClassToSystem}\ ) & (21, 138) \\
\quad \setminus (\mathit{enrolled}, \mathit{tested}, \mathit{enrolled}', \mathit{tested}')\ ) & \\
\quad \lor\ \mathit{UnknownClass} & (138)
\end{array}
$$

$$
\begin{array}{ll}
\mathit{CSTest} \mathrel{\widehat=} (\ (\ \mathit{Test} \land \mathit{ClassToSystem}\ ) & (21, 138) \\
\quad \setminus (\mathit{enrolled}, \mathit{tested}, \mathit{enrolled}', \mathit{tested}')\ ) & \\
\quad \lor\ \mathit{UnknownClass} & (138)
\end{array}
$$

$CSLeave \mathrel{\widehat{=}} ((Leave \wedge ClassToSystem)$ (21, 138)
$\quad \setminus (enrolled, tested, enrolled', tested'))$
$\quad \vee UnknownClass$ (138)

$CSEnquire \mathrel{\widehat{=}} ((Enquire \wedge ClassToSystem)$ (19, 138)
$\quad \setminus (enrolled, tested, enrolled', tested'))$
$\quad \vee UnknownClass$ (138)

The reader should calculate the declaration parts of the schemas and expressions used here to see that they define the correct interface.

Promotion is a very useful and common technique for presenting specifications. The reader should consult Wordsworth (1989) and Houston and Wordsworth (1990) for more examples.

5.6.3 Other varieties of promotion

Promotion can be applied to other methods of aggregation. For instance the simpler type that is being promoted might be organized into a stack, modelled by a sequence, and the operations on that type might be required to operate only on the head of the sequence. Suppose S is the schema that defines the simpler type, and suppose that the larger state is defined by the following schema:

StackState

$stack: \mathbf{seq}\ S$

The schema to promote operations on S to be operations on the head of the sequence is as follows:

Stack_promote

$\Delta StackState$
ΔS

$stack \neq \langle\rangle$
$\theta S = \mathbf{head}\ stack$
$\theta S' = \mathbf{head}\ stack'$
$\mathbf{tail}\ stack = \mathbf{tail}\ stack'$

An operation on S can only be promoted to an operation on *StackState* if there is an S in the sequence. The head of the sequence is the S affected by the operation. The rest of the sequence is unchanged.

There is an example of using a stack in this way in King (1990b).

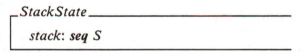

Another way of creating aggregates is by making sets. Suppose S is the schema that defines the simpler type, and suppose that the larger state is defined by the following schema:

```
┌─ SetState ──────────────────────────
│ set: ℙ S
└─────────────────────────────────────
```

The schema to promote operations on S to be operations on an element of the set is as follows:

```
┌─ Set_promote ───────────────────────
│ ΔSetState
│ ΔS
├──────────
│ θS ∈ set
│ set' = (set \ {θS}) ∪ {θS'}
└─────────────────────────────────────
```

An operation on S can only be promoted to an operation on *SetState* if there is an S in the set. The operation is applied to an arbitrary member of the set, though the precondition of the operation might influence which member of the set is chosen.

5.7 More schema operations

5.7.1 Schema piping

To introduce the next technique of building larger schemas from smaller ones, we consider an operating system that manages a number of printers, and allows its many users to create files for printing and queue them to printers. Printers are known by name, and are divided into groups, all the printers in a group having similar facilities (paper size etc.). We are to specify a facility that allows a user to queue a file to any printer in a group. The user supplies the file and names the group, and the operating system chooses the printer and queues the file. We introduce given sets for the names of printers, for the names of groups and for files.

[*PrinterName*, *GroupName*, *File*]

For the purpose of this specification, a printer can be regarded as a sequence of files waiting to be printed:

Printer == **seq** *File* (140)

The printer management environment needs to take account of how the printers are organized into groups, and what files are queued to the printers:

Printers

$printers: GroupName ⇻ \mathbb{P}\ PrinterName$	(140, 140)
$queue: PrinterName ⇻ Printer$	(140, 141)

$$printers\ \textit{partitions}\ \mathbf{dom}\ queue$$
$$\forall gn: \mathbf{dom}\ printers \bullet printers\ gn \neq \varnothing$$

The names in the groups are all the printers we have, and no name is in more than one group. (This is what *partitions* means. If you have forgotten the definition, look it up in the index.) Every group has at least one printer in it. The situation is illustrated by the following:

pagemode
- *pp1* $\langle file1, file2, file3 \rangle$
- *pp2* $\langle\rangle$
- *pp2* $\langle file4, file5 \rangle$

linemode
- *lm1* $\langle file6, file7 \rangle$
- *lm2* $\langle file8 \rangle$

impactquarto
- *qu1* $\langle file9, file10 \rangle$
- *qu2* $\langle\rangle$

impactstandard
- *st1* $\langle\rangle$
- *st2* $\langle file11 \rangle$

Here, *pagemode*, *linemode* etc. are the names of the groups, while *pp1*, *lm1*, etc. are the names of the printers. The diagram shows a sequence of files associated with each printer. In some cases there are no files in the sequence, since no work is waiting to be printed on a particular printer.

We look at two aspects of the operation of queueing a file, given only the name of the group, and we first write a schema that selects a printer from a group. We shall treat the selected printer as an output of this schema.

SelectPrinter

$\Delta Printers$	(141)
$gn?: GroupName$	(140)
$pn!: PrinterName$	(140)

$gn? \in \mathbf{dom}\ printers$
$pn! \in printers\ gn?$
$printers' = printers$

The input group name must be a valid group name, the printer selected is a printer in that group, and the organization of printers into groups is unchanged. This schema is not suitable for offering as an operation, since it leaves undecided what happens to the *queue* component of *Printers*. This is not an accident, but is something that will be determined by the next aspect of this operation, which is the queueing of a file to a named printer. This behaviour is non-deterministic, since it does not specify the criteria for choosing the printer; it specifies only that the printer shall be one from the group identified by the input group name.

The queueing of a file to a selected printer is specified next. In this schema we must have the printer name and the file as inputs.

QueueFile

$\Delta Printers$	(141)
$file?: File$	(140)
$pn?: PrinterName$	(140)

$pn? \in \mathbf{dom}\ queue$
$queue' = queue \oplus \{pn? \mapsto (queue\ pn?) ^\frown \langle file? \rangle\}$

The input printer name must be one for which we have a printer. The input file is added to the selected printer after the other files. This schema is not suitable for offering as an operation, since it leaves undecided what happens to the *printer* component of *Printers*. However, it can be combined with *SelectPrinter* to specify the required operation of queueing a file by group name. The combination technique is called **schema piping**, and we present the notation and then explain its significance:

$QueueByGroup \mathrel{\widehat{=}} SelectPrinter \gg QueueFile$ (142, 142)

The sign '$\gg$' is the symbol for schema piping. The result of piping two schemas is a new schema constructed as follows.

(1) The outputs of the first schema are matched with the inputs of the second schema. An output matches an input if, when the output name is stripped of its '!' and the input name is stripped of its '?', the names are the same. For each matching output and its corresponding input, a name not otherwise in scope is chosen, and both are renamed to it.

(2) The schemas are combined by schema conjunction, and the new names are hidden.

(3) Any inputs and unmatched outputs of the first schema, and any outputs and unmatched inputs of the second schema remain in the signature of the result.

Applying these rules to the above example we see that the declaration part of *QueueByGroup* is as follows:

$\Delta Printers$	(141)
gn?: *GroupName*	(140)
file?: *File*	(140)

It is encouraging to see that this schema has only the group name and the file as its inputs. The predicate part of *QueueByGroup* is as follows.

$$
\begin{array}{ll}
gn? \in \mathbf{dom}\ printers & \\
printers' = printers & \\
(\ \exists pn: PrinterName & (140)\\
\bullet\ (\ pn \in printers\ gn? & \\
\quad \wedge\ queue' = queue \oplus \{pn \mapsto (queue\ pn) ^\frown \langle file? \rangle\}\ )\ ) &
\end{array}
$$

The predicate part has been simplified as follows. A single name *pn* has been used for the common value of *pn!* and *pn?*, and the hiding has been done by using the existential quantifier. The predicates that do not contain the bound variable have been moved outside the quantifier.

In this example the two schemas specify operations on the same state.

- The first fixes the change to only one part of the state – it says that the relation between group names and the printers in the groups is not changed. It exposes some information from that part of the state (the name of the printer that is selected), and leaves unspecified what happens to the rest of the state.
- The second schema changes only the other part of the state, absorbing the printer name that was exposed in the first schema. It leaves unspecified what happens to the rest of the state.

Schema conjunction completes the picture by bringing the two schemas together. While it is not necessary for the schemas that take part in piping to partition the state in this way, they must not interfere with one another. Interference would have occurred if for instance *SelectPrinter* had been specified with $\Xi Printers$, since this would have contradicted the predicate in *QueueFile* that says that *queue'* and *queue* are different values.

5.7.2 Renaming

Sometimes it is convenient to rename the variables in a schema. The renaming affects the occurrences of variables in the declaration part and in the predicate part. The notation is as follows:

$$NewNamesClass \mathrel{\widehat=} Class\ [members\ /\ enrolled,\ passed\ /\ tested] \qquad (14)$$

is equivalent to the following:

NewNamesClass

$members, passed: \mathbb{P}\ Student$ (14)

$passed \subseteq members$
$\#\ members \leq size$

The renaming list is enclosed in square brackets, and the entries in the list are separated by commas. Each entry in the list consists of the new name and the old separated by the renaming symbol '/' (read 'for').

5.7.3 Schema composition

Another method of building new schemas from old is **schema composition**, and we illustrate this by reconsidering the problem of queueing files to printers from p. 140. We propose to change the state *Printers* by adding a new component *selected* to the declaration part and a predicate to the predicate part, using the following definition:

PrintersExt

$Printers$ (141)
$selected: PrinterName$ (140)

$selected \in \mathbf{dom}\ queue \lor queue = \varnothing$

We now rewrite the schema that selects a printer to use the new state component. Only the *selected* component is allowed to change.

$$
\begin{array}{|ll}
\multicolumn{2}{l}{\textit{SelectPrinterExt}} \\
\hline
\Delta \textit{PrintersExt} & (145) \\
\Xi \textit{Printers} & (141) \\
\textit{gn?}: \textit{GroupName} & (140) \\
\hline
\textit{gn?} \in \mathbf{dom}\ \textit{printers} & \\
\textit{selected}' \in \textit{printers gn?} & \\
\hline
\end{array}
$$

The new value of the *selected* component is one of the printers in the named group.

We now rewrite the schema that queues the file to the selected printer:

$$
\begin{array}{|ll}
\multicolumn{2}{l}{\textit{QueueFileExt}} \\
\hline
\Delta \textit{PrintersExt} & (145) \\
\textit{file?}: \textit{File} & (140) \\
\hline
\textit{printers}' = \textit{printers} & \\
\textit{queue}' = \textit{queue} \oplus \{\textit{selected} \mapsto (\textit{queue selected}) ^\frown \langle \textit{file?} \rangle\} & \\
\hline
\end{array}
$$

The input file is queued to the printer named in the *selected* component. The ending value of *selected* is not specified.

The new operation is defined as follows.

$$
\begin{array}{ll}
\textit{QueueByGroupExt} \mathrel{\widehat{=}} & \\
\quad \textit{SelectPrinterExt} \mathbin{⨾} \textit{QueueFileExt} & (145, 145)
\end{array}
$$

The very fat semicolon '⨾' is the symbol for schema composition. The meaning of schema composition is as follows. First we note that the dashed names of the first schema must match the undashed names of the second; that is to say if we remove the dashes from all the dashed names in the first schema, we have exactly the same names, neither more nor less, than the undashed names in the second schema. This is certainly true of the above expression, since the two schemas are both defined on the same state. The signature of the new schema is the inputs and outputs of both, together with the undashed variables of the first and the dashed variables of the second. The property is constructed as follows:

- The property of the first schema is included, but all the dashed names are redecorated with a decorator not used in either schema.

- The property of the second schema is included, but all the undashed names are decorated with the same decorator as was used in the first schema.
- The newly decorated names are hidden with an existential quantifier.

For schemas X, Y with common state S, the composition is defined as

$$\exists S_0 \bullet X[\_{}_0 / \_{}'] \wedge Y[\_{}_0 / \_\,]$$

In this expression we have an example of a notation for **systematic renaming**, in which all the names of a certain kind are to be renamed in a certain way. All the dashed names in X are to be renamed with subscript zero, and all the undashed names in Y are to be renamed with subscript zero. Systematic renaming is not part of the Z language, but is a useful syntactic notation that I have used here and elsewhere in this book.

We now calculate the declaration part of the composition of *SelectPrinterExt* and *QueueFileExt* to be the following:

$\Delta PrintersExt$ (145)
$gn?: GroupName$ (140)
$file?: File$ (140)

The predicate part is as follows:

$$\begin{aligned}
&(\ \exists PrintersExt_0 && (145)\\
&\bullet (\ gn? \in \mathbf{dom}\ printers\\
&\quad \wedge selected_0 \in printers\ gn?\\
&\quad \wedge queue_0 = queue\\
&\quad \wedge printers_0 = printers\\
&\quad \wedge printers' = printers_0\\
&\quad \wedge queue' = queue_0\\
&\qquad\qquad \oplus \{selected_0 \mapsto ((queue_0\ selected_0) \frown \langle file? \rangle)\}\ )\ )
\end{aligned}$$

and this can be simplified using the one-point rule to give

$$\begin{aligned}
&gn? \in \mathbf{dom}\ printers\\
&printers' = printers\\
&(\ \exists selected_0: printers\ gn?\\
&\bullet queue' = queue \oplus \{selected_0 \mapsto ((queue\ selected_0) \frown \langle file? \rangle)\}\ )
\end{aligned}$$

The reader should compare this with the predicate part derived on p. 143 for schema piping, and observe that it is the same apart from the name of the bound variable.

The reader might be tempted to think that schema composition makes precise the idea 'do what the first schema specifies and then do what the second schema specifies', but this is not the case. The notion 'do one thing, and then do another' is not a specification notion, but a programming notion, and it is explored in detail in Chapter 7.

5.7.4 Generic schema definitions

The idea of a generic definition discussed in Chapter 4 can be applied to schema definitions. Suppose we wish to write a specification dealing with different kinds of resources, each kind of resource having its own name type. We could define a generic resource manager schema as follows. The generic parameter *RName* is the type of names resources and the generic parameter *RType* is the type of the resources.

```
┌─RManager[RName, RType]────────────
│ resmap: RName ⇸ RType
│ known: ℙ RName
├──────────
│ known = dom resmap
└───────────────────────────────────
```

For each resource manager, *known* is the set of names for which there are corresponding resources.

We can define a generic operation as follows:

```
┌─RInquire[RName, RType]────────────
│ ΞRManager[RName, RType]                    (147)
│ rnam?: RName
│ resp!: YesNo                               (33)
├──────────
│ resp! = yes ⇔ rnam? ∈ known
└───────────────────────────────────
```

The response is *yes* if and only if the input name is a known resource name.

Other operations can be similarly defined. These definitions can be reused in various different contexts by supplying appropriate sets for the generic parameters.

Theorems about schemas with generic parameters can be proved by generic theorems. Thus to assert that *RInquire* returns a response of *no* when the input resource name is not known we could write a theorem as follows:

$$[RName, RType]\ RInquire[RName, RType] \qquad (147)$$
$$\vdash rnam? \notin known \Rightarrow r! = no$$

Generic parameters can be prefaced to any theorem, whether reference is made to a generic schema or not. Thus the assertion that any set is a member of its own power set could be written as a theorem as follows:

$$[S] \vdash S \in \mathbb{P}\, S$$

5.8 Writing good specifications

The reader of a specification is very much at the mercy of the writer, so this section aims to persuade writers to bear the reader in mind. The mathematical language reviewed in the earlier part of this book is very powerful, and it has many ways of saying the same thing. Writers should always choose the simplest way of saying something. It is the writer's duty to organize the specification so that simple things can be simply said. Another important point is to make a lot of use of informal text. I have seen Z specifications with hardly a line of informal text – 'This is the specification; I'll put the English in later' is just not good enough. Specifications are intended to be understood, to educate and to inform. In short, they are for precise communication of ideas. We want our specifications to be so simple that no one can doubt that we are all talking about the same thing. A good grasp of the mathematical basis is not sufficient to make a good writer. A fluent and persuasive pen with more than a hint of poetry in it is also needed.

In laying out a specification, some informal summary of the scope of what is being specified should come first. It is important here to establish a sound technical vocabulary that will be made precise in the specification proper.

The given sets should be introduced next, and the writer's choice of given sets should be justified. Data types and important constants should be described here. If the values of some of these sets and constants are determined during the installation procedure for the product being specified, this should be made clear.

In introducing the state schema it is often necessary to refer informally to the operations in order to justify the components of the state and the models chosen for them. When a specification is being researched, it is the interplay between state and operations that determines what the content of the state must be. The initial value of the state is specified next, and any dependence on the installation procedure should be explained.

Before specifying the schemas that contribute to operations on this state, it is best to explain the inputs and outputs that will appear in the declaration parts of the schemas. The input and output names should be related informally to the physical means available to the user for providing them in the interface. For instance, if a programming interface is being specified it should be clear which parameter in a parameter list is being referred to. In a programming language in which the call statements can have keywords to identify the parameters it might be convenient to use the keyword (appropriately decorated with ! or ?) as the name of the input or output value. If the interface is a display screen the references will be to fields on the display, and perhaps to keys that the operator might press.

Many of the operation schemas will be partial, since an operation often has several aspects, each of which will be separately specified. The aspects of an operation should be described roughly in order of their desirability. The most desired ('correct') aspects should be described first, and the least desired ('error') aspects last. The preconditions of the partial operations should be summarized so that the reader can see at a glance what cases are covered. The actual operations of the interface are then built from the partial operations using the techniques described earlier in this chapter.

We now examine, or at least record, suggested formats for presenting specifications of different complexity, beginning with the class manager's assistant. The layout of the specification is analysed in Table 5.6.

Table 5.6 Example layout of a simple specification.

(1)	Given sets, data types, constants	
(2)	State	
(3)	Initial state	Uses (2)
	Operations	
(4)	Partial 'correct'	
(5)	Partial 'error'	
(6)	Combined	Uses (4) and (5)

If the specification were of the class management system, we should include the whole of the class manager's assistant, noting however that (6) was not the interface, but was a collection of operations from which the interface would be built, and then we should extend it as in Table 5.7.

Table 5.7 Example layout of a simple specification with promotion.

(7)	Promoted state	From (2)
(8)	Initial promoted state	
	Operations	
(9)	Operations to create and destroy instances of the state	Uses (3)
(10)	New error cases	
(11)	Promoted operations	Uses (6)

Sometimes the state can be partitioned into two parts that are more or less independent. The format of Table 5.8 is recommended.

Table 5.8 Example layout of a specification with partitioned state.

(1)	Given sets, data types, constants	
(2)	State A	
(3)	Initial state A	Uses (2)
	Operations on A	
(4)	Partial 'correct'	
(5)	Partial 'error'	
(6)	Combined	Uses (4) and (5)
(7)	State B	
(8)	Initial state B	Uses (7)
	Operations on B	
(9)	Partial 'correct'	
(10)	Partial 'error'	
(11)	Combined	Uses (9) and (10)
(12)	Complete state	Uses (2) and (7)
(13)	Complete initial state	Uses (3) and (8)
(14)	Complete operations	Uses (6) and (11)

Lastly, we give a format in Table 5.9 for a specification in which a number of things, identified by name, are to be managed, but these things are of two different kinds, though the operations on them are similar.

Table 5.9 Example layout of a specification with partitioned state and promotion.

(1)	Given sets, data types, constants	
(2)	State A	
(3)	Initial state A	Uses (2)
	Operations on A	
(4)	Partial 'correct'	
(5)	Partial 'error'	
(6)	Combined	Uses (4) and (5)
(7)	State B	
(8)	Initial state B	Uses (7)
	Operations on B	
(9)	Partial 'correct'	
(10)	Partial 'error'	
(11)	Combined	Uses (9) and (10)
(12)	Complete state with As and Bs	Uses (2) and (7)
(13)	Complete initial state	Uses (3) and (8)
(14)	Management operations to create and destroy As and Bs	Uses (3) and (8)
(15)	New errors	
(16)	Promotion schema for As, leaving Bs unchanged	
(17)	Promotion schema for Bs, leaving As unchanged	
(18)	Complete operations	From (6), (11), (14), (15), (16) and (17)

5.9 Inspecting specifications

The specification to be used as the basis for development of software should be inspected by the users and the developers to record their agreement that the specification represents a reasonable compromise between what the customer would like and what the developer wishes to supply. This inspection should be a formal meeting of the kind commonly used in the later phases of software development. The reader is referred to Fagan (1976) for background information about the role of inspections in the development process. The inspection of a specification is arranged to validate the formal specification against the informal requirements that led to its being drawn up. The term 'verification', which refers to the comparison of two precise descriptions to see that one is a correct refinement of another, cannot be used here, since only one of the descriptions is precise.

The comparison involves three kinds of text that need to be defined.

informal text The natural language, pictures, charts, tables etc. in the Z specification document

formal text The mathematical part of the Z specification document

informal description The requirements statement that gave rise to the writing of the Z specification document

The participants in an inspection should include at least the following:

- A moderator to chair the inspection meeting and record problems.
- At least two inspectors, one to represent the customer and one to represent the development organization. The inspectors need to have a good grasp of the formal notation.
- A reader to read the specification document. As readers can tire, it might be a good idea to have two of these.
- The author of the specification document.

It is preferable not to combine any of these roles, so at least six people are needed.

Now we can present a checklist of questions for use in preparing for inspections.

(1) Informal text:

- Is the technical vocabulary in the informal text used in a consistent manner?

- Is that technical vocabulary consistent with what is usually found in discussions of this subject?
- Are charts, diagrams and summary listings used to good effect?
- Is the informal text easy to read?

(2) The relation of the formal text to the informal text:

- Is the balance between formal text and informal text satisfactory? (There is often too much formal and not enough informal.)
- Is the vocabulary of the informal text reflected in the names used in the formal text?
- Does the informal text give convincing examples of the way the interface might be used?

(3) The formal text:

- Is the formal text free of syntax, scope and type errors? (This is not an issue if a tool to check syntax, scope and type is available.)
- Are the state components few in number?
- Have the devices of the schema calculus been used to good effect in presenting the model?
- Are the predicates in the state short, easily understood and few in number?
- Are all the invariants on the state documented?
- Is the consistency of the abstract state proved?
- Are the operations easily explained in terms of the model?
- Are the operations in the interface total, and if not are the preconditions well documented?

(4) The relation of the formal text to the informal description:

- Does the formal text reveal missing information in the informal description?
- Does the formal text demonstrate understanding of all the aspects of the operations?
- Does the formal text capture the documented requirements?

- Does the formal text over-specify the requirements by making decisions that are not justified?

Not all these questions are of the same size or importance. In particular, the penultimate question is crucial; encouraging answers to the others are of no value if the answer to this one is 'no'.

Exercises

Some of the exercises below ask the reader to write specifications in Z. If the reader is one of a group of students, then the writing of the specification should be a team effort. Ideally a class works in groups of three or four, each group writing its own specification, and then presenting it to the whole class. Presentations can be supported by visual aids showing the formal text while the presenter adds the informal text that should surround the mathematics. Informal visual aids like tables, diagrams and cartoons can be used. Alternatively, specifications could be made into proper documents by using a text entry and formatting system, distributed for review, and then inspected as described above on p. 152. This latter approach is more time-consuming, and uses more computing power and terminal time, but is a useful introduction for undergraduates to industrial practice.

(5.1) The exercises to Chapter 3 introduced some informal notions of a banking system. Write a schema to describe the state of the banking system to include the sets described there, and the relation

$$balance: AcctNo \mathrel{+\!\!\!\!\to} \mathbb{Z} \qquad (271)$$

where integers are to represent sums of money. (Negative values represent loans from the bank to the customer.) Document an initial abstract state.

(5.2) Write the schemas needed to formalize the requirements for the following operations of phase 1 of the library management system. Informal descriptions were given on p. 107.

- add a borrower
- delete a book
- delete a borrower
- lend a book
- return a book

Document the preconditions of the schemas in a table, and then construct specifications of the robust operations using schema disjunction. Write your own definition of the type *LMSResponse*.

(5.3) The informal descriptions of the operations of the banking system shown in Table 5.10 should be formalized using the methods of this chapter.

Table 5.10 Informal description of banking operations.

Inputs	**Processing**	**Outputs**
Open a deposit account		
amount	If there are no account numbers left, then the response is 'No more account numbers'. If the amount offered is negative, then the response is 'Overdrawn balances are not allowed in deposit accounts'. Otherwise the account is opened in the input amount with an unused account number chosen by the system, and the response is 'Account opened'. The account number chosen is displayed.	response, account number
Open a current account		
amount	If there are no account numbers left, then the response is 'No more account numbers'. Otherwise the account is opened in the input amount with an unused account number chosen by the system, and the response is 'Account opened'. The account number chosen is displayed.	response, account number
Close an account		
account number	If the account number is not active, then the response is 'Not an active account number'. If the account number is active, but is a current account that is overdrawn, then the response is 'Deposit the stated amount to clear', and the output amount is the amount to be paid in to clear the account. Otherwise the account is removed from the records, the closing balance is output, and the response is 'Account closed'.	response, amount

Inputs	Processing	Outputs
Make a deposit or a withdrawal		
account number, amount	If the account number is not active, then the response is 'Not an active account number'. If the account is a deposit account that would become overdrawn, the response is 'Overdrawn balance not allowed', and an output amount is given to show the current balance of the account. Otherwise the balance of the account is changed according to the amount, positive amounts representing deposits, and negative amounts representing withdrawals, and the response is 'Transaction complete'.	response, amount

(5.4) Modify your specification in the light of a new requirement, changing the response to making a deposit or a withdrawal as follows:

- If the amount was positive, the response is to be 'Deposit completed'
- If the amount was negative, the response is to be 'Withdrawal completed'

(5.5) Modify your specification in the light of a new requirement that the bank shall remain solvent, i.e. the sum of all the balances, positive and negative, shall never be negative. Amend the informal description of the state and operations as well as the schemas that specify the state and operations. (You will have to invent your own requirements about what responses will be issued when an attempt is made to break the bank.)

(5.6) The following are the informal requirements for an oil terminal control system, a simple system to control the allocation of berths to tankers in an oil terminal.

An oil terminal has a number of berths at which tankers can discharge their cargoes. When an approaching tanker asks for permission to dock, the controller will ask the system to allocate a berth for it to use. If no berth is free, the system will tell the controller so, and the tanker will be queued in the approach to the terminal. The system assumes that there is enough queueing space for any number of tankers. On docking, a tanker occupies the allocated berth and unloads its cargo. When it is ready to leave, the controller will notify the system so that the berth is ready for reuse, and the tanker is deleted from the system. A tanker's leaving a berth might mean that a queueing tanker can come and occupy it. The system will identify the tanker at the head of the queue to the controller, and allocate the berth to the tanker. The system has enquiry facilities so that the controller can get information about which tankers are queueing, which berths are occupied and by which tankers, and which berths are free.

Identify ambiguities and inconsistencies in these requirements, and record them in the form of questions directed to the person supplying the requirements. Obtain or invent clarifications, and then construct a tabular description of these requirements in the manner of Table 5.2 on p. 108. Write a Z specification to formalize the requirements.

(5.7) Specify a printer management system based on the fragments used as an example on p. 140.

(5.8) What are the signature and property of the schema *Time_sharing* on p. 102?

(5.9) What are the signatures and properties of the following schemas? (You may assume that *RB* is established elsewhere as the name of a type.)

$$X \triangleq [x\colon \mathbb{Z}]$$

$$Y \triangleq [x\colon \mathbb{Z};\ y\colon \mathbb{N}]$$

$$RBQ \triangleq [rbqueue\colon \mathbf{seq}\ RB \mid \#\ rbqueue > 0]$$

(5.10) Show that removing $s? \in enrolled$ from the schema *Testok* on p. 17 does not change its precondition.

Table 5.11 gives the informal requirements for phase 3 of the library management system, in which reservation of titles by borrowers is to be supported.

(5.11) Write a specification of phase 3 of the library management system reusing as much as possible of the phase 2 specification.

Table 5.11 Informal description of library operations for phase 3.

Inputs	**Processing**	**Outputs**
Delete a book		
book	If the title of this book has been reserved by a borrower then the response is 'Borrowers waiting', and the book is not removed from the library system.	response
Delete a borrower		
person	Any reservations made by this borrower are cancelled.	response
Lend a book		
book, person	If the book is a reserved title, and this borrower is not the first borrower waiting for this title, then the response is 'Book reserved'.	response
Return a book		
book	If the book is a title that has borrowers waiting, and there are fewer instances of this title waiting for their borrowers than there are borrowers, then the response is 'Book reserved'.	response
Reserve a title		
title, person	If the title is not one owned by the library, then the response is 'Title not available'. If the person is not a borrower, then the response is 'Not a borrower'. If this borrower already has a reservation for this title, then the response is 'Book already reserved by this borrower'. Otherwise the title is reserved to the borrower, and the response is 'Book reserved'.	response

(5.12) Continue the specification of the two-class system by specifying the remaining operation on 'Z for Beginners' and all the operations on 'Z Advanced'. Write an informal description of the interface offered to the manager of the two classes.

The following exercises refer to the promotion of operations of the class manager's assistant into the class management system.

(5.13) Partial operations to add and remove classes in the class management system were specified on p. 137. Write schemas to make them robust, and specify the robust forms.

(5.14) Write the definition of the type *CSResponse* used in the promotion of the class manager's assistant to the class management system.

Chapter 6
Data design

Summary: Direct and indirect data design – two views of a software object – concrete state – forward simulation – concrete initial state, its existence and verification – concrete operations and their verification – linked lists – indirect data design – documenting assumptions about interfaces – inspecting data designs.

In this chapter the class manager's assistant is the main source of examples, and we investigate different ways of implementing it.

6.1 Principles of data design

The abstract objects and operations of the specification have to be represented by data structures and algorithms available on computers. The software engineer's skill lies in constructing these concrete representations of the abstract specification within the constraints imposed by development schedules, hardware and software available for the implementation etc. The first stage in this process is the choice of data structures to represent the abstract data objects of the specification.

6.1.1 Modes of data design

There are primarily two modes of data design: direct and indirect. In direct data design the implementer chooses data structures of the target programming language, and organizes them to represent the abstract objects of the specification. In indirect data design the implementer chooses abstract data types such as files, trees or other structures and uses these to represent the abstract objects of the specification. These abstract data types might already be implemented, or the data design step might produce, as part of its documentation, specifications of the abstract data types to be developed. For instance, if we were implementing the class manager's assistant, and a package for implementing sets were available on the chosen computer, our concrete state might just be two instances of the abstract data type for sets. The instances might correspond to *enrolled* and *tested*, or they might correspond to *tested* and $enrolled \setminus tested$.

6.1.2 Abstract and concrete views

The abstract state of the specification represents the user's view of the data he or she is using. The software engineer must provide a concrete representation of the data, and algorithms for the operations.

In Figure 6.1 there are illustrated two views of the class manager's assistant. The abstract view is the view we wish to encourage the class manager to take. This view sees the class as two sets that can be manipulated by the four operations, and the operations are the only way the class manager can have any effect on the two sets. These sets stand in a certain relationship to one another, and this relationship is maintained by the operations. The concrete view is that of the implementer of the class manager's assistant, who sees concrete structures of the programming environment that will be used to implement the software. The implementer's duty is to provide four algorithms that will manipulate the concrete structures so that

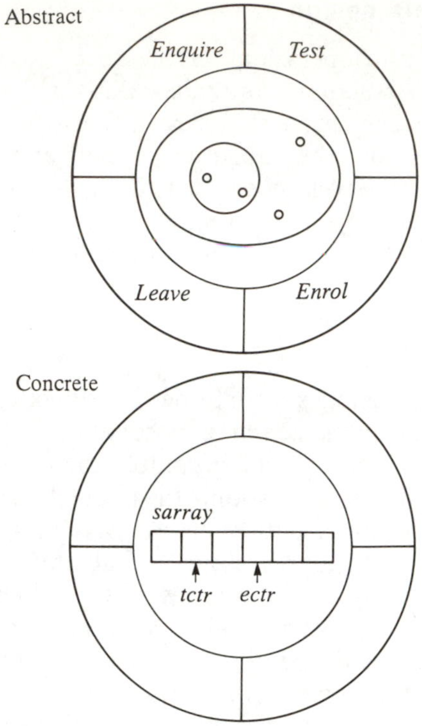

Figure 6.1 Abstract and concrete views.

the class manager cannot tell the difference between what the specification promised and what has been provided.

6.2 An example of direct data design

6.2.1 Environment

In a direct data design of the class manager's assistant, we shall use concrete structures found in many programming languages. We suppose the reader has some acquaintance with programming languages like Pascal, though these languages are not discussed in detail in this book until the next chapter. The following considerations guided our choice.

- The problem is not very complicated.
- We needed an example of direct data design for this chapter.
- We have a programmer who needs experience in writing simple programs from specifications.

- Saving and restoring data in storage is a feature of the operating system of the intended hardware, so the operational problem of making the data persist from day to day can be solved even if we choose an in-storage solution.

6.2.2 Concrete state data

We have chosen to represent the class by an array of students and two counters. This representation is the **concrete state** for this data design. We shall model the notion of an array by a total function relating the valid indexes (in this case *1..size*) to values of *Student*. Since *Student* is a given set, its values are suitable for passing across an interface as parameters, so we suppose that they are suitable for storing in the cells of an array in Pascal.

DClass

$sarray: (1..size) \rightarrow Student$ (14)
$ectr: 0..size$
$tctr: 0..size$

$tctr \leq ectr$
$\forall i, j: 1..ectr \mid i \neq j \bullet sarray\ i \neq sarray\ j$

It is our intention that the tested set shall be represented by the segment of the array up to *tctr*, and the enrolled set by the segment of the array up to *ectr*, but we shall make this more precise shortly. We have put some constraints on the counters, and the contents of the array. The value of *tctr* will never exceed the value of *ectr*, and there are to be no duplicate entries in the array up to *ectr*. We put no constraints on the contents of the array beyond *ectr*.

The relation between the abstract and concrete states explained informally above is made precise in the **forward simulation**, which explains how the abstract state is to be found from the concrete state. We record it in a schema that brings together the abstract state *Class* and the concrete state *DClass*.

The forward simulation for this data design is as follows.

DSim

Class (14)
DClass (163)

$enrolled = \{i: 1..ectr \bullet sarray\ i\}$
$tested = \{i: 1..tctr \bullet sarray\ i\}$

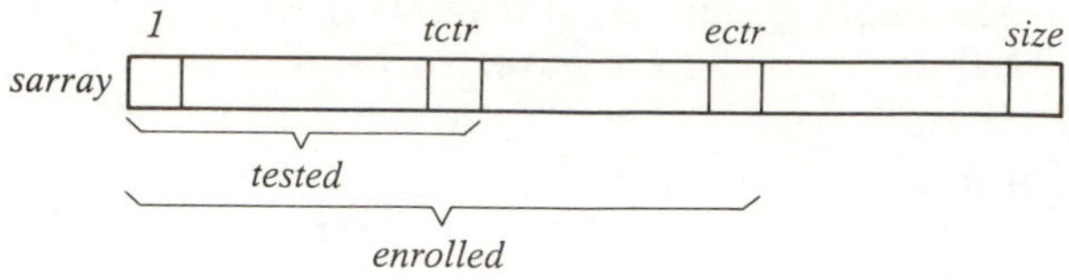

Figure 6.2 Forward simulation for the direct data design.

The set *enrolled* is the set of students in the cells of the array up to *ectr*, and the set *tested* is the set of students in the cells of the array up to *tctr*.

The forward simulation is illustrated by Figure 6.2.

The forward simulation from concrete to abstract is many – one, since many different concrete states represent the same abstract state. It is very common in data design to find that the forward simulation is many – one, and could therefore be documented as a function:

$$abstr: DClass \rightarrow Class \qquad (163, 14)$$

$$(\ \forall dc: DClass \bullet \qquad (163)$$
$$(\ (abstr\ dc).enrolled = \{i: 1..dc.ectr \bullet dc.sarray\ i\}$$
$$\wedge\ (abstr\ dc).tested = \{i: 1..dc.tctr \bullet dc.sarray\ i\}\ )\ )$$

When the forward simulation is a function, it is often called the **abstraction function** for the data design.

Certain design decisions have been made that are worth reviewing:

- A single array has been chosen rather than two arrays.
- Counters are used to delimit the parts of the array rather than flagging the array entries.
- The active array entries are at the low index end.
- The tested students come first and the enrolled students after, rather than the other way round.
- No duplicates are allowed in the active part of the array.
- We do not specify an ordering of students in the active part of the array.

6.2.3 Concrete initial state

We have to specify a **concrete initial state**, that is to say a state of the concrete data structures that will be established when the class manager's assistant is first switched on.

DInit	
$DClass'$	(163)
$ectr' = 0$	

Initially the value of $ectr'$ is zero, and the value of the array is of no interest. It is easy to see that $tctr' = 0$.

We have a proof obligation to show that

$$\vdash \exists DClass' \bullet DInit, \qquad (163, 165)$$

i.e. that a concrete initial state can be found. To do this it is only necessary to find a value $tctr'$ that satisfies the constraints, and zero is such a value. This remark establishes the existence of a concrete initial state, and hence the consistency of the concrete state. There are in fact many concrete initial states for this data design, since the contents of the array are not specified, and unless the given set *Student* contains only one value, there are many possible array values that could be used in a concrete initial state. We should be careful to avoid speaking or writing about 'the concrete initial state', since there are many of them.

We now have another proof obligation to show that any concrete initial state is correct, i.e. that according to the forward simulation, any concrete initial state represents an abstract initial state. Formally the requirement is expressed by the theorem

$$DInit \vdash \exists Class' \bullet (\ ClassInit \land DSim'\ ) \qquad (165, 14, 15, 164)$$

To prove this theorem we first expand the conclusion as follows:

$\exists enrolled', tested' : \mathbb{P}\ Student \bullet$

(1)	$(\ tested' \subseteq enrolled'$	From $Class'$
(2)	$\land\ \#\ enrolled' \leq size$	From $Class'$
(3)	$\land\ enrolled' = \varnothing$	From $ClassInit$
(4)	$\land\ tctr' \leq ectr'$	From $DSim'$
(5)	$\land\ (\ \forall i, j: 1..ectr' \mid i \neq j$ $\bullet\ sarray'\ i \neq sarray'\ j\ )$	From $DSim'$

(6) $\wedge$ *enrolled'* = {*i*: *1..ectr'* • *sarray' i*} From *DSim'*

(7) $\wedge$ *tested'* = {*i*: *1..tctr'* • *sarray' i*}) From *DSim'*

The obvious choice for *enrolled'* and *tested'* are the empty set, and this reduces the conclusion to the following:

(8) (*tctr'* ≤ *ectr'* From (4)

(9) $\wedge$ (∀*i*, *j*: *1..ectr'* | *i* ≠ *j*
• *sarray' i* ≠ *sarray' j*) From (5)

(10) $\wedge$ Ø = {*i*: *1..ectr'* • *sarray' i*} From (6)

(11) $\wedge$ Ø = {*i*: *1..tctr'* • *sarray' i*}) From (7)

(8) and (9) are in the predicate part of *DInit*, which is the hypothesis. (10) and (11) follow since *ectr'* =*0* and *tctr'*≤*ectr'* are in *DInit*.

6.2.4 Enrolling a student

We now write specifications of the effects of the operations on concrete states, using the schema calculus to present the specifications just as we did with the operations on abstract states. In the case of the operation to enrol a student we shall use a decomposition that corresponds to the decomposition of the abstract operation into *Enrolok*, *NoRoom* and *AlreadyEnrolled*. First we describe the behaviour that produces the response *success*. Note that the declaration part of this schema must have the same inputs and outputs as *Enrolok*, and only the state schema can have changed.

```
┌─DEnrolok──────────────────────────
│ ΔDClass                                  (163)
│ s?: Student                              (14)
│ r!: Response                             (14)
├───────────
│ ∀i: 1..ectr • sarray i ≠ s?
│ ectr < size
│ tctr' = tctr
│ ectr' = ectr + 1
│ sarray' = sarray ⊕ {ectr' ↦ s?}
│ r! = success
└───────────────────────────────────
```

Table 6.1 records the intended correspondence between abstract and concrete predicates.

Table 6.1 Abstract and concrete predicates.

Abstract	**Concrete**
$s \notin enrolled$	$\forall i: 1..ectr \bullet sarray\ i \neq s?$
$\# enrolled < size$	$ectr < size$
$tested' = tested$ $enrolled' = enrolled \cup \{s?\}$	$tctr' = tctr$ $ectr' = ectr + 1$ $sarray' = sarray \oplus \{ectr' \mapsto s?\}$
$r! = success$	$r! = success$

The predicate $sarray' = sarray \oplus \{ectr' \mapsto s?\}$ captures exactly the notion of assigning $s?$ to the cell of the array whose index is $ectr'$. Figure 6.3 illustrates this design.

Note that this specification permits no rearrangement of the array elements, not even in the unused part. Consider however the following:

DEnrolok1

$$\Delta DClass \qquad (163)$$
$$s?: Student \qquad (14)$$
$$r!: Response \qquad (14)$$

$$\forall i: 1..ectr \bullet sarray\ i \neq s?$$
$$ectr < size$$
$$tctr' = tctr$$
$$ectr' = ectr + 1$$
$$(1..tctr) \lhd sarray' = (1..tctr) \lhd sarray$$
$$\{i: 1..ectr' \bullet sarray'\ i\} = \{i: 1..ectr \bullet sarray\ i\} \cup \{s?\}$$
$$r! = success$$

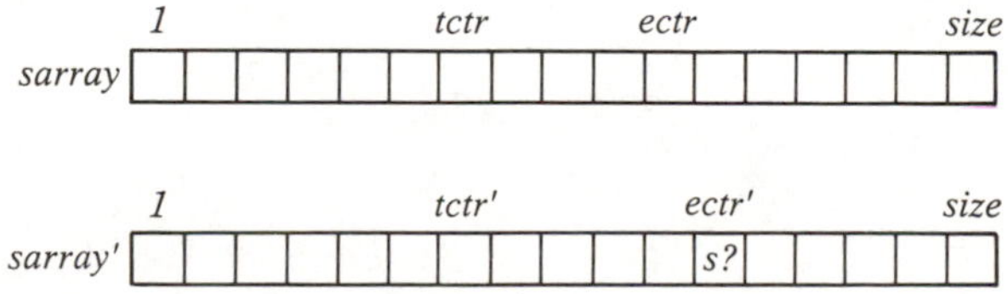

Figure 6.3 Enrolling a student – direct design.

This schema provides the same function as *DEnrolok*, that is it correctly implements what was required in the abstract operation, but it allows some rearrangement of the array. The new predicates can be interpreted as follows. The array is unchanged up to *tctr*. Between $tctr + 1$ and $ectr + 1$ all the old students are still there, and there is a new one, *s?*. Beyond $ectr + 1$ anything might happen. This kind of non-determinism allows the designer of the algorithm a freedom that might be exploited in algorithm design.

The other cases of enrolling a student are dealt with in the same way:

DNoRoom

$\Xi DClass$	(163)
$r!: Response$	(14)

$ectr = size$
$r! = noroom$

DAlreadyEnrolled

$\Xi DClass$	(163)
$s?: Student$	(14)
$r!: Response$	(14)

$\exists i: 1..ectr \bullet sarray\ i = s?$
$r! = alreadyenrolled$

Neither of these schemas permits any change to any part of the array.

The concrete version of the operation to enrol a student is now specified:

$DEnrol \mathrel{\widehat=}$
$\quad DEnrolok \lor DNoRoom \lor DAlreadyEnrolled$ (166, 168, 168)

The reader should now be able to specify the concrete operations to test a student and discharge a student, and is required to do so in the exercises.

6.2.5 Correctness of operation refinement

The notion that *DEnrol* implements *Enrol* is informally explained by saying that the operator of the interface (the class manager) can maintain a consistent view of the abstract state while the computer system actually manipulates the concrete state. There are two formal statements of correctness that we now examine:

$$(\mathbf{pre}\ Enrol) \land DSim \vdash \mathbf{pre}\ DEnrol \qquad (21, 164, 168)$$

$$(\mathbf{pre}\ Enrol) \land DSim \land DEnrol \qquad (21, 164, 168)$$
$$\vdash \exists Class' \bullet (\ Enrol \land DSim'\ ) \qquad (14, 21, 164)$$

These two statements constitute a proof obligation on the writer of the data design.

The first rule is the **safety condition**. It expresses that fact that if the operator thinks that the proposed input and current abstract state satisfy the precondition of the abstract operation, then the proposed input and the concrete state must satisfy the precondition of the concrete operation.

The second rule is the **liveness condition**. It expresses the fact illustrated in Figure 6.4. The concrete representation is in a state *DClass* when the operator introduces the input *s?* and attempts to enrol a student. The operator thinks that the system is in an abstract state *Class*, related to *DClass* by the forward simulation *DSim*, and the proposed input and current state satisfy the precondition of the operation. The operator expects the effect to be a new abstract state *Class'*, and an output response r_1, where *Class*, *s?*, *Class'* and r_1 are related by *Enrol*. In fact the concrete representation moves to a new concrete state *DClass'*, and produces a response r_2, where *DClass*, *s?*,

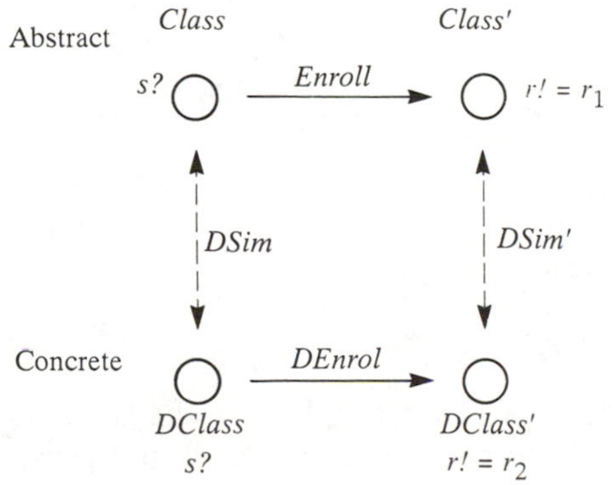

Figure 6.4 Correctness of concrete operations.

DClass' and r_2 are related by *DEnrol*. The correctness requirement is that

- r_1 and r_2 are equal, and
- *Class'* is related to *DClass'* by *DSim'*.

6.2.6 Proof of correctness of enrolling a student

We prove first the safety condition that

$$(\textbf{\textit{pre}}\ Enrol) \wedge DSim \vdash \textbf{\textit{pre}}\ DEnrol \qquad (21, 164, 168)$$

Note that ***preDEnrol*** is the disjunction of ***preDEnrolok***, ***preDNoRoom*** and ***preDAlreadyEnrolled***. These three schemas have in common the invariant on the concrete state, and three predicates whose disjunction is true:

$$\forall i: 1..ectr \bullet sarray\ i \neq s?$$

$$ectr = size$$

$$\exists i: 1..ectr \bullet sarray\ i = s?$$

But the invariant on the concrete state is in the hypothesis, since it is part of *DSim*, so the theorem is proved.

Now we must prove the liveness condition

$$(\textbf{\textit{pre}}\ Enrol) \wedge DSim \wedge DEnrol \qquad (21, 164, 168)$$
$$\vdash \exists Class' \bullet (\ Enrol \wedge DSim'\ ) \qquad (14, 21, 164)$$

The proof can be done by considering cases, and it is important to partition the proof according to the cases of the concrete operation. In this example the specification of the concrete operation has been organized so that the cases of the abstract and concrete operations are the same, but had they been different, the cases of the concrete operation would have been used. The cases can be characterized by the values of the response:

(1) $r! = noroom$

(2) $r! = success$

(3) $r! = alreadyenrolled$

We shall do the first two cases, and leave the third as an exercise.

First we collect the predicates of the hypothesis, adding the first case assumption to simplify *DEnrol*, as follows:

(1)	$tested \subseteq enrolled$	From ***pre****Enrol* and *DSim*
(2)	$\# enrolled \leq size$	From ***pre****Enrol* and *DSim*
(3)	$tctr \leq ectr$	From *DSim* and *DEnrol*
(4)	$(\forall i, j: 1..ectr \mid i \neq j$ $\bullet\ sarray\ i \neq sarray\ j)$	From *DSim* and *DEnrol*
(5)	$enrolled = \{i: 1..ectr \bullet sarray\ i\}$	From *DSim*
(6)	$tested = \{i: 1..tctr \bullet sarray\ i\}$	From *DSim*
(7)	$sarray \in (1..size) \rightarrow Student$	From *DSim* and *DEnrol*
(8)	$ectr \in 0..size$	From *DSim* and *DEnrol*
(9)	$tctr \in 0..size$	From *DSim* and *DEnrol*
(10)	$ectr = size$	From *DEnrol*, in this case
(11)	$r! = noroom$	From *DEnrol*, in this case
(12)	$ectr' = ectr$	From *DEnrol*, in this case
(13)	$tctr' = tctr$	From *DEnrol*, in this case
(14)	$sarray' = sarray$	From *DEnrol*, in this case

Then we expand the conclusion, which is an existential quantification, using the first case assumption to simplify *Enrol*, as follows:

$\exists tested', enrolled': \mathbb{P}\ Student \bullet$

(15)	$(tested' \subseteq enrolled'$	From *Class'*, *Enrol* and *DSim'*
(16)	$\wedge\ \# enrolled' \leq size$	From *Class'*, *Enrol* and *DSim'*
(17)	$\wedge\ sarray' \in (1..size) \rightarrow Student$	From *DSim'*
(18)	$\wedge\ ectr' \in 0..size$	From *DSim'*
(19)	$\wedge\ tctr' \in 0..size$	From *DSim'*
(20)	$\wedge\ tested' = \{i: 1..tctr' \bullet sarray'\ i\}$	From *DSim'*
(21)	$\wedge\ enrolled' =$ $\{i: 1..ectr' \bullet sarray'\ i\}$	From *DSim'*
(22)	$\wedge\ tctr' \leq ectr'$	From *DSim'*
(23)	$\wedge\ (\forall i, j: 1..ectr' \mid i \neq j$ $\bullet\ sarray'\ i \neq sarray'\ j)$	From *DSim'*

(24)	$\wedge$ *tested* $\subseteq$ *enrolled*	From *Enrol*
(25)	$\wedge$ # *enrolled* $\leq$ *size*	From *Enrol*
(26)	$\wedge$ # *enrolled* = *size*	From *Enrol*, in this case
(27)	$\wedge$ *enrolled'* = *enrolled*	From *Enrol*, in this case
(28)	$\wedge$ *tested'* = *tested*	From *Enrol*, in this case
(29)	$\wedge$ *r!* = *noroom*)	From *Enrol*, in this case

Next we apply the one-point rule to eliminate the existential quantifier using predicates (27) and (28) as follows:

(30)	*tested* $\subseteq$ *enrolled*	From (15), (27) and (28)
(31)	# *enrolled* $\leq$ *size*	From (16) and (27)
(32)	*sarray'* $\in$ (*1..size*) $\rightarrow$ *Student*	From (17)
(33)	*ectr'* $\in$ *0..size*	From (18)
(34)	*tctr'* $\in$ *0..size*	From (19)
(35)	*tested* = {*i*: *1..tctr'* • *sarray' i*}	From (20) and (28)
(36)	*enrolled* = {*i*: *1..ectr'* • *sarray' i*}	From (21) and (27)
(37)	*tctr'* $\leq$ *ectr'*	From (22)
(38)	($\forall$*i*, *j*: *1..ectr'* | *i* $\neq$ *j* • *sarray' i* $\neq$ *sarray' j*)	From (23)
(39)	# *enrolled* = *size*	From (26)
(40)	*r!* = *noroom*	From (29)

Now all the predicates (30) to (40) are deducible from (1) to (14) as follows:

(30) from (1)
(31) from (2)
(32) from (7) and (14)
(33) from (8) and (12)
(34) from (9) and (13)
(35) from (6), (13) and (14)
(36) from (5), (12) and (14)
(37) from (3), (12) and (13)
(38) from (4), (12) and (14)
(39) from (5), (4) and (10)
(40) from (11)

This concludes the proof for the case $r! = noroom$. Because the correspondence between the concrete and abstract states is straightforward, the deductive steps in this proof are fairly simple. The difficulty of the proof lies in first finding a strategy, and then handling the large number of predicates involved. With a more elaborate forward simulation the deductive steps will be more complicated. The case chosen is also a simple case, since the state does not change. In the next case the state changes, and we shall see that the deductive process is slightly more demanding.

Now we consider the case in which $r! = success$, documenting the hypotheses as follows:

(1)	$tested \subseteq enrolled$	From ***pre****Enrol* and *DSim*
(2)	$\# enrolled \leq size$	From ***pre****Enrol* and *DSim*
(3)	$tctr \leq ectr$	From *DSim* and *DEnrol*
(4)	$(\forall i, j: 1..ectr \mid i \neq j$ $\bullet\ sarray\ i \neq sarray\ j)$	From *DSim* and *DEnrol*
(5)	$enrolled = \{i: 1..ectr \bullet sarray\ i\}$	From *DSim*
(6)	$tested = \{i: 1..tctr \bullet sarray\ i\}$	From *DSim*
(7)	$sarray \in (1..size) \rightarrow Student$	From *DSim* and *DEnrol*
(8)	$ectr \in 0..size$	From *DSim* and *DEnrol*
(9)	$tctr \in 0..size$	From *DSim* and *DEnrol*
(10)	$\forall i: 1..ectr \bullet sarray\ i \neq s?$	From *DEnrol*, in this case
(11)	$ectr < size$	From *DEnrol*, in this case
(12)	$tctr' = tctr$	From *DEnrol*, in this case
(13)	$ectr' = ectr + 1$	From *DEnrol*, in this case
(14)	$sarray' =$ $sarray \oplus \{ectr' \mapsto s?\}$	From *DEnrol*, in this case
(15)	$r! = success$	From *DEnrol*, in this case

Then we expand the conclusion, which is an existential quantification, using the first case assumption to simplify *Enrol*, as follows:

$$\exists tested', enrolled': \mathbb{P}\ Student \bullet$$

(16)	$(\ tested' \subseteq enrolled'$	From *Class'*, *Enrol* and *DSim'*

(17)	$\land \# enrolled' \leq size$	From *Class'*, *Enrol* and *DSim'*
(18)	$\land sarray' \in (1..size) \rightarrow Student$	From *DSim'*
(19)	$\land ectr' \in 0..size$	From *DSim'*
(20)	$\land tctr' \in 0..size$	From *DSim'*
(21)	$\land tested' = \{i: 1..tctr' \bullet sarray'\ i\}$	From *DSim'*
(22)	$\land enrolled' =$ $\{i: 1..ectr' \bullet sarray'\ i\}$	From *DSim'*
(23)	$\land tctr' \leq ectr'$	From *DSim'*
(24)	$\land (\forall i, j: 1..ectr' \mid i \neq j$ $\bullet sarray'\ i \neq sarray'\ j)$	From *DSim'*
(25)	$\land tested \subseteq enrolled$	From *Enrol*
(26)	$\land \# enrolled \leq size$	From *Enrol*
(27)	$\land s? \notin enrolled$	From *Enrol*, in this case
(28)	$\land \# enrolled < size$	From *Enrol*, in this case
(29)	$\land enrolled' = enrolled \cup \{s?\}$	From *Enrol*, in this case
(30)	$\land tested' = tested$	From *Enrol*, in this case
(31)	$\land r! = success)$	Case assumption

Next we apply the one-point rule to eliminate the existential quantifier using predicates (29) and (30), as follows:

(32)	$tested \subseteq enrolled \cup \{s?\}$	From (16), (29) and (30)
(33)	$\# (enrolled \cup \{s?\}) \leq size$	From (17) and (29)
(34)	$sarray' \in (1..size) \rightarrow Student$	From (18)
(35)	$ectr' \in 0..size$	From (19)
(36)	$tctr' \in 0..size$	From (20)
(37)	$tested = \{i: 1..tctr' \bullet sarray'\ i\}$	From (21) and (30)
(38)	$enrolled \cup \{s?\} =$ $\{i: 1..ectr' \bullet sarray'\ i\}$	From (22) and (29)
(39)	$tctr' \leq ectr'$	From (23)
(40)	$(\forall i, j: 1..ectr' \mid i \neq j$ $\bullet sarray'\ i \neq sarray'\ j)$	From (24)

(41) $s? \notin enrolled$ From (27)

(42) $\# enrolled < size$ From (28)

(43) $r! = success$ From (31)

Now all the predicates (32) to (43) are deducible from (1) to (15) as follows:

(32) from (1)
(33) from (4), (5) and (11)
(34) from (14), (7), (11) and (10)
(35) from (13), (8) and (11)
(36) from (9) and (12)
(37) from (6), (12), (14), (3) and (13)
(38) from (5), (13) and (14)
(39) from (3), (12) and (13)
(40) from (4), (10) and (14)
(41) from (5) and (10)
(42) from (5) and (11)
(43) from (15)

This concludes the proof for the case $r! = success$. The proof for the case $r! = alreadyenrolled$ is left as an exercise.

6.3 Some concrete data structures

In the first part of this chapter we showed how to record a decision that a certain concrete structure, an array and two counters, were to be used to represent a certain abstract structure, two sets. In the second part of this chapter we shall show how to make such a record when more elaborate structures are selected. We choose in particular the linked list.

6.3.1 Using linked lists

We consider the means of describing in Z a common structure used in refining operating system software, namely a singly-linked list. Figure 6.5 illustrates the kind of situation we are going to describe.

We need some given sets for the pointers, and the kind of data that is to be stored in the blocks in the linked list.

$[Pointer, Data]$

There is no need to be more specific about the nature of a pointer except to say that we need a special value, a pointer that doesn't point at anything.

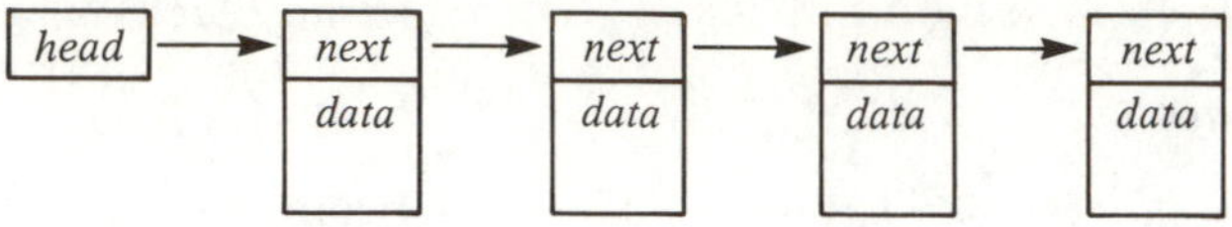

Figure 6.5 Refinement using a singly-linked list.

| $nil\_pointer: Pointer$ (175)

Now we define the type of the blocks in the list.

Block

$next: Pointer$ (175)
$data: Data$ (175)

There is no constraint that can be placed on the values of *pointer* or *data*.

To describe the way in which blocks are linked we need a starting pointer (*head*) and some auxiliary ideas, namely the relation between pointers and the blocks they address (*block_at*), and the idea of the sequence of pointers (*pointers*) that is derived from the way in which the blocks are chained together.

Queue

$head: Pointer$ (175)
$block\_at: Pointer \rightarrowtail\!\!\!\!\rightarrow Block$ (175, 176)
$pointers: \mathbf{seq}\ Pointer$ (175)

$nil\_pointer \notin \mathbf{dom}\ block\_at$
$\mathbf{ran}\ pointers = \mathbf{dom}\ block\_at$
$\#\, pointers = \#\, \mathbf{ran}\ pointers$
$pointers = \langle\rangle \Leftrightarrow head = nil\_pointer$
$(\, pointers \neq \langle\rangle \Rightarrow$
$\quad (\, \mathbf{head}\ pointers = head$
$\quad \wedge\ (block\_at\ (\mathbf{last}\ pointers)).next = nil\_pointer$
$\quad \wedge\ (\ \forall\ i: 1..(\#pointers - 1)$
$\qquad \bullet\ (block\_at\ (pointers\ i)).next = pointers\ (i + 1)\ )\ )\ )$

The nil pointer does not address a block. The pointers in the sequence are exactly those that address the blocks in the linked list. The length of the sequence of pointers is the number of distinct pointers, so there are no duplicates. There are no blocks in the linked list if and only if the head pointer is the nil pointer. If there are pointers in the sequence, then the head pointer is the first pointer in the sequence, the *next* pointer of the block addressed by the last in the sequence is the nil pointer, and each block except the last has the pointer to the next block as its *next* component.

This schema contains three components:

head represents a pointer that must be maintained as part of the data structure used by the programs that manipulate the linked list.

block_at represents the collection of storage areas that make up the linked list. They too are part of the data structure used by the programs that manipulate the linked list.

pointers is a much more abstract thing. It is not part of the concrete data structure, instead it is a notion that was introduced to explain how the blocks and pointers must be organized to create a linked list.

In the schema these things have the same status – they are just its components – but in the implementation, *head* and *block_at* will be part of the concrete data structure, while *pointers* will not. We shall call the former **actual components** of the design, and the latter **notional components**.

We now illustrate how to specify an operation that adds a block to the top (head end) of the list. The operation changes the linked list, and we shall need to speak about the new block, so we introduce it into the declaration part. The new pointer that addresses the new block must be input, and so must the data to go into the block.

Add_to_head

$\Delta Queue$ (176)
$Block$ (176)
$new\_pointer?: Pointer$ (175)
$data?: Data$ (175)

$new\_pointer? \notin \mathbf{dom}\ block\_at$
$data = data?$
$pointers' = \langle new\_pointer? \rangle \frown pointers$
$block\_at' = block\_at \oplus \{new\_pointer? \mapsto \theta Block\}$ (176)

The new pointer must not be one that already addresses a block in the list. The data in the new block will be the input data. The list is reorganized in such a way that the sequence of pointers is unchanged except that the new pointer is now at the top. The new pointer will address the new block, and all the other pointers address the same blocks as before.

It is interesting to note that all other changes entailed in adding the new block at the head of the queue need not be explicitly stated. For instance, the new value of *head* can be seen to be *new_pointer?*

$$Add\_to\_head \vdash head' = new\_pointer?$$

by the following deduction.

(1)	$pointers' \neq \langle\rangle \Rightarrow$ $head' = \mathbf{head}\ pointers'$	From $\Delta Queue$
(2)	$pointers' = \langle new\_pointer? \rangle \mathbin{\char94} pointers$	From *Add_to_head*
(3)	$pointers' \neq \langle\rangle$	From (2)
(4)	$head' = \mathbf{head}\ pointers$	From (1) and (3)
(5)	$head' = new\_pointer?$	From (2) and (4)

The fact that *new_pointer?* cannot be *nil_pointer* is also implicit in the schema. We can state this fact as a theorem:

$$Add\_to\_head \vdash new\_pointer? \neq nil\_pointer \qquad (177)$$

The proof of this theorem is left as an exercise.

6.4 An example of indirect data design

In indirect data design, instead of relying solely on the resources of the target language, we choose to enrich the language with abstract data types. These data types might be pre-written packages, or they might be specified as part of the design process and then developed in parallel with the completion of the algorithm design. As an example we shall show how to record a design of the class manager's assistant using the following package.

6.4.1 The limited set specification

Users of the limited set specification can declare variables of the following two-valued type:

$$Indic ::= found \mid notfound$$

We define a state that will be referred to informally as a student-set with the following schema. The *ss* component is the set of students. The *max* component is a natural number.

$$\begin{array}{|l} \hline \textit{StudentSet} \\ ss: \mathbb{P}\ \textit{Student} \\ max: \mathbb{N} \\ \hline \#\, ss \leq max \\ \hline \end{array}$$ (14)

There can never be more than *max* students in the set.

The initial value of a student-set is specified as follows.

$$\textit{InitStudentSet} \mathrel{\widehat=} [\textit{StudentSet}' \mid ss' = \varnothing]$$ (179)

When a variable of this type is created, the set is empty, but no guarantee is made about the maximum value.

The first operation we specify is one to set the value of the maximum size. The new size is input.

$$\begin{array}{|l} \hline \textit{SetMax} \\ \Delta \textit{StudentSet} \\ new?: \mathbb{N} \\ \hline new? \geq \#\, ss \\ max' = new? \\ ss' = ss \\ \hline \end{array}$$ (179)

It is the user's responsibility to make sure that the new maximum is at least the current size of *ss*. The new maximum is installed, and the set is unchanged.

An operation is provided so that the user can find the current size of the set:

$$\textit{FindSize} \mathrel{\widehat=} [\Xi \textit{StudentSet};\ cur!: \mathbb{N} \mid cur! = \#\, ss]$$ (179)

The current size of the set is reported in *cur!*.

The user can add a member to the set.

$$\begin{array}{|l} \hline \textit{AddStudent} \\ \Delta \textit{StudentSet} \\ s?: \textit{Student} \\ \hline \#\, ss < max \\ ss' = ss \cup \{s?\} \\ max' = max \\ \hline \end{array}$$ (179) (14)

It is the user's responsibility to make sure that there is room for another student. The new student is added. (If the student is already there, the set is not changed.)

A member can be deleted.

RemoveStudent

$\Delta StudentSet$ (179)
$s?: Student$ (14)

$ss' = ss \setminus \{s?\}$
$max' = max$

The student is removed and the maximum is unchanged. (If the student is not there, the set is unchanged.)

We can find out if a student is present in the set.

TryStudent

$\Xi StudentSet$ (179)
$s?: Student$ (14)
$ind!: Indic$ (178)

$ind! = found \Leftrightarrow s? \in ss$

The output indicator will be *found* if and only if the student is in the set. Since the only other value of the indicator is *notfound*, that must be the value of the indicator if the student is not in the set.

The operations are summarized in Table 6.2.

Table 6.2 Summary of operations for the limited set specification.

Operation	Input	Precondition	Output
SetMax	$new?: \mathbb{N}$	$new? \geq \# ss$	none
FindSize	none	true	$cur!: \mathbb{N}$
AddStudent	$s?: Student$	$\# ss < max$	none
RemoveStudent	$s?: Student$	true	none
TryStudent	$s?: Student$	true	$ind!: Indic$

6.4.2 Concrete state data

We propose to use two instances of the *StudentSet* type to implement the class manager's assistant. The intention, made precise in the forward simulation *ISim* below, is to use one for those tested and one for those enrolled but not tested.

```
┌ IClass ───────────────────────────
│ yes, no: StudentSet                          (179)
├───────────
│ yes.max = size
│ no.max = size
│ yes.ss ∩ no.ss = ∅
└───────────────────────────────────
```

Each instance will have a maximum size equal to the maximum size of the class. The two instances will have no members in common.

The two components of the concrete state will be informally referred to as the yes-set and the no-set.

The forward simulation for this refinement is as follows:

```
┌ ISim ─────────────────────────────
│ Class                                        (14)
│ IClass                                       (181)
├───────────
│ enrolled = yes.ss ∪ no.ss
│ tested = yes.ss
└───────────────────────────────────
```

The enrolled students are represented by the union of the yes-set and the no-set. The yes-set represents the tested students.

6.4.3 Concrete initial state

The initial value is as follows.

```
┌ IInit ────────────────────────────
│ IClass'                                      (181)
├───────────
│ yes'.ss = ∅
│ no'.ss = ∅
└───────────────────────────────────
```

The sets are initially empty, and their maximum sizes are both *size*.

The consistency of this state is easy to prove, but we must show its correctness by proving the following theorem:

$$IInit \vdash \exists Class' \bullet (\ ClassInit \wedge ISim'\ ) \qquad (181, 14, 15, 181)$$

We begin by writing down the conclusion in detail.

$\exists enrolled', tested' : \mathbb{P}\ Student \bullet$

(1)	$(\ tested' \subseteq enrolled'$	Invariant of *ClassInit*
(2)	$\wedge\ \#\ enrolled' \leq size$	Invariant of *ClassInit*
(3)	$\wedge\ enrolled' = \varnothing$	From *ClassInit*
(4)	$\wedge\ enrolled' = yes'.ss \cup no'.ss$	From *ISim'*
(5)	$\wedge\ tested' = yes'.ss$	From *ISim'*
(6)	$\wedge\ yes'.max = size$	From *ISim'*
(7)	$\wedge\ no'.max = size$	From *ISim'*
(8)	$\wedge\ yes'.ss \cap no'.ss = \varnothing\ )$	From *ISim'*

Simplifying with the one-point rule, using predicates (4) and (5), gives the following:

(9) $yes'.ss \subseteq yes'.ss \cup no'.ss$

(10) $\#\ (yes'.ss \cup no'.ss) \leq size$

(11) $yes'.ss \cup no'.ss = \varnothing$

(12) $yes'.max = size$

(13) $no'.max = size$

(14) $yes'.ss \cap no'.ss = \varnothing$

We justify these from the hypothesis *IInit* as follows.

(9) is a theorem of set theory
(10), (11), (14) since $yes'.ss$ and $no'.ss$ are both empty, according to *IInit*
(12), (13) are both predicates of *IInit*, since it includes *IClass'*

6.4.4 Enrolling a student

The concrete form of this operation will be given in three parts, like the abstract form. First the case where it works.

IEnrolok

$\Delta IClass$	(181)
$s?: Student$	(14)
$r!: Response$	(14)

$s? \notin (yes.ss \cup no.ss)$
$\# (yes.ss \cup no.ss) < size$
$yes' = yes$
$no'.ss = no.ss \cup \{s?\}$
$no'.max = no.max$
$r! = success$

The input student must not be in the yes-set or in the no-set. There must be room for another. The yes-set is unchanged, and the student is added to the no-set without changing its maximum size.

Next the case where there is no room.

INoRoom

$\Xi IClass$	(181)
$r!: Response$	(14)

$\# (yes.ss \cup no.ss) = size$
$r! = noroom$

If there is no room, the response is *noroom*.

Lastly the case where the student is already enrolled.

IAlreadyEnrolled

$\Xi IClass$	(181)
$s?: Student$	(14)
$r!: Response$	(14)

$s? \in yes.ss \lor s? \in no.ss$
$r! = alreadyenrolled$

If the student is already in one of the sets, the response is *alreadyenrolled*.

Now we put them together:

$IEnrol \mathrel{\widehat{=}}$
$IEnrolok \lor INoRoom \lor IAlreadyEnrolled$ (183, 183, 183)

To prove the correctness of this refinement we consider first the safety condition.

$$\textit{pre Enrol} \wedge \textit{ISim} \vdash \textit{pre IEnrol} \qquad (21, 181, 184)$$

Since *IEnrol* is total, we need only find the invariants on the concrete state, and these are in *ISim*.

The liveness condition is as follows:

$$\textit{pre Enrol} \wedge \textit{ISim} \wedge \textit{IEnrol} \qquad (21, 181, 184)$$
$$\vdash \exists \textit{Class}' \bullet (\textit{Enrol} \wedge \textit{ISim}')$$
$$(14, 21, 181)$$

We examine first the case in which $r! = success$, and expand the conclusion of the theorem as follows.

$\exists enrolled', tested' : \mathbb{P}\ Student \bullet$

(1)	$(\ tested' \subseteq enrolled'$	Invariant of *Class'*
(2)	$\wedge\ \#\ enrolled' \leq size$	Invariant of *Class'*
(3)	$\wedge\ tested \subseteq enrolled$	From *Enrol*
(4)	$\wedge\ \#\ enrolled \leq size$	From *Enrol*
(5)	$\wedge\ s? \notin enrolled$	From *Enrol*, in this case
(6)	$\wedge\ \#\ enrolled < size$	From *Enrol*, in this case
(7)	$\wedge\ enrolled' = enrolled \cup \{s?\}$	From *Enrol*, in this case
(8)	$\wedge\ tested' = tested$	From *Enrol*
(9)	$\wedge\ r! = success$	From *Enrol*, in this case
(10)	$\wedge\ yes'.max = size$	From *ISim'*
(11)	$\wedge\ no'.max = size$	From *ISim'*
(12)	$\wedge\ yes'.ss \cap no'.ss = \varnothing$	From *ISim'*
(13)	$\wedge\ enrolled' = yes'.ss \cup no'.ss$	From *ISim'*
(14)	$\wedge\ tested' = yes'.ss$	From *ISim'*
(15)	$\wedge\ \#\ yes'.ss \leq size$	From *ISim'*
(16)	$\wedge\ \#\ no'.ss \leq size\ )$	From *ISim'*

Next we transform the conclusion by applying the one-point rule, using predicates (7) and (8).

(17)	$tested \subseteq enrolled \cup \{s?\}$	From (1)

(18)	$\# enrolled \cup \{s?\} \leq size$	From (2)
(19)	$tested \subseteq enrolled$	From (3)
(20)	$\# enrolled \leq size$	From (4)
(21)	$s? \notin enrolled$	From (5)
(22)	$\# enrolled < size$	From (6)
(23)	$r! = success$	From (9)
(24)	$yes'.max = size$	From (10)
(25)	$no'.max = size$	From (11)
(26)	$yes'.ss \cap no'.ss = \emptyset$	From (12)
(27)	$enrolled \cup \{s?\} = yes'.ss \cup no'.ss$	From (13)
(28)	$tested = yes'.ss$	From (14)
(29)	$\# yes'.ss \leq size$	From (15)
(30)	$\# no'.ss \leq size$	From (16)

We now expand the hypothesis to see what we have to work on.

(31)	$tested \subseteq enrolled$	From ***pre*** *Enrol* and *ISim*
(32)	$\# enrolled \leq size$	From ***pre*** *Enrol* and *ISim*
(33)	$yes.max = size$	From *ISim* and *IEnrol*
(34)	$no.max = size$	From *ISim* and *IEnrol*
(35)	$yes.ss \cap no.ss = \emptyset$	From *ISim* and *IEnrol*
(36)	$\# yes..ss \leq size$	From *ISim*
(37)	$\# no..ss \leq size$	From *ISim*
(38)	$enrolled = yes.ss \cup no.ss$	From *ISim*
(39)	$tested = yes.ss$	From *ISim*
(40)	$yes'.max = size$	From *IEnrol*
(41)	$no'.max = size$	From *IEnrol*
(42)	$yes'.ss \cap no'.ss = \emptyset$	From *IEnrol*
(43)	$s? \notin (yes.ss \cup no.ss)$	From *IEnrol*, in this case
(44)	$\# (yes.ss \cup no.ss) < size$	From *IEnrol*, in this case
(45)	$yes' = yes$	From *IEnrol*, in this case

(46) $no'.ss = no.ss \cup \{s?\}$ From *IEnrol*, in this case

(47) $r! = success$

The conclusion (17) to (30) can be justified by the hypothesis (31) to (47) as follows:

(17) from (31)
(18) from (32)
(19) from (31)
(20) from (32)
(21) from (38) and (43)
(22) from (38) and (44)
(23) from (47)
(24) from (40)
(25) from (41)
(26) from (42)
(27) from (38), (45) and (46)
(28) from (39) and (45)
(29) from (36) and (45)
(30) from (46), (37) and (44)

The remaining cases, and the specifications of the concrete forms of the other operations, are left as exercises.

6.4.5 Documenting assumptions in indirect data design

It sometimes happens that a system is to be implemented using components from a supplier who does not provide precise specifications. The reader will understand that from what has been said earlier in this chapter that verification of a system using such components is not possible. It might appear that in such circumstances the use of a formal design method is of no value, but this is not the case. The software engineer who is required to undertake such a refinement should use a Z specification to document the assumptions made about the externally-provided components. The specification should be sufficient to allow the design to be verified. It should be used as the basis of discussions with the supplier of the component to assess the risk of the development.

6.5 Inspecting data designs

The inspection of a data design is a comparison of two documents, both with a formal content, namely the specification and the data design. The purpose of the inspection is to establish that

- the data design is correct with respect to the specification, and
- the design decisions that give rise to it are appropriate for the development being undertaken.

We need the same sort of participants as in an inspection of a specification, but now the inspectors represent the specifiers and the developers.

Since the data design includes a specification – the specification of the concrete state and the operations on it – many of the questions listed on p. 152 for inspecting specifications apply to data designs. However, the two considerations listed above give rise to new questions.

(1) Is the appropriateness of the concrete state apparent from the informal text?

- Is it simply related to the abstract state? (Look at the forward simulation.)
- If the forward simulation is complex, is the choice of concrete state justified by the non-functional requirements of the specification?

(2) Has appropriate use been made of non-determinism in the specifications of the concrete operations?

(3) Are the proof obligations for correctness clearly stated?

- Initial concrete state (p. 165)
- Safety of each concrete operation (p. 169)
- Liveness of each concrete operation (p. 169)

(4) Are the proofs clearly presented in sufficient detail to be convincing?

(5) Has appropriate use been made of indirect data design?

- Does the design reuse components of this or related developments?
- Are the specifications of the subsidiary abstract data types clearly presented?
- Where components without formal specifications are to be used, are the assumptions about the behaviour of these components clearly documented, and in accordance with their informal descriptions?

Exercises

The following exercises refer to the direct design of the class manager's assistant.

(6.1) Write the concrete form of the specification of the operation to test a student.

(6.2) Write the concrete form of the specification of the operation to discharge a student.

(6.3) Complete the proof of the correctness of the operation to enrol a student by considering the case $r! = alreadyenrolled$.

(6.4) Write the concrete form of the operation to enquire about a student, and prove it correct.

The following exercises refer to the use of linked lists.

(6.5) Prove the theorem

$$Add\_to\_head \vdash new\_pointer? \neq nil\_pointer$$

(6.6) Prove that the value of the *next* component of the new block after the operation *Add_to_head* is *head*.

(6.7) Specify an operation to add a block to the end of the list.

(6.8) Specify an operation to delete a block given the pointer that addresses it.

The following exercises refer to the indirect design of the class manager's assistant.

(6.9) Complete the proof of the correctness of the operation to enrol a student.

(6.10) Specify the concrete form of the operation to enquire about a student.

(6.11) Specify the concrete form of the operation to test a student.

(6.12) Specify the concrete form of the operation to discharge a student.

Chapter 7
Algorithm design

Summary: Programming languages and specification languages contrasted – concepts of common imperative languages – structured programming – stepwise refinement – informal description of Dijkstra's guarded command language – using schemas to describe programs – two views of the refinement relation – program states – the assignment statement – the alternation control structure – the sequence control structure – local variables – the initialized iteration control structure – algorithm design for indirect data design – inspecting algorithm designs – reverse engineering

7.1 Programming languages in software development

Z is a specification language, and it allows us to express a model of some part of the world in a way that helps software suppliers to communicate in a precise way with their customers. This communication is rendered possible only by use of abstraction, i.e. replacing notions that have many associated complications with simpler ones in which only essential properties remain. The skill of the specifier lies in choosing these abstractions and organizing them in a convincing way.

A programming language like Pascal is full of complications that are inescapable. The programmer has to consider the state of machine storage, the instructions to be executed, and the order in which they are to be presented to the processor. Though I list these considerations one after the other on the page, there is in reality no separation between them to ease the burden. A programming language in which we could first write down all the instructions needed to accomplish a task, and then quite separately decide what order we wanted to put them in, is impossible. A programming language has, however, one distinct advantage over a language like Z: it can be compiled and executed to give a customer a solution to his problems. While Z is good (much better than the programming language) for making the notions of the system precise for the customer, it must eventually give way to the programming language in the development process.

Z has no notion of the order of doing things. It can express what it means to do *A* (where *A* is a schema describing an operation), but it cannot say 'do *A* first, then *B*', or 'if the value in this program variable is greater that zero, do *A*, but if not, do *B*'. These things are the bread and butter of programming languages. We could extend Z in order to include these notions, but we prefer to import them from a simple programming language.

In this chapter we shall begin by studying a simple programming language, Dijkstra's guarded command language, and see how the behaviour of programs can be summarized using schemas. Then we shall study ways of refining the concrete specifications produced in data design into programs.

7.1.1 Common programming language concepts

Most of the target languages of contemporary program development have much in common, and before exploring the guarded command language we look at the basic notions of such programming languages (Cobol, Fortran, Pascal, Ada etc.).

The notion of a **variable** is very common. In a programming language a variable is a store in which different values can appear from time to time. The contents of variables can be read, i.e. extracted for use elsewhere without changing the contents of the store, and written, i.e. changed to a new value. In most programming languages each variable has a **type**, which controls the values that can appear in it. Each variable is introduced in a **declaration** which names the variable and identifies its type.

Variables can be organized into **data structures** like **arrays**, in which a finite collection of variables of the same type can be given a single name and referred to by an index, usually a natural number, or **records**, in which a number of variables of different types are brought together under an single name.

Programming languages allow an **expression** to be computed from the current values in the variables, and the value so computed can be stored in a variable by an **assignment statement**. The assignment statement is one way of getting things done in a programming language. The other way is usually to get another program to do some work for you. In this scheme, a program is packaged into a **procedure** which includes a mechanism for the program to have access to values and variables supplied from elsewhere. A program wishing to use the services of a procedure will use a **call statement** of the appropriate programming language, making available in the statement the values of some of its variables, and in some cases the variables themselves for the called procedure to work on. Values and variables exposed in this way are called **parameters** of the call.

Assignment statements and calls to procedures are tied together by **control structures** of the kind illustrated in the **flow charts** of Figure 7.1.

The rectangular boxes represent assignments or calls, or other control structures. The diamonds represent **boolean expressions**, i.e. programming language expressions whose values are true or false. The arrows point the direction of flow of control. The circles are collectors of flow of control. The boxes, diamonds and circles are called the **nodes** of the flow chart.

The control structures illustrated in the figure have popular names:

(1) is the **sequence** control structure

(2) is the **if-then** control structure

(3) is the **if-then-else** control structure

(4) is the **do-while** control structure

(5) is the **do-until** control structure

(6) is the **initialized do-while** control structure

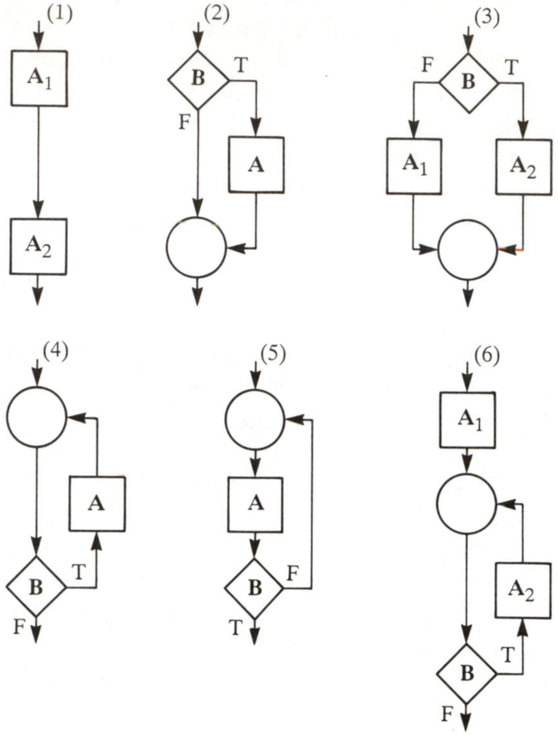

Figure 7.1 Flow charts of simple control structures.

7.1.2 Structured programming and stepwise refinement

The idea of **structured programming** is that programs should be built from a limited number of easily understood control structures. The allowed control structures form a **basis set** for a system of structured programming. Different systems have different basis sets. Structured programming favours **proper programs**, i.e. programs in which

- there is only one node at which control can flow in,
- there is only one node from which control can flow out, and
- every node is on a path to the way out.

All the flow charts in Figure 7.1 are flow charts of proper programs. Three of them, sequence, if-then-else, and initialized do-while, are sufficient for constructing any proper program, and they will form the basis set for a system of structured programming that will be presented later in this chapter.

In **stepwise refinement** the development of a program from a specification is presented as a series of replacements of boxes by control structures, starting from a single box representing the specification. The function of each box is successively elaborated until the boxes contain only assignment statements or calls that are easily implemented in the target language.

In Figure 7.2, command **A** has been replaced by a sequence. The first element of the sequence ($\mathbf{A}_1$) has been replaced by an if-then-else, and the second ($\mathbf{A}_2$) by an initialized do-while.

It should be emphasized that stepwise refinement is a method of recording design decisions, not a method of producing designs. In practice, a programmer faced with a specification of any complexity will consider various possible designs, and might write a few code fragments, or a complete prototype, before making any decisions about the design approach. These activities are all part of planning the design. For the refinement illustrated in the previous figure, the programmer may have considered possibilities well beyond (c) before deciding that (b) is an appropriate first step in the refinement of (a).

The practice of stepwise refinement relies on good planning of the implementation before recording is begun, and on the recognition of the **design quiescent points** in the development at which subsequent design decisions will not upset those already made.

7.2 An algorithmic notation – the guarded command language

7.2.1 The guarded command language

The guarded command language was introduced by Dijkstra (1975) and expounded as a means of developing programs by Gries (1981) and elsewhere. It provides a framework for recording the refinement of specifications into programs. It has only three simple control structures – sequence, alternation and iteration. These three are generalizations of the sequence, if-then-else and do-while constructs described above. The commands that are organized into programs by these three constructs can be

- assignment statements of the form

  $$x := \mathbf{E}$$

  where x is a program variable, **E** an expression built from values of program variables, and ':=' is the assignment symbol.
- specifications to be further refined
  - in-line, or by

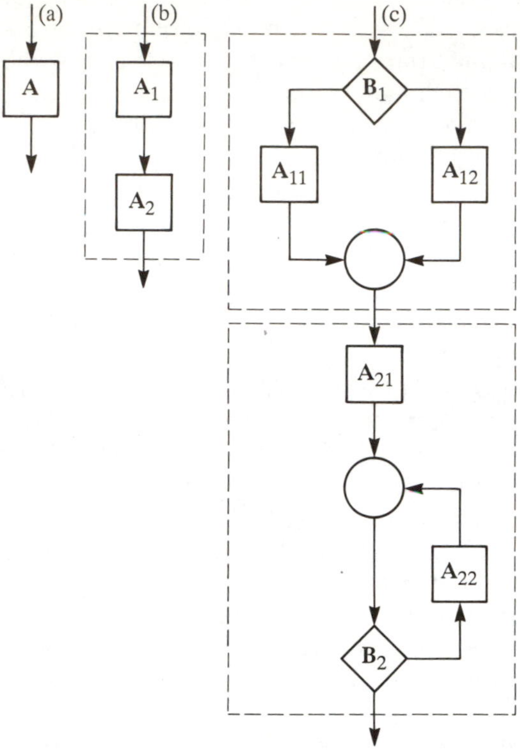

Figure 7.2 Stepwise refinement as successive replacement.

  - calls to other programs.

- two special commands: ***skip*** and ***abort***. The command ***skip*** does nothing; the command ***abort*** is entirely unpredictable in its effect – it might never complete.

7.2.2 Declarations and commands

The kinds of data available to a program in the guarded command language depend on the target language of the program, on the given sets of the specification being refined, and on the abstract types used in the refinement. In the programs to refine the operations of the class manager's assistant using the direct data design, we might expect to see any of the following declarations:

s: *Student*	given set of specification
where: *0..size*	type in target language

sarray: ***array***(*1..size*) ***of*** *Student*	array type (target language) and given set of the specification

It should be observed that declarations in the guarded command language are declarations of program variables. The names of these variables persist through the program as their values change. Specifications on the other hand use distinct names (undashed and dashed) to denote the values of the program variables before and after the program has been executed.

The kinds of command available to a program in the guarded command language depend on the target language of the program, and on the abstract types used in the refinement. In the programs to refine the operations of the class manager's assistant using the direct data design, we might expect to see any of the following commands:

$where := 0$	assignment statement
$sarray(1) := s$	assignment statement to an array element
Search	specification of an operation to be refined

In the last case we should expect to find a definition of the schema *Search*.

7.2.3 Sequence control structure

A sequence of commands may be presented in horizontal or vertical format:

$$x := x + 1; y := y - 1$$

or

$$x := x + 1;$$
$$y := y - 1$$

The semicolon is used to separate the commands. It should not be confused with the fat semicolon for composition of relations, nor with the very fat semicolon for composition of schemas.

In a sequence control structure the commands are executed unconditionally in the order in which they appear. The sequence control structure (1) in Figure 7.1 would be recorded as

$$\mathbf{A}_1; \mathbf{A}_2$$

in the guarded command language.

7.2.4 Alternation control structure

In an alternation control structure a number of commands are presented. Each command is prefaced by a boolean expression called a **guard**. The guards are intended to correspond to the boolean expressions of the target language. A command will be executed only if its guard is true.

In the following simple example the alternation control structure is bounded by the signs ***if*** and ***fi***. There are only two guarded commands; the sign '□' is the guarded command separator. In the first guarded command, $x \leq y$ is the guard and $z := x$ is the command. The guard arrow '→' separates the guard from the command.

$$\textbf{\textit{if}}\ x \leq y \rightarrow z := x \ \Box \ x \geq y \rightarrow z := y\ \textbf{\textit{fi}}$$

There may be as many guarded commands as you like in an alternation control structure. When there are several they are usually displayed vertically as follows.

$x, y, s \colon \mathbb{Z}$

$\textbf{\textit{if}}\ x < y \rightarrow s := -1$
$\Box\ x = y \rightarrow s := 0$
$\Box\ x > y \rightarrow s := 1$
fi

The rules for the alternation control structure are as follows.

(1) When execution reaches the ***if***, the guards must all be defined. If any guard is undefined, the result of the execution is not specified.

(2) When execution reaches the ***if***, at least one of the guards must be true. The result of the execution is undefined if all the guards are false.

(3) Exactly one of the commands that have a true guard will be executed, and execution will continue with the command after the ***fi***. If more than one guard is true, it is not specified which of the eligible commands will be executed.

The if-then and if-then-else constructs illustrated in Figure 7.1 are represented by the following guarded command language programs:

$$\textbf{\textit{if}}\ \mathbf{B} \rightarrow \mathbf{A} \ \Box \ \neg \mathbf{B} \rightarrow \textbf{\textit{skip}}\ \textbf{\textit{fi}}$$

$$\textbf{\textit{if}}\ \mathbf{B} \rightarrow \mathbf{A}_1 \ \square\ \neg\mathbf{B} \rightarrow \mathbf{A}_2\ \textbf{\textit{fi}}$$

Note that for an if-then structure, the guarded command language requires the use of a guard that covers the if-test false case, and this should guard the special command ***skip***.

7.2.5 Iteration control structure

In an iteration control structure a number of commands are presented. As in the alternation control structure, each command has a guard. A command will be executed only if its guard is true.

In the following simple example the iteration control structure is bounded by the signs ***do*** and ***od***. There is only one guarded command. The boolean expression $z<x \wedge z<y$ is the guard and $z:=z+1$ is the command.

$$\textbf{\textit{do}}\ z < x \wedge z < y \rightarrow z := z + 1\ \textbf{\textit{od}}$$

There may be as many guarded commands as you like in an iteration control structure. When there are several they are usually displayed vertically, as in the alternation control structure.

The rules for the iteration control structure are as follows.

(1) When execution reaches the ***do***, the guards must all be defined. If any guard is not defined, the result of the execution is not specified.

(2) When execution reaches the ***do***, if all the guards are false, then execution continues at the command after the ***od***.

(3) Exactly one of the commands that have a true guard will be executed, and execution will continue at the ***do***. If more than one guard is true, it is not specified which of the eligible commands will be executed.

The do-while control structure illustrated in Figure 7.1 would be represented by the following guarded command language program.

$$\textbf{\textit{do}}\ \mathbf{B} \rightarrow \mathbf{A}\ \textbf{\textit{od}}$$

In the programming system to be developed later in this chapter, the initialized do-while will be used, and in the guarded command language this is recorded using a sequence of commands, the last of which is the iteration control structure. The initialized do-while illustrated in Figure 7.1 would be represented by the following guarded command language program:

$$\mathbf{A}_1;\ \textbf{\textit{do}}\ \mathbf{B} \rightarrow \mathbf{A}_2\ \textbf{\textit{od}}$$

7.2.6 Method of recording

At each stage of recording an algorithm refinement we record only one step of refinement. Thus to record the design decisions illustrated in Figure 7.2 we would record the first step (a) to (b) as follows.

$$A \sqsubseteq A_1; A_2$$

The sign '$\sqsubseteq$' is to be read 'is refined by', and its meaning will be made precise in later sections of this chapter. A, A_1, and A_2 are the names of schemas that specify the actions **A**, $\mathbf{A}_1$, and $\mathbf{A}_2$ in the flow charts (a) and (b). To record the design decisions from (b) to (c) we need two records:

$$A_1 \sqsubseteq \textit{if}\ \mathbf{B}_1 \rightarrow A_{11} \ \square\ \neg \mathbf{B}_1 \rightarrow A_{12}\ \textit{fi}$$

records the refinement of A_1 into the if-then-else construct, and

$$A_2 \sqsubseteq A_{21};\ \textit{do}\ \mathbf{B}_2 \rightarrow A_{22}\ \textit{od}$$

records the refinement of A_2 into the initialized do-while.

The record thus consists of a number of program fragments, and to get a complete program for A it is necessary to bring these fragments together. However, such a bringing together of fragments is not necessary to record the refinement, and it could be done in a purely mechanical way by a suitable design tool.

7.2.7 Schemas and programs

Z schemas can be used to summarize the function of programs in the guarded command language. The values of the program variables before and after the execution of the program make up the declaration part of the schema, and the predicate part expresses the relation between those values induced by the execution of the program.

The process of deducing a description of the function of a program from the program itself is an exercise in abstraction. It can be pursued by the method of **stepwise abstraction**, which consists of abstracting the function of single assignment statements or calls, then abstracting the function of the control structures in which they are used, and so on until the function of the entire program has been discovered.

The following simple example shows how an assignment statement might be abstracted. Suppose that a programming language has a natural number type *Nat*, whose values are from zero to some maximum *maxnat*, and suppose that the effect of adding *1* to a natural number variable is to increase it by *1*, except when its value is *maxnat*, when the result is unpredictable. The assignment statement in the following program fragment

$x, y: Nat$
$x := x + 1$

has the following abstract description:

```
Increase_x_carefully
  x, x', y, y': 0..maxnat
  ─────────
  x < maxnat
  y' = y
  x' = x + 1
```

The precondition tells us that this program's behaviour is not guaranteed if the value in x is *maxnat* when the program is executed.

The schema *Increase_x_carefully* is a **description** of the behaviour of the program fragment. It is also a specification that is satisfied by this program, but not the only such specification. It is in fact the strongest specification that the program can satisfy in the sense that if the predicate part were strengthened by adding new predicates that were not a consequence of the old predicates, then the program would fail to satisfy it.

There are many other specifications that the program satisfies, indeed every program acting only on program variables x and y as declared satisfies

```
Do_anything
  x, x', y, y': 0..maxnat
```

which says 'Do whatever you like to the values of the program variables, subject only to the type constraint'.

7.3 Specifications and refinements

The implementer of a concrete operation must produce a program. Data design provides a specification of what the program is to do, and various explicit or implicit instructions about how it is to be done. The specification (a schema or a schema expression) describes

- The state on which the program is to operate
- The inputs to be supplied by the caller of the program
- The outputs to be returned by the program
- The preconditions that the writer of the program can assume

- The postconditions that the outputs and the final state must satisfy

The program is correct if, under the preconditions described in the specification, every possible behaviour of the program is allowed by the specification. In circumstances not allowed by the preconditions, the program can exhibit any behaviour (including failure to terminate).

The program is not correct if, under the preconditions described in the specification, it might exhibit a behaviour not allowed by the specification.

These notions can be made more precise as follows: Suppose *Spec* is a schema describing a specification and *Ref* is a schema describing the action of a program. To show that *Ref* is a correct implementation of *Spec* we have the following proof obligations.

pre *Spec* $\vdash$ ***pre*** *Ref*	Any circumstance acceptable to *Spec* must be acceptable to *Ref*. (This is the safety condition.)
(***pre*** *Spec*) $\wedge$ *Ref* $\vdash$ *Spec*	In any circumstance acceptable to *Spec*, the behaviour of *Ref* must be allowed by *Spec*. (This is the liveness condition.)

In this situation we shall write

$$Spec \sqsubseteq Ref$$

The sign '$\sqsubseteq$' is the sign of the **refinement** relation.

The first rule can be paraphrased by saying that a refinement can weaken the precondition, where weakness is meant in the sense described on p. 48. A refinement can apply to a wider range of circumstances than the specification requires, so a specification that says that an integer input will be positive can be satisfied by a refinement that accepts positive or negative input. The second rule can be paraphrased by saying that a refinement can strengthen the postcondition. A refinement can choose a more limited range of outcomes than the specification allows. A refinement of the enrol operation from the class manager's assistant could, in the case when the class is full and the input student is already enrolled, choose always to make the response *noroom*, though the specification allows either *noroom* or *alreadyenrolled*.

7.3.1 Examples of refinements

The following specification requires the natural number state variable x to be reduced, provided it is greater than zero:

$$\begin{array}{|l}\hline \textit{Decrease} \\ x, x' : \mathbb{N} \\ \hline x > 0 \land x' < x \\ \hline \end{array}$$

A program described by the following schema is a correct refinement of the specification *Decrease*.

$$\begin{array}{|l}\hline \textit{Downone} \\ x, x' : \mathbb{N} \\ \hline x' = x - 1 \\ \hline \end{array}$$

To prove this we should show that

$$\textbf{\textit{pre}}\ \textit{Decrease} \vdash \textbf{\textit{pre}}\ \textit{Downone}$$

which is

$$[x : \mathbb{N} \mid x > 0] \vdash x > 0$$

since *Downone* has $x > 0$ as its precondition, even though this is not explicit in the schema. This is clearly true. In addition we must show

$$(\textbf{\textit{pre}}\ \textit{Decrease}) \land \textit{Downone} \vdash \textit{Decrease}$$

which is

$$[x, x' : \mathbb{N} \mid x > 0 \land x' = x - 1] \vdash x > 0 \land x' < x$$

and this follows since $x - 1 < x$ when x is a natural number greater than 0.

7.3.2 Specifications and refinements as relations

A specification of an operation can be regarded as defining a relation between the possible values of inputs and starting state (the from-set) and the possible values of outputs and ending state (the to-set). The following specification of an operation on a single program variable x

$$\begin{array}{|l}\hline \textit{Decrease\_x} \\ x, x' : 0..5 \\ \hline x' < x \\ \hline \end{array}$$

requires only that the value of x be decreased. It corresponds to the relation

$$\{x, x' : 0..5 \mid x > 0 \land x' < x \bullet x \mapsto x'\}$$

The domain of this relation is $1..5$, and this corresponds to the precondition of the schema. Notice that the specification places no requirements on the behaviour of an implementation when the value in x is 0.

A program can also be regarded as defining a relation. The alternation command in the following program

$$x: 0..5$$
$$\textbf{\textit{if}}\ x > 0 \rightarrow x := x - 1 \ \square\ x = 0 \rightarrow \textbf{\textit{skip fi}}$$

defines the relation

$$\{0 \mapsto 0, 1 \mapsto 0, 2 \mapsto 1, 3 \mapsto 2, 4 \mapsto 3, 5 \mapsto 4\}$$

The domain of this relation is $0..5$.

The idea that the program implements the specification can be formalized as follows. If *Srel* is a specification relation, and if *Rrel* is a relation that describes the behaviour of a program, then the program refines the specification provided that the safety condition

$$\textbf{dom}\ Srel \subseteq \textbf{dom}\ Rrel$$

and the liveness condition

$$(\ \textbf{dom}\ Srel \lhd Rrel\ ) \subseteq Srel$$

are both true.

For the above program and specification we have

$$Srel == \{x, x' : 0..5 \mid x > 0 \land x' < x \bullet x \mapsto x'\}$$

$$Rrel == \{0 \mapsto 0, 1 \mapsto 0, 2 \mapsto 1, 3 \mapsto 2, 4 \mapsto 3, 5 \mapsto 4\}$$

The domains of the relations satisfy the first condition, since

$$1..5 \subseteq 0..5$$

Also we have

$$\mathbf{dom}\ Srel \lhd Rrel = \{1 \mapsto 0,\ 2 \mapsto 1,\ 3 \mapsto 2,\ 4 \mapsto 3,\ 5 \mapsto 4\}$$

and this is a subset of *Srel*.

7.4 Program states and assignment

7.4.1 Program spaces and program states

The declarations in a program establish the program variables that the commands of the program can work with. A **program space** is a collection of program variables whose values are subject to restrictions of type, and perhaps other constraints. Thus the following program declarations

sarray: ***array***(*1..size*) ***of*** *Student*; (14)
s: *Student*; (14)
r: *Response*; (14)
ectr, *tctr*: *0..size*

establish a program space defined by the following schema:

EnrolSpace

sarray: *1..size* → *Student* (14)
ectr, *tctr*: *0..size*
s: *Student* (14)
r: *Response* (14)

Such a schema would be constantly referred to in recording the design of a program to implement the operation to enrol a student using the direct data refinement of the previous chapter.

Before we present the design of the algorithm for that operation we need to establish some conventions about how the inputs and outputs of the schema *DEnrol* are to be represented as program variables. The example of a program space above hints at a simple convention based on removing the '*!*' and the '*?*' from the names. We can make this precise by first considering the following schema that introduces the program variables.

Identify_s_and_r

s?, *s*, *s'*: *Student* (14)
r!, *r*, *r'*: *Response* (14)

$s? = s$
$r! = r'$

This schema makes precise that the starting value of the program variable s will be the value of the input $s?$, and the value of the output $r!$ will be the ending value of the program variable r. To make this schema suitable for the algorithm refinement of *DEnrol* we need to combine it with *DEnrol* and hide the input and output variables as follows:

$$DEnrolProg \mathrel{\widehat{=}} (\ DEnrol \land Identify\_s\_and\_r\ ) \setminus (s?, r!) \qquad (168, 204)$$

It will help in the refinement to make similar transformations of the disjuncts of *DEnrol*:

$$DEnrolokProg \mathrel{\widehat{=}} (\ DEnrolok \land Identify\_s\_and\_r\ ) \setminus (s?, r!) \qquad (166, 204)$$

$$DNoRoomProg \mathrel{\widehat{=}} (\ DNoRoom \land Identify\_s\_and\_r\ ) \setminus (s?, r!) \qquad (168, 204)$$

$$DAlreadyEnrolledProg \mathrel{\widehat{=}} (\ DAlreadyEnrolled \land Identify\_s\_and\_r\ ) \setminus (s?, r!) \qquad (168, 204)$$

7.4.2 Using the assignment statement

The assignment statement is used to refine specifications in which just one variable in the program state is to change, and the new value is easily computed in the target language.

Suppose the program space is defined by

$$PSpace \mathrel{\widehat{=}} [x, y, z: 0..maxnat]$$

so there are three program variables. The effect of the assignment statement

$$x := y + z$$

is precisely described by the following schema:

```
┌─ Assign_1 ─────────────────────────
│ ΔPSpace                                  (204)
├──────────────
│ x' = y + z
│ y' = y
│ z' = z
└────────────────────────────────────
```

Note that this schema has a precondition, namely that the sum of y and z must not exceed *maxnat*.

More generally, if the program state is given by the schema

```
┌─GenPSpace──────────────────────────
│ x: T
│ Others
└────────────────────────────────────
```

where x does not occur in *Others*, and if **E** is an expression of type T in the values of x and the components of *Others*, then the effect of

$$x := \mathbf{E}$$

is precisely described by the following schema:

```
┌─Assign_2───────────────────────────
│ ΔGenPSpace                              (205)
│ ΞOthers
├──────────
│ x' = E
└────────────────────────────────────
```

Returning to the program space *PSpace* above, we see that the assignment

$$x := y + z$$

can be used to refine many specifications on this program space, not just *Assign_1*. For instance it refines

```
┌─Forget_z───────────────────────────
│ ΔPSpace                                 (204)
├──────────
│ x' = y + z
│ y' = y
└────────────────────────────────────
```

in which x is to be changed as before, y is to remain unchanged, but the final value of z is not specified. We can prove that this assignment satisfies this specification by showing that the schema that describes the assignment (*Assign_1*) is a refinement of the specification. We do this using rules established in this chapter.

We must show that

$$\textbf{pre}\ Forget\_z \vdash \textbf{pre}\ Assign\_1 \qquad (205, 205)$$

$$(\textbf{pre}\ Forget\_z) \wedge Assign\_1 \vdash Forget\_z \qquad (205, 205, 205)$$

The first theorem is the safety condition. We notice that the preconditions of the two schemas are the same, namely

$$y + z \leq maxnat$$

For the liveness condition we must show that

$$[x, y, z, x', y', z': 0..maxnat$$
$$\mid y + z \leq maxnat \wedge x' = y + z \wedge y' = y \wedge z' = z]$$
$$\vdash x' = y + z \wedge y' = y$$

which is straightforward, since the conjuncts in the conclusion are both present among the conjuncts in the hypothesis.

7.5 The alternation control structure

7.5.1 Using the alternation control structure

Suppose S is a specification on a program space, and A_1 and A_2 are operations on the same space. Suppose $\mathbf{B}_1$ and $\mathbf{B}_2$ are boolean expressions defined on the variables in the space, and are computable in the target language. We shall say that

$$S \sqsubseteq \textit{if}\ \mathbf{B}_1 \rightarrow A_1 \ \Box\ \mathbf{B}_2 \rightarrow A_2\ \textit{fi}$$

when certain proof obligations are satisfied. Before stating the proof obligations we must establish some conventions of notation. The schemas B_1 and B_2 are defined on the same space as S, and their predicate parts are logically equivalent to the boolean expressions $\mathbf{B}_1$ and $\mathbf{B}_2$. The proof obligations are as follows:

$\textbf{\textit{pre}}\ S \vdash B_1 \vee B_2$	Any circumstance acceptable to S must make at least one of the guards true. (This is the safety condition.)
$S \wedge B_1 \sqsubseteq A_1$	When $\mathbf{B}_1$ is true, A_1 must be a refinement of S. (This is the first liveness condition.)
$S \wedge B_2 \sqsubseteq A_2$	When $\mathbf{B}_2$ is true, A_2 must be a refinement of S. (This is the second liveness condition.)

These proof obligations can be extended to cover alternations with several guarded commands, but we shall not describe them here.

7.5.2 Example of refinement by alternation

For a simple example of refinement by an alternation, consider the following specification of a program to find the positive difference of two numbers. The program space is *PSpace* defined previously in this chapter with three variables *x*, *y* and *z*, all drawn from *0..maxnat*.

$$\begin{array}{|l}
\hline
\textit{PosDiff} \\
\Delta PSpace \\
\hline
z' = x - y \lor z' = y - x \\
x' = x \\
y' = y \\
\hline
\end{array} \qquad (204)$$

This is a total operation. We propose the following program

$$\textit{if}\ x \geq y \rightarrow z := x - y \ \Box\ y \geq x \rightarrow z := y - x\ \textit{fi}$$

as a refinement of the specification. To verify it we replace the two assignment statements by their descriptions.

$$\begin{array}{|l}
\hline
\textit{Assign_xmy} \\
\Delta PSpace \\
\hline
x \geq y \\
z' = x - y \\
x' = x \\
y' = y \\
\hline
\end{array} \qquad (204)$$

$$\begin{array}{|l}
\hline
\textit{Assign_ymx} \\
\Delta PSpace \\
\hline
y \geq x \\
z' = y - x \\
x' = x \\
y' = y \\
\hline
\end{array} \qquad (204)$$

Now we are to show that

$$\begin{array}{ll}
\textit{PosDiff} \sqsubseteq & (207) \\
\quad \textit{if}\ x \geq y \rightarrow \textit{Assign_xmy} & (207) \\
\quad \Box\ y \geq x \rightarrow \textit{Assign_ymx} & (207) \\
\quad \textit{fi} &
\end{array}$$

The safety condition is

$$\textbf{pre}\ PosDiff \vdash x \geq y \lor y \geq x \qquad (207)$$

which is valid since both sides are true.

The first liveness condition is

$$[PosDiff \mid x \geq y] \sqsubseteq Assign\_xmy \qquad (207, 207)$$

and the safety condition for this refinement is

$$\textbf{pre}\ [PosDiff \mid x \geq y] \vdash \textbf{pre}\ Assign\_xmy \qquad (207, 207)$$

which is valid since the predicate in the conclusion is present in the hypothesis. The liveness condition for this refinement is

$$\textbf{pre}\ [PosDiff \mid x \geq y] \land Assign\_xmy \qquad (207, 207)$$
$$\vdash PosDiff \land x \geq y \qquad (207)$$

which is valid since the predicate in the conclusion is present in the hypothesis.

The proof of the second liveness condition, namely

$$[PosDiff \mid y \geq x] \sqsubseteq Assign\_ymx \qquad (207, 207)$$

is left as an exercise.

7.5.3 Refining a disjunction with an alternation

The reader might have noticed that *PosDiff* is the same as the disjunction of *Assign_xmy* and *Assign_ymx*, and the guards are actually the preconditions of the disjuncts. This observation leads to a general rule:

$$A_1 \lor A_2 \sqsubseteq \ \textbf{if}\ \textbf{pre}\ A_1 \rightarrow A_1 \ \Box\ \textbf{pre}\ A_2 \rightarrow A_2\ \textbf{fi}$$

(Here the schemas $\textbf{pre}\ A_1$ and $\textbf{pre}\ A_2$ are being used in place of the corresponding boolean expressions.) We might further observe that $A_1 \lor A_2$ is not only a specification satisfied by the program, but is actually a description of the program behaviour.

We shall prove the refinement by checking the three conditions. The safety condition is

$$\textbf{pre}(A_1 \lor A_2) \vdash (\textbf{pre}\ A_1) \lor (\textbf{pre}\ A_2)$$

which is valid since the conclusion and the hypothesis are logically equivalent.

The first liveness condition is

$$(A_1 \lor A_2) \land \textbf{pre}\ A_1 \sqsubseteq A_1$$

and this requires the safety and liveness checks for refinement. The safety condition is

$$\textit{pre}((A_1 \vee A_2) \wedge \textit{pre}\ A_1) \vdash \textit{pre}\ A_1$$

and the hypothesis is $(\textit{pre}\ A_1) \wedge ((\textit{pre}\ A_1) \vee \textit{pre}\ A_2)$, from which the conclusion can be drawn. The liveness condition is

$$\textit{pre}((A_1 \vee A_2) \wedge \textit{pre}\ A_1) \wedge A_1 \vdash A_1 \vee A_2$$

and since A_1 is in the hypothesis, thc conclusion can be drawn at once.

The proof of the other liveness condition is left as an exercise.

7.5.4 Refining a disjunction to an if-then-else

In a disjunction of schemas, if the precondition of one is computable in the target language, then an if-then-else is easily constructed. Suppose that $A_1 \vee A_2$ is to be refined, and the precondition of A_1 is easily computed, then

$$A_1 \vee A_2 \sqsubseteq \ \textit{if pre}\ A_1 \rightarrow A_1 \ \Box\ \neg(\textit{pre}\ A_1) \rightarrow A_2\ \textit{fi}$$

and this can be translated into an if-then-else. To show that this refinement is correct, we must prove the safety condition

$$\textit{pre}\ (A_1 \vee A_2) \vdash (\textit{pre}\ A_1) \vee \neg(\textit{pre}\ A_1)$$

the first liveness condition

$$(A_1 \vee A_2) \wedge \textit{pre}\ A_1 \sqsubseteq A_1$$

and the second liveness condition

$$(A_1 \vee A_2) \wedge \neg(\textit{pre}\ A_1) \sqsubseteq A_2$$

The safety condition is immediate, since the conclusion is a tautology.

The first liveness condition involves showing that

$$\textit{pre}((A_1 \vee A_2) \wedge \textit{pre}\ A_1) \vdash \textit{pre}\ A_1$$

which is true since the conclusion appears in the hypothesis. In addition we have to show that

$$\textit{pre}((A_1 \vee A_2) \wedge \textit{pre}\ A_1) \wedge A_1 \vdash (A_1 \vee A_2) \wedge \textit{pre}\ A_1$$

which is left as an exercise.

For the second liveness condition we first note that

$$(A_1 \vee A_2) \wedge \neg(\textit{pre}\ A_1)$$

is the same as

$$(A_1 \wedge \neg(\mathbf{pre}\ A_1)) \vee (A_2 \wedge \neg(\mathbf{pre}\ A_1))$$

and the first disjunct is a contradiction, so we have to prove

$$(A_2 \wedge \neg(\mathbf{pre}\ A_1)) \sqsubseteq A_2$$

This proof is also left as an exercise.

7.5.5 Refinement of the enrol operation

In a previous section of this chapter we converted the concrete operation to enrol a student (*DEnrol*) into a schema *DEnrolProg* with three disjuncts with the preconditions shown in Table 7.1.

Table 7.1 Preconditions of schemas for enrolling (direct).

Schema	Page	Precondition
DEnrolokProg	204	$(\forall i: 1..ectr \bullet (sarray\ i) \neq s)$ $\wedge\ ectr < size$
DNoRoomProg	204	$ectr = size$
DAlreadyEnrolledProg	204	$\exists i: 1..ectr \bullet (sarray\ i) = s$

The easiest precondition to deal with is that of *DNoRoomProg*, so we give a name to *DEnrolokProg* ∨ *DAlreadyEnrolledProg*:

DEnoughRoom ≙
DEnrolokProg ∨ *DAlreadyEnrolledProg* (204, 204)

Using the result of the previous section, we can refine *DEnrolProg* as follows:

DEnrolProg ⊑ (204)
if $ectr = size \rightarrow$
| *DNoRoomProg* (204)
□ $ectr < size \rightarrow$
| *DEnoughRoom* (210)
fi

The refinement has decided to resolve the non-determinism in the specification, which did not determine the behaviour when both

$ectr = size$ and $\exists i$: *1..ectr* • (*sarray i*) = *s*. We have chosen to limit the application of *DAlreadyEnrolled* to situations in which $ectr = size$ does not apply.

The refinement of *DEnrolProg* is complete, since the specifications *DEnoughRoom* and *DNoRoomProg* have been documented.

The refinement of *DNoRoomProg* is easy.

$$DNoRoomProg \sqsubseteq r := noroom \qquad (204)$$

The refinement of *DEnoughRoom* will be pursued on p. 216.

7.6 The sequence control structure

7.6.1 Using the sequence control structure

If a sequence of two specifications (A_1; A_2) is offered as a refinement of a third (S), we shall record this by writing

$$S \sqsubseteq A_1; A_2$$

To verify this refinement we have the following proof obligations.

pre $S \vdash$ ***pre*** A_1	Any circumstance acceptable to the specification must be acceptable to the first program. (This is the first safety condition.)
pre $S \wedge A_1 \vdash$ (***pre*** A_2)'	Any circumstance resulting from the first program being run in circumstances acceptable to the specification must be acceptable to the second program. (This is the second safety condition.)
pre $S \wedge A_1 \wedge A_2'$ $\vdash S[\_'' / \_']$	Running A_1 and then A_2 starting in circumstances acceptable to the specification must produce a result acceptable to the specification. (This is the liveness condition.)

(The notation (***pre*** A_2)' is not a Z notation, but an instance of systematic renaming. All the variables of ***pre*** A_2 are to be decorated with a dash.)

Figure 7.3 shows the states and the schemas that relate them. It illustrates the need for the decoration of ***pre*** A_2 in the second safety condition, and the renaming of the variables in S.

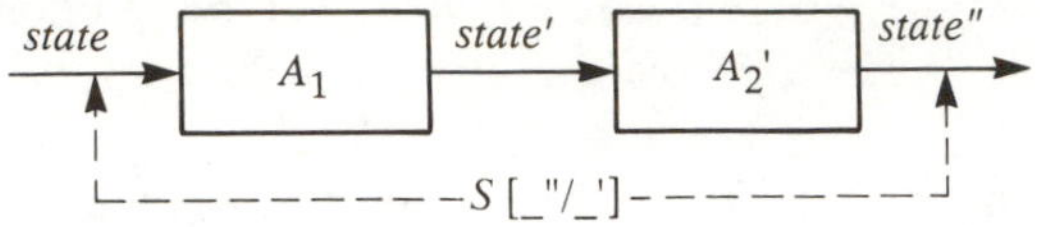

Figure 7.3 Verifying refinement into a sequence of programs.

7.6.2 Example of refinement by sequence

As a simple example of the use of this rule, consider the following program state

$$XState \mathrel{\widehat=} [x: 0..maxnat]$$

and the following specification:

$$UpTwo \mathrel{\widehat=} [\Delta XState \mid x' = x + 2] \qquad (212)$$

We note that the specification has $x + 2 \leq maxnat$ as its precondition. This specification is to be refined by the following sequence:

$$x := x + 1; x := x + 1$$

The schema describing each assignment statement is as follows:

$$Increase\_x \mathrel{\widehat=}$$
$$[\Delta XState \mid x + 1 \leq maxnat \wedge x' = x + 1] \qquad (212)$$

Here the precondition has been made explicit.

The first safety condition is

$$[XState \mid x + 2 \leq maxnat] \vdash x + 1 \leq maxnat \qquad (212)$$

which is a correct deduction. The second safety condition is

$$[XState \qquad (212)$$
$$\mid x + 2 \leq maxnat \wedge x + 1 \leq maxnat \wedge x' = x + 1]$$
$$\vdash x' + 1 \leq maxnat$$

which is also a correct deduction. The liveness condition is

$$[XState; XState'' \qquad (212, 212)$$
$$\mid x + 2 \leq maxnat \wedge x + 1 \leq maxnat$$
$$\wedge x' = x + 1 \wedge x'' = x' + 1]$$
$$\vdash x'' = x + 2$$

which is also a correct deduction.

7.6.3 Replacing commands in a sequence

If a specification has been refined into a sequence, either of the commands in the sequence can be replaced by something that refines it without upsetting the correctness of the first refinement step. Suppose

$$S \sqsubseteq A_1; A_2$$

and

$$A_2 \sqsubseteq A_3$$

We shall show that

$$S \sqsubseteq A_1; A_3$$

as follows:

(1)	$\textit{pre}\ S \vdash \textit{pre}\ A_1$	Since $S \sqsubseteq A_1; A_2$
(2)	$(\textit{pre}\ S) \wedge A_1 \vdash (\textit{pre}\ A_2)'$	Since $S \sqsubseteq A_1; A_2$
(3)	$(\textit{pre}\ S) \wedge A_1 \wedge A_2' \vdash S[\_''/\_']$	Since $S \sqsubseteq A_1; A_2$
(4)	$\textit{pre}\ A_2 \vdash \textit{pre}\ A_3$	Since $A_2 \sqsubseteq A_3$
(5)	$(\textit{pre}\ A_2) \wedge A_3 \vdash A_2$	Since $A_2 \sqsubseteq A_3$
(6)	$(\textit{pre}\ S) \wedge A_1 \vdash (\textit{pre}\ A_3)'$	From (2) and (4)
(7)	$(\textit{pre}\ S) \wedge A_1 \wedge A_3'$ $\vdash (\textit{pre}\ S) \wedge A_1 \wedge (\textit{pre}\ A_2)' \wedge A_3'$	From (2)
(8)	$(\textit{pre}\ S) \wedge A_1 \wedge A_3'$ $\vdash (\textit{pre}\ S) \wedge A_1 \wedge A_2'$	From (7) and (5)
(9)	$(\textit{pre}\ S) \wedge A_1 \wedge A_3' \vdash S[\_''/\_']$	From (8) and (3)

The required conclusions are (1), (6) and (9).

7.6.4 Operations on partitioned states

A sequence program is a natural choice when separate parts of a state are to be acted upon in an independent manner. Suppose that

$$PartState \mathrel{\widehat{=}} PartA \wedge PartB$$

and *PartA* and *PartB* have no declarations in common, and *OpA* is an operation on *PartA* and *OpB* is an operation on *PartB*. The operation $OpA \wedge OpB$ on the whole of *PartState* can be refined by amended operations *OpAx* and *OpBx* as follows:

$$OpAx \mathrel{\widehat=} [\Delta PartState; \Xi PartB; OpA]$$

$$OpBx \mathrel{\widehat=} [\Delta PartState; \Xi PartA; OpB]$$

OpAx is the operation *OpA* extended to act on the whole state, but leaving the parts of the state not in *OpA* unchanged. *OpBx* is similarly defined.

We have to prove that

$$OpA \wedge OpB \sqsubseteq OpAx; OpBx$$

First we show that because the state is partitioned,

$$\textbf{pre}(OpA \wedge OpB) \vdash (\textbf{pre}\ OpA) \wedge (\textbf{pre}\ OpB),$$

and prove this result as follows:

(1)	$\textbf{pre}(OpA \wedge OpB)$	Hypothesis
(2)	$\exists PartState' \bullet$ $(OpA \wedge OpB)$	From (1) by definition of the precondition operator
(3)	$\exists PartA' \bullet$ $(\exists PartB' \bullet$ $(OpA \wedge OpB))$	From (2) by definition of *PartState*
(4)	$\exists PartA' \bullet$ $(OpA \wedge \exists PartB' \bullet OpB)$	From (3) since *OpA* does not contain any of the variables in *PartB'*
(5)	$(\exists PartA' \bullet OpA) \wedge$ $(\exists PartA' \bullet$ $(\exists PartB' \bullet OpB))$	From (4) by distribution of existential quantification over conjunction
(6)	$(\exists PartA' \bullet OpA)$ $\wedge (\exists PartB' \bullet OpB)$	From (5) since the second conjunct is a quantification over variables that do not occur there
(7)	$(\textbf{pre}\ OpA) \wedge (\textbf{pre}\ OpB)$	From (6) by the definition of the precondition operator

The first safety condition is

$$\textbf{pre}(OpA \wedge OpB) \vdash \textbf{pre}\ OpAx$$

and this follows from the observation that

$$\textbf{pre}\ OpA \vdash \textbf{pre}\ OpAx$$

The second safety condition is

$$\textit{pre}(OpA \wedge OpB) \wedge OpAx \vdash (\textit{pre}\ OpBx)'$$

and we prove this as follows:

(8)	$\textit{pre}(OpA \wedge OpB) \wedge OpAx \vdash (\textit{pre}\ OpA) \wedge (\textit{pre}\ OpB) \wedge OpAx \wedge \Xi PartB$	From the precondition result above, and the fact that $\Xi PartB$ is part of the definition of $OpAx$
(9)	$\textit{pre}(OpA \wedge OpB) \wedge OpAx \vdash (\textit{pre}\ OpB) \wedge \Xi PartB$	By dropping the first and third conjuncts
(10)	$\textit{pre}(OpA \wedge OpB) \wedge OpAx \vdash (\textit{pre}\ OpB)'$	From (9)

The liveness condition is

$$\textit{pre}(OpA \wedge OpB) \wedge OpAx \wedge OpBx' \vdash (OpA \wedge OpB)[\_'' / \_']$$

and this is proved as follows:

(11)	$\textit{pre}(OpA \wedge OpB) \wedge OpAx \wedge OpBx' \vdash (\textit{pre}\ OpA) \wedge (\textit{pre}\ OpB) \wedge OpA \wedge \Xi PartB \wedge OpB \wedge \Xi PartA$	By replacing $OpAx$ and $OpBx$ by their definitions
(12)	$\textit{pre}(OpA \wedge OpB) \wedge OpAx \wedge OpBx' \vdash (OpA \wedge OpB)[\_'' / \_']$	From (11) by dropping some conjuncts

7.6.5 Introducing local variables

A sequence program is often chosen to implement a specification when the preconditions of a disjunction need work to be done to evaluate them. The first program decides which case we are in and the second takes appropriate action. We need to be able to introduce **local variables** to communicate between the programs. Suppose A is a schema specifying an operation on a program state, and x is a variable of type X not in the program state. In these circumstances we can assert that

$$A \sqsubseteq$$
$$x\colon X$$
$$[A;\ x, x'\colon X]$$

The refinement of the modified command can do anything it likes to the new variable x. To establish this we need only note that the predicate part of the horizontal schema expression is exactly the same as the predicate part of A. The proof obligations then reduce to

$$\textbf{pre}\ A \vdash \textbf{pre}\ A$$

and

$$(\textbf{pre}\ A) \wedge A \vdash A$$

which are immediate.

7.6.6 Further refinement of the enrol operation

We propose a refinement of *DEnoughRoom* as follows:

DEnoughRoom ⊑ (210)
where: *0..(size + 1)*
DEnoughRoomX (216)

The extension of *DEnoughRoom* is defined in the usual way.

```
┌─DEnoughRoomX──────────────────
│ where, where': 0..(size + 1)
│ DEnoughRoom                        (210)
└───────────────────────────────
```

Now we propose that

DEnoughRoomX ⊑ (216)
Search; (217)
Decide (217)

where *Search* and *Decide* are to be specified.

The program to implement *Search* will not change the state of *DClass* but will set the variable *where* to index an occurrence of *s* in the active part of the array, if there is one, and to *ectr + 1* if there isn't. Hence the following specification is recorded for *Search*.

```
┌─SearchState───────────────────
│ DClass                             (163)
│ where: 0..(size + 1)
│ s: Student                         (14)
│ r: Response                        (14)
└───────────────────────────────
```

Search

$\Delta SearchState$ (216)
$\Xi DClass$ (163)

$((\forall i: 1..ectr \bullet (sarray\ i) \neq s \wedge where' = ectr + 1)$
$\vee ((sarray\ where') = s \wedge where' \in 1..ectr))$
$s' = s$

For *Decide* we can supply the following definition:

Decide

$\Delta SearchState$ (216)
$DEnoughRoom$ (210)

$where \leq ectr \Leftrightarrow (\exists i: 1..ectr \bullet (sarray\ i) = s)$

The proof that this refinement into a sequence is correct is left as an exercise.

The refinement of *Decide* by an alternation is as follows:

Decide $\sqsubseteq$ (217)
if $where \leq ectr \rightarrow$
  $r := alreadyenrolled$
$\square$ $where > ectr \rightarrow$
  $ectr := ectr + 1;$
  $sarray(ectr) := s;$
  $r := success$
fi

7.7 The iteration control structure

7.7.1 Using the initialized do-while control structure

Iteration programs are often appropriate when aggregates (arrays, lists) are to be processed. They often appear when predicates that are not directly computable (especially predicates with quantifiers) are to be decided. The reader might have guessed that the *Search* command specified above as part of the refinement of the enrol operation is a case in point. The form of iteration program we shall study is the initialized do-while, whose form in the guarded command language is as follows.

Initial; ***do*** **B** → *Body* ***od***

Initial is the initialization program, **B** the while-test, and *Body* is the loop body. The correct recording of the refinement of a specification into an initialized do-while needs specifications for all these things, and for two others as follows:

- The loop **invariant**, a weakening of the specification that is easy to implement (for initialization) and suitable for strengthening (by the negation of the while-test) by means of the loop. The invariant embodies design decisions about the roles of the program variables in the loop. It must be the designer's intention that the invariant will be true every time the while-test is made.
- The **bound function**, an upper bound on the number of iterations left when the while-test is made. The bound function must depend on the values of the program variables, and must be defined when the while-test is made. It must have a value that is an integer.

Some of the important relationships among these things are illustrated in Figure 7.4. In this figure, *Initial* represents the initialization program, *Invar* represents the invariant relation, *Guard* represents the while-test and *Body* represents the specification of the loop body. Only the bound function has no representation in the figure.

7.7.2 Recording an invariant and a bound function

Z can be used to record the loop invariant, since the invariant is a relation between the values of the program variables at two points in the execution of the program: the values before the program begins executing, and the values when the while-test is made. We shall use undashed names for the former and dashed names for the latter.

Our notions about how we propose to use an initialized loop to implement a specification *Spec* are made precise by recording the invariant and the bound function. Suppose *Invar* is a schema on two states X and X' defining the invariant, and *bf* a natural number function on one state X defining the bound function.

$$bf: X \nrightarrow \mathbb{N}$$

If these are well chosen, we should be able to complete the recording to satisfy the following proof obligations:

- Initialization – set values in the variables that satisfy the invariant. Choose *Initial*, a schema on X and X', so that the initialization refines the invariant.

$$\textbf{\textit{pre Spec}} \vdash \textbf{\textit{pre Init}}$$

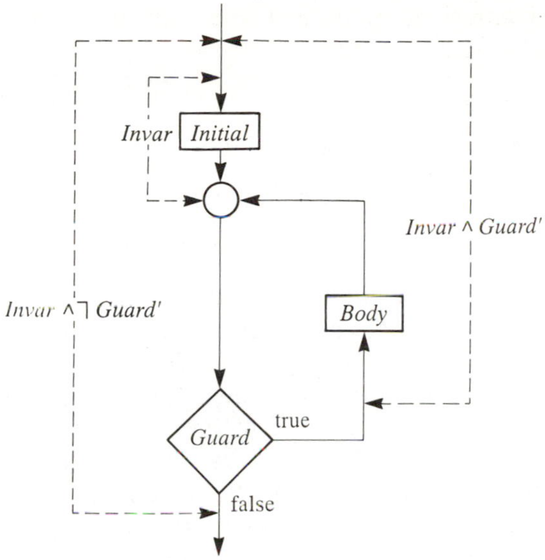

Figure 7.4 Components of an initialized loop.

$$(\textbf{pre}\ Spec) \land Initial \vdash Invar$$

- Final condition – choose *Guard*, a schema on one state *X* that will force the invariant to be an implementation of the specification when the guard is false.

$$(\textbf{pre}\ Spec) \land Invar \land \neg Guard' \vdash Spec$$

- Termination – make sure that, if the guard is true in a state satisfying the invariant, the bound function is strictly positive, and is reduced by the proposed body.

$$(\textbf{pre}\ Spec) \land Invar \land Guard' \vdash bf\ \theta X' > 0$$

$$(\textbf{pre}\ Spec) \land Invar \land Guard' \land Body' \vdash bf\ \theta X'' < bf\ \theta X'$$

- Preservation – make sure that, if the guard is true, the body is safe, and will preserve the invariant.

$$(\textbf{pre}\ Spec) \land Invar \land Guard' \vdash (\textbf{pre}\ Body)'$$

$$(\textbf{pre}\ Spec) \land Invar \land Guard' \land Body' \vdash Invar\ [\_''/\_']$$

The specification of the body of the loop must have the following properties:

- The while-test is true in the starting state
- The invariant holds for the starting state
- The invariant holds for the ending state
- The state change reduces the bound function

This method of deriving the initialization, guard and body from the invariant and bound function is generally to be preferred to guessing the program and then verifying it. Verification involves finding an invariant and a bound function, and showing that the given loop could be built from them. Failure to find an invariant and a bound function from which the given loop can be built is not sufficient to tell us that the program is incorrect. It might just be the case that our understanding of the loop is not as well developed as that of the loop's author. Hence it is very important that the invariant and bound function be documented when the loop is being constructed.

7.7.3 Example of refinement by initialized do-while

We take as a simple example the problem of summing the elements of an array of integers. First we need to specify precisely what we mean by the sum of the elements of an array, and we use the following axiomatic description for the sum of a sequence of integers, since our model of an array is just a sequence of fixed size.

$$sumseq: \textbf{seq}\ \mathbb{Z} \rightarrow \mathbb{Z}$$

$$\begin{array}{l} (\ \forall si: \textbf{seq}\ \mathbb{Z} \\ \bullet\ (\ (\ si = \langle\rangle \wedge sumseq\ si = 0\ ) \\ \quad \vee\ (\ si \neq \langle\rangle \wedge sumseq\ si = (\textbf{head}\ si)\ +\ (sumseq\ (\textbf{tail}\ si))\ )\ ) \end{array}$$

Now we introduce a program space that includes the array to be summed and the variable to hold the answer. The value n is a constant greater than zero, the size of the array.

SumSpace

$$\begin{array}{l} intarr: 1..n \rightarrow \mathbb{Z} \\ s: \mathbb{Z} \end{array}$$

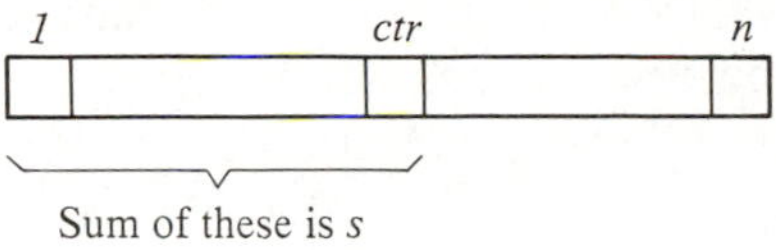

Figure 7.5 Invariant for summing an integer array.

Now we specify the program:

Addup
$\Delta SumSpace$ (220)

$intarr' = intarr$
$s' = sumseq\ intarr$

The array will not be changed by the program, and the program will terminate with the sum of the elements of the array in s.

There are various ways in which we could solve this problem, but the one we shall pursue is to go through the array from the lowest numbered cell, adding up the elements as we go. For this we need a counter *ctr*, and we refine the specification as follows.

$Addup \sqsubseteq$ (221)
$ctr: 0..n$
$AddupExt$ (221)

with the following definition for *AddupExt*:

$AddupExt \mathrel{\widehat{=}} [Addup; ctr, ctr': 0..n]$ (221)

Each time the while-test is made we expect s to contain the sum of all the elements in the segment of the array up to *ctr*. This intention is illustrated by Figure 7.5.

The invariant is made precise in the following schema.

Addup_invar
$\Delta SumSpace$ (220)
$ctr, ctr': 0..n$

$s' = sumseq((1..ctr') \lhd intarr')$
$ctr' \leq n$
$intarr' = intarr$

Here the undashed variables represent the values of the program variables before the program begins, while the dashed variables represent the values of the program variables at the time the while-test is evaluated. The intention about the value of *s* is recorded in the first predicate. The second predicate reiterates the fact that *ctr* will never exceed *n*. We record in the third predicate the intention that the array will always have its initial value every time the while-test is made.

Having presented an invariant, we must fix the initialization program. This must implement the invariant, and it must be easy to program. We cannot change *intarr*, but we can choose any values we like for *s* and *ctr*. Let us take the easy way out, and make them both zero.

```
┌─ Addup_init ──────────────────────────────
│ ΔSumSpace                                          (220)
│ ctr, ctr': 0..n
├───────────────
│ intarr' = intarr
│ s' = 0
│ ctr' = 0
└───────────────────────────────────────────
```

It is an easy matter to prove the theorems

$$\textbf{pre}\ Addup \vdash \textbf{pre}\ Addup\_init \qquad (221, 222)$$

$$\textbf{pre}\ Addup \wedge Addup\_init \vdash Addup\_invar \qquad (221, 222, 222)$$

and it is left as an exercise. Also as an exercise the reader can show that

$$\begin{array}{l} Addup\_init \sqsubseteq \\ \quad s := 0; \\ \quad ctr := 0 \end{array} \qquad (222)$$

Now let us calculate the while-test for the loop by considering how the invariant must be strengthened to make it implement the specification. In this case the invariant will implement the specification when $ctr' = n$, so the while-test is the negation of the corresponding boolean expression on values of program variables, namely

$$ctr \neq n$$

To assure termination we need to find a bound function, an

expression with an integer for its value that we intend to decrease each time we go through the loop body. Bearing in mind our informal intention, the natural choice is

$n - ctr$

Now we can construct a specification of the body as follows.

```
┌─Addup_body──────────────────────────────
│ ΔSumSpace                                          (220)
│ ctr, ctr': 0..n
├──────────
│ ctr < n
│ s = sumseq((1..ctr) ◁ intarr)
│ s' = sumseq((1..ctr') ◁ intarr')
│ ctr' ≤ n
│ intarr' = intarr
│ ctr' = ctr + 1
└─────────────────────────────────────────
```

The predicates in the body can be analysed as follows:

- The first predicate says that when the body is entered, the while-test is true.
- The second predicate says that when the body is entered, *s* contains the sum of the elements of the array up to the starting value of *ctr*. (This is part of the invariant for the starting state.)
- The third predicate says that when the body ends, *s* contains the sum of the elements of the array up to the ending value of *ctr*. (This is part of the invariant for the ending state.)
- The fourth predicate says that the ending value of *ctr* cannot exceed *n*. (This is part of the invariant for the ending state.)
- The fifth predicate says that the body does not change the array. (This is derived from the invariant for the starting state, and the invariant for the ending state.)
- The last predicate is to reduce the bound function. We have chosen to make the reduction in the bound function exactly one, in accordance with our informal intention of examining each element of the array in turn.

Some of the predicates can be combined and simplified to give the following version of the specification of the body.

Addup_body

$\Delta SumSpace$ (220)
$ctr, ctr' : 0..n$

$ctr < n$
$s' = s + intarr(ctr')$
$intarr' = intarr$
$ctr' = ctr + 1$

and this can be implemented by the following program:

$Addup\_body \sqsubseteq$ (224)
$ctr := ctr + 1;$
$s := s + intarr(ctr)$

as the reader can verify.

7.7.4 Completing the refinement of the enrol operation

At first sight it might seem that an initialized do-while would be a suitable choice for refining *Search*. We could use the program variable *where* as a counter in the loop, and increase *where* steadily as we search for the student *s*. Each time the while-test is made, there will be no occurrence of the student in the array so far. Figure 7.6 summarizes the proposed strategy.

A first guess at the termination condition is that *where* has passed *ectr*, or *sarray(where)* is the required student. This, however, presents us with two practical problems.

- *ectr* might be zero
- *ectr* might be *size*, and *sarray*(*where*) is not defined if *where* is $ectr + 1$

For a first refinement step we propose to separate the first case, using the following alternation.

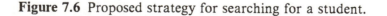

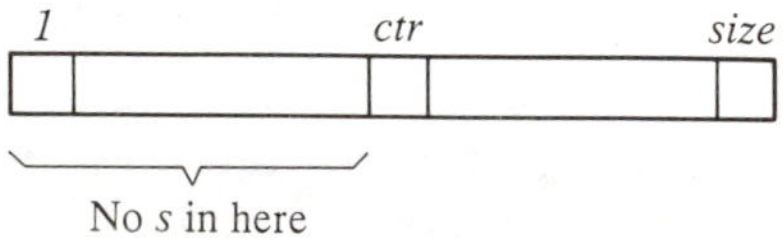

Figure 7.6 Proposed strategy for searching for a student.

$Search \sqsubseteq$ (217)
$\quad \textit{if } ectr = 0 \rightarrow where := 1$
$\quad \Box ectr > 0 \rightarrow Search1$ (225)
$\quad \textit{fi}$

where

$Search1 \mathrel{\hat{=}} [Search \mid ectr > 0]$ (217)

and the verification of this refinement is left to the reader. The implementer of *Search1* is entitled to assume that the value of the program variable *ectr* is greater than zero when the program starts.

To deal with the second problem we propose to increase *where* until it gets to the *ectr* value, but not let it go beyond. This design decision is made precise as follows.

$Search1 \sqsubseteq Search2; Search3$ (225, 225, 226)

The commands in this sequence are specified as follows:

Search2

$\Delta SearchState$ (216)
$\Xi DClass$ (163)

$ectr > 0$
$((\, sarray\ where' = s \wedge where' \in 1..(ectr-1)\,)$
$\vee ((\, \forall i: 1..(ectr-1) \bullet sarray\ i \neq s\,) \wedge where' = ectr\,))$
$s' = s$

The writer of this program can assume that the value of the program variable *ectr* is greater than zero when the program starts. The value of the program variable *where* is to be set to index an occurrence of *s* if there is one in the range *1..ectr−1*, otherwise it is to be set to *ectr*. The array and the values in *ectr* and *tctr* are to be unchanged.

Search3

$\Delta SearchState$ (216)
$\Xi DClass$ (163)

$ectr > 0$
$where \leq ectr$
$((\, sarray\ where = s \wedge where' = where\,)$
$\vee (\, sarray\ where \neq s \wedge where' = where + 1\,))$
$s' = s$

The writer of the program for *Search3* can assume that the value of the program variable *ectr* is greater than zero when the program starts, and that the value of *where* does not exceed the value of *ectr*. If *where* is indexing an occurrence of *s*, do nothing, otherwise increase *where* by one.

The reader is invited to verify this refinement of *Search1*, and the following refinement of *Search3*.

$$
\begin{array}{l}
Search3 \sqsubseteq \\
\mathbf{if}\ sarray(where) \neq s \rightarrow \\
\quad where := where + 1 \\
\Box\ sarray(where) = s \rightarrow \mathbf{skip} \\
\mathbf{fi}
\end{array}
\qquad (226)
$$

Now we can get down to the business of developing the initialized do-while for searching for the student. The strategy is the same as first proposed, but the specification is a bit different.

Search2_invar

$\Delta SearchState$	(216)
$\Xi DClass$	(163)

$$
\begin{array}{l}
ectr > 0 \\
where' \leq ectr \\
s' = s \\
\forall i: 1..(where'-1) \bullet sarray'\ i \neq s
\end{array}
$$

The bound function that suggests itself is *ectr−where*. The invariant tells us that $where' \leq ectr$, so the bound is always defined and always greater than or equal to zero.

We choose *Search2_init* to be an easily programmed implementation of *Search2_invar*,

$$where := 1$$

For the final condition we look for a predicate that will turn *Search2_invar* into an implementation of *Search2*. We choose

$$where' = ectr \vee sarray(where') = s$$

because when we add it to *Search2_invar* we get the following:

Search2_invar_ext

$\Delta SearchState$	(216)
$\Xi DClass$	(163)

$ectr > 0$
$where' \leq ectr$
$s' = s$
$\forall i: 1..(where'-1) \bullet sarray'\ i \neq s$
$where' = ectr \vee sarray\ where' = s$

The while-test is the boolean expression corresponding to the negation of the chosen predicate,

$$where < ectr \wedge sarray(where) \neq s$$

Now we construct the body of the loop.

Search2_body

$\Delta SearchState$	(216)
$\Xi DClass$	(163)

$ectr > 0$
$where < ectr$
$sarray\ where \neq s$
$\forall i: 1..(where-1) \bullet sarray\ i \neq s$
$where \leq ectr$
$\forall i: 1..(where'-1) \bullet sarray'\ i \neq s$
$where' \leq ectr$
$where' = where + 1$

This is refined by

$$where := where + 1$$

7.8 Algorithms for indirect data designs

The foregoing examples of algorithm design were based on a direct data design, that is a design that used only primitive data types of typical target programming languages. In the chapter on data design, when the notion of indirect data design was introduced, we spoke of enriching the target programming language with abstract data types.

The programming language has to be extended in two ways:

- Declaring variables of the new type
- Using the operations of the new type

How these facilities are introduced into particular programming languages depends on the language in question. In Ada, for instance, this kind of extension is a primary feature of the language. In other languages things might not be so easy, and often some kind of preprocessing has to be used to convert statements that declare variables and use the operations into statements of the language that call procedures supplied by the provider of the abstract data type. For the purposes of this chapter we need only establish some conventions about the notation to be used to augment the guarded command language.

7.8.1 Declaring variables

In the indirect refinement of the class manager's assistant, two instances of *StudentSet* were required. The declarations of the guarded command language can be used provided that we allow schemas to be used as data types. We declare the yes-set and the no-set as follows.

yes: *StudentSet*; (179)
no: *StudentSet* (179)

These declarations introduce two program variables. The provider of the package must say what guarantees about the initial values are to be given. In this case, the values of these variables the first time they appear in the program will be the initial value of *StudentSet*, *InitStudentSet*, defined on p. 179.

The limited set specification also introduced the type *Indic* and the two values *found* and *notfound*. We need to declare variables of this type, and to use *found* and *notfound* in assignment statements and boolean expressions in guards. The following are sample declarations.

indx: *Indic*; (178)
indy: *Indic* (178)

7.8.2 Using the operations

The operations *SetMax*, *FindSize*, *AddStudent*, *RemoveStudent* and *TryStudent* have to be made available in the guarded command language. We propose to extend the language with statements of the following form:

SetMaxC(**set**, **num**)

will apply the *SetMax* operation using whatever program variable is supplied for **set** as the *StudentSet*, and the value of the program variable supplied for **num** as the input *new?*.

FindSizeC(**set**, **num**)

will apply the *FindSize* operation using whatever program variable is supplied for **set** as the *StudentSet*, and will return the output *cur!* in the program variable supplied for **num**.

AddStudentC(**set**, **s**)

will apply the *AddStudent* operation using whatever program variable is supplied for **set** as the *StudentSet*, and the value of the program variable supplied for **s** as the input *s?*.

RemoveStudentC(**set**, **s**)

will apply the *RemoveStudent* operation using whatever program variable is supplied for **set** as the *StudentSet*, and the value of the program variable supplied for **s** as the input *s?*.

TryStudentC(**set**, **s**, **ind**)

will apply the *TryStudent* operation using whatever program variable is supplied for **set** as the *StudentSet*, the value of the program variable supplied for **s** as the input *s?*, and will return the output *ind!* in the program variable supplied for **ind**.

When one of these commands is used in the program we can say what its effect is to be. Consider the following declarations and statement.

yes: *StudentSet*; (179)
s: *Student*; (14)
indy: *Indic* (178)
TryStudentC(*yes*, *s*, *indy*)

The meaning of the command can be made precise in terms of the schemas of the limited set package. First we need a schema to convert operations on the anonymous *StudentSet* into operations on *yes*. We introduce the values of the program variable *yes* before and after the operation, and relate them to the starting and ending values of the *StudentSet*.

YesOperation

$yes, yes': StudentSet$	(179)
$\Delta StudentSet$	(179)
$yes = \theta StudentSet$	(179)
$yes' = \theta StudentSet'$	(179)

Now we define a new version of the *TryStudent* operation, introducing the other program variables.

TryStudentYes

$TryStudent$	(180)
$YesOperation$	(230)
$s, s': Student$	(14)
$indy, indy': Indic$	(178)
$s? = s$	
$s' = s$	
$ind! = indy'$	

The current value of the program variable *s* is to be used in the role assigned in the specification to *s?*. The value of that program variable will not change. The value of the program variable *indy* will be the value the specification promises for *ind!*.

To say precisely what the effect of the command is, we need to do a bit of tidying, since the declaration part of *TryStudentYes* is too big. It is in fact as follows:

$ss, ss': \mathbb{P} Student$	(14)
$max, max': \mathbb{N}$	
$s?: Student$	(14)
$ind!: Indic$	(178)
$yes, yes': StudentSet$	(179)
$s, s': Student$	(14)
$indy, indy': Indic$	(178)

We should have only the values of the program variables, so we must hide the auxiliary variables to produce the following precise description of the command.

$$\exists \Delta StudentSet \bullet (\ TryStudentYes \setminus (s?, ind!)\ ) \qquad (179, 230)$$

7.8.3 An algorithm for enrolling a student

To prepare the specification of *IEnrol* for algorithm refinement, we need to make use of the schema *Identify_s_and_r* introduced earlier.

$IEnrolProg \mathrel{\widehat=}$
$(IEnrol \land Identify\_s\_and\_r) \setminus (r!, s?)$ (184, 204)

$IEnrolokProg \mathrel{\widehat=}$
$(IEnrolok \land Identify\_s\_and\_r) \setminus (r!, s?)$ (183, 204)

$INoRoomProg \mathrel{\widehat=}$
$(INoRoom \land Identify\_s\_and\_r) \setminus (r!, s?)$ (183, 204)

$IAlreadyEnrolledProg \mathrel{\widehat=}$
$(IAlreadyEnrolled \land Identify\_s\_and\_r) \setminus (r!, s?)$ (183, 204)

We observe that *IEnrolProg* is the same as the following schema expression:

$IEnrolokProg \lor INoRoomProg$ (231, 231)
$\lor\ IAlreadyEnrolledProg$ (231)

It is therefore useful to examine the preconditions of these schemas (Table 7.2).

Table 7.2 Precondition of schemas for enrolling (indirect).

IEnrolokProg	$s \in (yes.ss \cup no.ss)$ $\land \#(yes.ss \cup no.ss) < size$
INoRoomProg	$\#(yes.ss \cup no.ss) = size$
IAlreadyEnrolledProg	$s \in yes.ss \lor s \in no.ss$

All these predicates require enquiries to be made to decide them, so we declare some variables to hold the results of the enquiries.

indy: *Indic* Will record whether the input student is in the yes-set

indn: *Indic* Will record whether the input student is in the no-set

cardy: $\mathbb{N}$ Will record the size of the yes-set

cardn: $\mathbb{N}$ Will record the size of the no-set

The first step of the refinement is to introduce the local variables to the scene.

$IEnrolProg \sqsubseteq$ (231)
$indy, indn: Indic;$ (178)
$cardy, cardn: 0..size$
$IEnrolX$ (232)

where *IEnrolX* is the following schema:

```
┌─ IEnrolX ─────────────────────────────────────
│ indy, indn, indy', indn': Indic                  (178)
│ cardy, cardn, cardy', cardn': 0..size
│ IEnrolProg                                       (231)
└───────────────────────────────────────────────
```

Several directions might now be followed, but we choose to decide everything first, and then take action.

$IEnrolX \sqsubseteq$ (232)
$DecideAll; IEnrolEasy$ (232, 233)

The operation *DecideAll* is specified as follows:

```
┌─ DecideAll ───────────────────────────────────
│ indy, indn, indy', indn': Indic                  (178)
│ cardy, cardn, cardy', cardn': 0..size
│ ΞIClass                                          (181)
│ s, s': Student                                   (14)
│ r, r': Response                                  (14)
├──────────
│ indy' = found ⇔ s ∈ yes.ss
│ indn' = found ⇔ s ∈ no.ss
│ cardy' = # yes.ss
│ cardn' = # no.ss
│ s = s'
└───────────────────────────────────────────────
```

The operation *IEnrolEasy* is specified as follows:

```
┌─ IEnrolEasy ──────────────────────────────────
│ IEnrolX                                          (232)
├──────────
│ indy = found ⇔ s ∈ yes.ss
│ indn = found ⇔ s ∈ no.ss
│ cardy = # yes.ss
│ cardn = # no.ss
└───────────────────────────────────────────────
```

The verification of this refinement is left to the reader.

We now present algorithms to implement these two specifications.

$$\begin{array}{l} \mathit{DecideAll} \sqsubseteq \\ \quad \mathit{TryStudentC}(\mathit{yes}, s, \mathit{indy}); \\ \quad \mathit{TryStudentC}(\mathit{no}, s, \mathit{indn}); \\ \quad \mathit{FindSizeC}(\mathit{yes}, \mathit{cardy}); \\ \quad \mathit{FindSizeC}(\mathit{no}, \mathit{cardn}) \end{array} \tag{232}$$

The verification of this refinement relies on the partitioning of the state into separate parts for the yes-set and the no-set, and the fact that each operation changes only one program variable.

$$\begin{array}{l} \mathit{IEnrolEasy} \sqsubseteq \\ \mathbf{if}\ \mathit{indy} = \mathit{found} \rightarrow r := \mathit{alreadyenrolled} \\ \square\ \ \mathit{indn} = \mathit{found} \rightarrow r := \mathit{alreadyenrolled} \\ \square\ \ \mathit{cardy} + \mathit{cardn} = \mathit{size} \rightarrow r := \mathit{noroom} \\ \square\ \ \mathit{indy} = \mathit{no} \wedge \mathit{indx} = \mathit{no} \wedge (\mathit{cardn} + \mathit{cardy}) < \mathit{size} \rightarrow \\ \mid\ \ \mathit{IEnrolokProg} \qquad (231) \\ \mathbf{fi} \end{array} \tag{233}$$

The verification of this refinement relies on the fact that the preconditions of the disjuncts of *IEnrolEasy* are equivalent to the guards in the alternation control structure.

We complete the algorithm design with the following program:

$$\mathit{IEnrolokProg} \sqsubseteq \mathit{AddStudentC}(\mathit{no}, s);\ r := \mathit{success} \tag{231}$$

7.9 Inspecting algorithm designs

The inspection of an algorithm design is a comparison of two documents, both with a formal content, namely the data design in which the algorithms were specified, and the algorithm design in which they are realized. The purpose of the inspection is to establish that

- the algorithm design is correct with respect to the data design, and
- the design decisions that give rise to it are appropriate for the development being undertaken.

The following questions should be asked for each algorithm design in a development.

- Has each step of the refinement been clearly documented?

- Are the proofs of correctness presented in sufficient detail to be convincing?
- Is the algorithm design natural, or otherwise justified by the non-functional requirements of the specification?
- If iteration is involved, are the initialization, guard, invariant, bound function and loop body clearly specified?
- Has any non-determinism in the specification of the algorithms been exploited to meet non-functional requirements?

More generally one should ask:

- Has sufficient reuse been made of subroutines common to several algorithms?

7.10 Reverse engineering

The precepts taught in this chapter have often been neglected in the past. Many a programmer has been faced with the task of making some modification to an existing algorithm that has not been recorded in the manner described above. Often all that is available to guide the programmer is a general informal statement of the intention of the system of which the algorithm is a part, and a program listing with comments in it. Even when the author of the program made an acceptable effort to say something of his or her intentions in the comments, later hands have generally not been so scrupulous for the welfare of the new reader. The programmer is therefore faced with the task of reconstructing, at least in part, the design rationale for the program. The term **reverse engineering** is often used to describe this procedure, and this section is intended to provide a reverse engineering method, or at least hints about how to construct one.

Reverse engineering is generally supposed to be a process that starts with a program and produces the specification of the program. Let us begin by saying that the expression 'the specification of the program' is one that has no denotation. Even the simplest program can be applied to implement many specifications, so the best we can hope to do is to derive 'a specification of the program'. But which one? Of course really we want 'the specification that caused this program to be written', but if it was not recorded at the time then the program itself is a bad place to start.

By way of example, consider the following program fragment,

$$x := x + 1$$

and consider what might have been the reason for writing it. Let us fix the environment by saying that in this programming language x is the name of a 3-bit register whose configurations are represented by the numbers from zero to seven, and that the manufacturer's description of this programming statement is the following set of ordered pairs.

$$bump == \{0 \mapsto 1,\ 1 \mapsto 2,\ 2 \mapsto 3,\ 3 \mapsto 4,\ 4 \mapsto 5,\ 5 \mapsto 6,\ 6 \mapsto 7,\ 7 \mapsto 0\}$$

This description advises us that the register wraps round quietly when the contents are seven.

The reader might suppose that this is all we wish to know in order to get a specification for the program fragment, and indeed this is a specification that the program fragment satisfies, but it gives no clue as to why the writer used this particular statement. For instance, the intention might have been to zero the register knowing that it contained the value 7; this specification could be formalized by the following relation.

$$spec1 == \{7 \mapsto 0\}$$

We can show that the relation *bump* is a refinement of *spec1* using the rules on p. 202.

$$\mathbf{dom}\ bump = 0..7$$

and

$$\mathbf{dom}\ spec1 = \{7\}$$

hence

$$\mathbf{dom}\ spec1 \subseteq \mathbf{dom}\ bump$$

as required by the safety condition. Similarly

$$\mathbf{dom}\ spec1 \lhd bump = \{7\} \lhd bump$$

and this is $\{7 \mapsto 0\}$, which is *spec1*, so

$$\mathbf{dom}\ spec1 \lhd bump \subseteq spec1$$

as required by the liveness condition.

Another specification that might have prompted the programmer to write the assignment statement is, given that the value of x is not 7, increase it by any amount. This specification is formalized by the relation

$$spec2 == \{i\colon 0..6;\ j\colon 1..7 \mid i < j \bullet i \mapsto j\}$$

This relation has 28 pairs in it, and it is also refined by *bump*.

Lastly we might mention a very unlikely specification, but still one that is refined by *bump*. It says that the program might do anything to x, including nothing. It is formalized by the relation

$$spec3 == 0..7 \times 0..7$$

which has 64 pairs.

There are clearly many thousands of specifications that are refined by *bump*, and the program itself can tell us nothing about which one was in the mind of the writer. To find out the specification that caused the program to be written we must work from outside the source statements of the program. We must enquire what users expect of this program, what documentation exists that might reveal its purpose, and we might even look at the informal comments that accompany the program statements.

The process of stepwise abstraction described on p. 198 can be used to get a description of the program's function, but this process can lead to spending large amounts of time revealing behaviour that is of no interest. Consider a **binary search** program. If you are not sure what this is, let me explain that it is a technique for searching an array of values for the occurrence of a particular value. The values must be ordered, and the contents of the array must be in ascending order of the values. The array can be searched much more quickly than in a linear search, as follows. On looking at the mid-point of the array, if the value there is greater than the value we are looking for, we can dismiss the upper half. If it is less than the value we are looking for, we can dismiss the lower half. We repeat this process on the remaining segment of the array. If an array of length 32 were to be searched one item after another, it would take an average of 16 comparisons to find the given value, or to conclude that it is not there, but with a binary search we can do the same work in at most 5 comparisons.

The problem with such a program from the reverse engineer's point of view is that it has a precondition, namely that the input array must be in ascending sequence. Attempts to discover the function by stepwise abstraction are bound to get bogged down in describing the behaviour of the program when this condition is not met. It is possible that the behaviour when the input array is in ascending sequence is so small a part of the total behaviour that we might never find it at all!

Exercises

(7.1) Complete the schema skeletons on the right to summarize the effect of the programs on the left. Hint: consider using the functions *max* and *min* defined in Chapter 4.

(a)

```
if x < y →
   | t: ℕ
   | t := x
   | x := y
   | y := t
□ x ≥ y → skip
fi
```

Prog1a

$x, x', y, y' : \mathbb{N}$

(b)

```
if x < y →
   | t: ℕ
   | t := x
   | x := y
   | y := t
□ x > y → skip
fi
```

Prog1b

$x, x', y, y' : \mathbb{N}$

(c)

```
z := 0
do z < x ∧ z < y →
   | z := z+1
od
```

Prog1c

$x, x', y, y', z, z' : \mathbb{N}$

(d)

```
z := 0
do z < x → z := z+1
□ z < y → z := z+1
od
```

Prog1d

$x, x', y, y', z, z' : \mathbb{N}$

(7.2) Write programs in the guarded command language to implement each of the following schemas.

(a)

Prog2a

$x, x', y, y' : \mathbb{N}$

$x' = y + 1$

$y' = y$

(b)

Prog2b

$x, x', y, y' : \mathbb{Z}$

$x' \geq 0$

$y' = y$

$x' = y \lor x' = -y$

(c)

$limit : \mathbb{N}$

$limit > 0$

Prog2c

$ar, ar' : (1..limit) \rightarrow \mathbb{Z}$

$p, p' : (0..limit)$

$\exists i : 1..limit \bullet (ar\ i) = 0$

$ar' = ar$

$(ar\ p') = 0$

(7.3) Show that for any specification S,

$$S \sqsubseteq S$$

(7.4) If A_1, A_2 and A_3 are specifications such that

$$A_1 \sqsubseteq A_2$$

and

$$A_2 \sqsubseteq A_3$$

show that

$$A_1 \sqsubseteq A_3$$

(7.5) Show that

$$Decrease\_x \sqsubseteq x := x - 1 \quad (202)$$

(7.6) Show that, for a suitable program state

$$DNoRoom \sqsubseteq r! := noroom \quad (168)$$

(Note that this assignment statement is total, i.e. its precondition is true.)

(7.7) Suppose that the following program state is given:

$$X \mathrel{\widehat{=}} [x, y: \mathbb{N}]$$

and suppose the following specifications of operations on it are given:

$$S \mathrel{\widehat{=}} [\Delta X \mid x' = y \wedge y' = x]$$

$$A_1 \mathrel{\widehat{=}} [\Delta X \mid x' = x + y \wedge y' = y]$$

$$A_2 \mathrel{\widehat{=}} [\Delta X \mid x' = y \wedge y' = x - y]$$

Show that

$$S \sqsubseteq A_1; A_2$$

(7.8) Continuing the previous question, if

$$A_3 \mathrel{\widehat{=}} [\Delta X \mid x' = x \wedge y' = x - y]$$

$$A_4 \mathrel{\widehat{=}} [\Delta X \mid x' = x - y \wedge y' = y]$$

show that

$$A_2 \sqsubseteq A_3; A_4$$

(7.9) Explain why the proof fails if the variables are declared to be of type *0..maxnat* rather than natural numbers.

(7.10) If

$$S \sqsubseteq A_1; A_2$$

and

$$A_1 \sqsubseteq A_3$$

show that

$$S \sqsubseteq A_3;\ A_2$$

(7.11) Prove the second liveness condition for the refinement of *PosDiff* on p. 208, namely

$$[PosDiff \mid y \geq x] \sqsubseteq Assign\_ymx \qquad (207, 207)$$

(7.12) State and prove the second liveness condition for the refinement

$$A_1 \vee A_2 \sqsubseteq \ \textit{\textbf{if pre}}\ A_1 \rightarrow A_1 \ \square\ \textbf{\textit{pre}}\ A_2 \rightarrow A_2\ \textbf{\textit{fi}}$$

introduced on p. 208.

(7.13) Refer to the notation of 'Refining a disjunction with an if-then-else' on p. 209, and prove

$$\begin{aligned}&\textbf{\textit{pre}}((A_1 \vee A_2) \wedge \textbf{\textit{pre}}\ A_1) \wedge A_1\\ &\vdash (A_1 \vee A_2) \wedge \textbf{\textit{pre}}\ A_1\end{aligned}$$

(7.14) Refer to the notation of 'Refining a disjunction with an if-then-else' on p. 209, and prove

$$A_2 \wedge \neg(\textbf{\textit{pre}}\ A_1) \sqsubseteq A_2$$

(7.15) Refer to the refinement of *DEnoughRoom* on p. 216, and prove it correct.

(7.16) Prove the theorems

$$\textbf{\textit{pre}}\ Addup \vdash \textbf{\textit{pre}}\ Addup\_init \qquad (221, 222)$$

$$\begin{aligned}&\textbf{\textit{pre}}\ Addup \wedge Addup\_init && (221, 222)\\ &\vdash Addup\_invar && (222)\end{aligned}$$

from p. 222.

(7.17) Prove the refinement

$$\begin{aligned}&Addup\_init \sqsubseteq && (222)\\ &\quad s := 0;\\ &\quad ctr := 0\end{aligned}$$

of p. 222.

(7.18) Verify the refinement of *Addup_body* on p. 224.

(7.19) Verify the refinement of *Search* on p. 225.

(7.20) Verify the refinement of *Search1* on p. 225.

(7.21) Verify the refinement of *Search3* on p. 226.

(7.22) Record a refinement of *DEnrolProg* on p. 204 in which reporting that a student is already enrolled takes precedence over reporting that the class is full.

(7.23) Record a refinement of *DTest* on p. 293 that reuses the *Search* operation specified on p. 217.

(7.24) Write down an invariant and a bound function to justify the correctness of the program in Exercise (7.1c) as a refinement of the schema *Prog1c*.

(7.25) Write down an invariant and a bound function to justify the correctness of the program in Exercise (7.1d) as a refinement of the schema *Prog1d*.

(7.26) Write down an invariant and a bound function to justify the correctness of the program in Exercise (7.2c) as a refinement of the schema *Prog2c*.

(7.27) If

$$Spec \sqsubseteq Init;\ \mathbf{do}\ Guard \rightarrow Body\ \mathbf{od}$$

with invariant *Invar* and bound function *bf*, and if

$$Body \sqsubseteq New$$

show that

$$Spec \sqsubseteq Init;\ \mathbf{do}\ Guard \rightarrow New\ \mathbf{od}$$

with the same invariant and bound function.

(7.28) Develop a program to set every element of an array of integers to zero.

(7.29) The positive natural number *size* is given:

$$size: \mathbb{N}$$

$$size > 0$$

A program is to operate on the following state containing an array of integers and two counters.

Pstate
$intarr: 1..size \rightarrow \mathbb{Z}$
$ctr, pos: 1..size$

The specification of the program is as follows:

Findmin	
$\Delta Pstate$	(242)
$intarr' = intarr$	
$\forall i: 1..size \bullet intarr\ i \geq intarr\ pos'$	

The program can do what it pleases with *ctr*. The final value of *pos* must, however, index an occurrence of the smallest integer in *intarr*.

Develop the program using the methods of this chapter.

(7.30) Make precise the definition of *RemoveStudentC* on p. 229 when **set** is *no* and **s** is *s*.

(7.31) Verify the refinement

$$IEnrolX \sqsubseteq DecideAll; IEnrolEasy \qquad (232, 232, 233)$$

on p. 232.

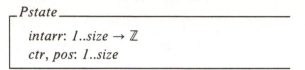

Appendix A
Specification of the oil terminal control system

A.1 Given sets and global constants

The specification has the following given sets:

- *Tanker* is the set of tankers
- *Berth* is the set of berths

$$[Tanker, Berth]$$

In any particular oil terminal there will be a certain set of berths available for tankers to use:

$$berths: \mathbb{P}\,Berth \qquad (244)$$

The following definition gives the values that the response to an operation can have.

$$OTCSResp ::= ok \mid wait \mid move\_tanker \mid known\_tanker \mid not\_at\_berth$$

A.2 State data for the oil terminal control system

The following information needs to be maintained:

- a queue of tankers waiting for berths
- a record of which tanker occupies which berth

The following requirements are to be met:

(1) A tanker cannot be in the queue and in a berth

(2) The tankers queueing will all be different

(3) No tanker will be queueing unless all the berths are full

(4) The tankers occupying berths will all be different

(5) Two tankers cannot occupy the same berth

Exercises

The following questions refer to the schema *Otcsys* below.

(A.1) For each of the numbered requirements, identify the line or lines in the schema that records it.

(A.2) What does the schema say about the contents of the set *known*?

(A.3) Which line of the schema introduces the relation between tankers and the berths they occupy?

Otcsys

$waiting: \mathbf{seq}\ Tanker$	(244)
$docked: Tanker \rightarrowtail\!\!\!\!\!\rightarrow Berth$	(244, 244)
$known: \mathbb{P}\,Tanker$	(244)

$$\mathbf{ran}\ waiting \cap \mathbf{dom}\ docked = \varnothing$$
$$\#\,waiting = \#\,(\mathbf{ran}\ waiting)$$
$$\#\,waiting > 0 \Rightarrow \mathbf{ran}\ docked = berths$$
$$\mathbf{ran}\ docked \subseteq berths$$
$$known = \mathbf{ran}\ waiting \cup \mathbf{dom}\ docked$$

A.3 Initializing the state data

This operation sets up an initial value of the system:

Initotc

$Otcsys'$	(245)

$$waiting' = \langle\rangle$$
$$docked' = \varnothing$$

The initial state clearly satisfies the predicates in the schema *Otcsys*:

$$\vdash \exists Otcsys' \bullet Initotc$$

Exercises

(A.4) Write an English sentence to describe the initial state.

(A.5) The initial value of the set *known* is not explicitly stated in *Initotc*. What is it?

(A.6) The user of the system wishes a modification to be made as follows:

> When the system is initialized the operator is to enter a list of tankers, and these are to be put in the queue.

The following schema formalizes the requirement:

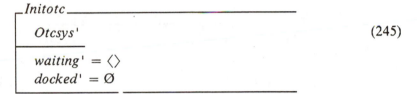

```
┌─Initotca──────────────────────────────
│ Otcsys'                                  (245)
│ q?: seq Tanker                           (244)
├──────────
│ waiting' = q?
│ docked' = Ø
└───────────────────────────────────────
```

Is this requirement consistent with the others?

(A.7) The user of the system wishes a modification to be made as follows:

> When the system is initialized the operator is to enter a list of tankers, and these are to be berthed. It is guaranteed that the length of the list will be not greater than the number of berths, and that the list of tankers will contain no duplicates. A list of berths will be output by the system.

The following schema formalizes the requirement:

```
┌─Initotcb──────────────────────────────
│ Otcsys'                                  (245)
│ q?: seq Tanker                           (244)
│ bs!: seq Berth                           (244)
├──────────
│ # q? ≤ # berths
│ # q? = # ran q?
│ waiting' = ⟨⟩
│ # bs! = # q?
│ docked' = {i: 1..#q? • (q? i) ↦ (bs! i)}
└───────────────────────────────────────
```

Is this requirement consistent with the others? How does the operator know which berth has been assigned to which tanker?

A.4 Operations — tankers arriving

Only tankers not already queueing or docked can ask permission to arrive. The first schema summarizes this.

$$
\begin{array}{|l}
\hline
\textit{Arrive0} \\
\hline
\Delta Otcsys \qquad (245) \\
a?: Tanker \qquad (244) \\
\hline
a? \notin known \\
\hline
\end{array}
$$

Two cases arise. If there is a free berth, the tanker is allocated to it:

$$
\begin{array}{|l}
\hline
\textit{Arrivenoq} \\
\hline
Arrive0 \qquad (247) \\
b!: Berth \qquad (244) \\
r!: OTCSResp \qquad (244) \\
\hline
\mathbf{ran}\ docked \neq berths \\
r! = ok \\
b! \in berths \setminus \mathbf{ran}\ docked \\
docked' = docked \oplus \{a? \mapsto b!\} \\
waiting' = waiting \\
\hline
\end{array}
$$

If there is no free berth, the tanker must be queued:

$$
\begin{array}{|l}
\hline
\textit{Arriveq} \\
\hline
Arrive0 \qquad (247) \\
r!: OTCSResp \qquad (244) \\
\hline
\mathbf{ran}\ docked = berths \\
r! = wait \\
waiting' = waiting ^\frown \langle a? \rangle \\
docked' = docked \\
\hline
\end{array}
$$

The successful arrive operation can now be defined as follows. (The possibility that the input tanker is already known to the system will be dealt with later.)

$$Arriveok \mathrel{\widehat{=}} Arriveq \lor Arrivenoq \qquad (247, 247)$$

Exercises

(A.8) Which predicate in *Arrivenoq* says that there are free berths?

(A.9) What in *Arrivenoq* tells you that there will be no queue of waiting tankers?

(A.10) Does the user of the operation *Arriveok* specify the berth to be allocated?

(A.11) How does the set *known* change under the *Arriveok* behaviour?

A.5 Operations — tankers leaving

A tanker can only apply to leave if it is at a berth:

Leave0

$\Delta Otcsys$ (245)
$a?: Tanker$ (244)

$a? \in \mathbf{dom}\ docked$

If there is no queue, the berth is freed:

Leavenoq

$Leave0$ (248)
$r!: OTCSResp$ (244)

$waiting = \langle\rangle$
$docked' = \{a?\} \lhd docked$
$waiting' = waiting$
$r! = ok$

If there is a queue the operation must output the berth and the tanker next to occupy it, and must update the docked function. A different response is required here.

Leaveq

Leave0	(248)
c!: *Tanker*	(244)
b!: *Berth*	(244)
r!: *OTCSResp*	(244)

$waiting \neq \langle\rangle$
$c! = \mathbf{head}\ waiting$
$b! = docked\ a?$
$docked' = (\{a?\} \lhd docked) \oplus \{c! \mapsto b!\}$
$waiting' = \mathbf{tail}\ waiting$
$r! = move\_tanker$

A successful leave operation can now be defined. (The possibility that the tanker is not at a berth when the operation is requested will be dealt with later.)

$Leaveok \mathrel{\hat=} Leaveq \vee Leavenoq$ (249, 248)

Exercises

(A.12) What happens to the set *known* in the *Leaveq* operation?

(A.13) Which predicate in *Leavenoq* says that there is no queue?

(A.14) Could the *Leaveq* specification apply to a situation in which some berths were free?

A.6 Operations – enquiries

The query operations are:

- *Queryq* Find out what tankers are in the queue
- *Queryb* Find out what tankers are occupying the berths

Queryq

$\Xi Otcsys$	(245)
q!: **seq** *Tanker*	(244)

$q! = waiting$

Queryb

$\Xi Otcsys$ (245)
$f!: Tanker \rightarrowtail\!\!\!\!\!\rightarrow Berth$ (244, 244)

$f! = docked$

A.7 Error conditions to be reported

The following preconditions on the operations will be removed to make the interfaces more robust. In each case a suitable response will be provided, and the state of the system will be left unchanged.

- Known tankers are unacceptable to *Arrive*
- Tankers not at berths are unacceptable to *Leave*

Knownt

$\Xi Otcsys$ (245)
$a?: Tanker$ (244)
$r!: OTCSResp$ (244)

$a? \in known$
$r! = known\_tanker$

Notatberth

$\Xi Otcsys$ (245)
$a?: Tanker$ (244)
$r!: OTCSResp$ (244)

$a? \notin \mathbf{dom}\ docked$
$r! = not\_at\_berth$

A.8 Final forms of the operations

Now the *Arrive* and *Leave* operations can be extended to their final forms.

$Arrive \mathrel{\widehat{=}} Arriveok \lor Knownt$ (247, 250)

$Leave \mathrel{\widehat{=}} Leaveok \lor Notatberth$ (249, 250)

Exercises

(A.15) A tanker already in the queue asks permission to dock, and the operator uses the *Arrive* operation to record this. What action does the system take?

(A.16) A tanker signals its intention to leave its berth. There are no tankers queueing. What action does the system take?

(A.17) A tanker arrives and is directed to a berth, but goes to another empty berth by mistake. Does this system help the operator to cope with that situation?

(A.18) A tanker in the queue gets tired of waiting, announces its intention to go elsewhere, and departs. Does this system help the operator to cope with that situation?

Appendix B
Summary tables

B.1 Symbols used

In the following table are all the symbols used as part of formal Z text in this book. The second column gives a very brief informal explanation of the symbol. The place in the text where the symbol is introduced and explained is given in the third column, which occasionally provides a second important reference.

Table B.1 Symbols used.

Sym	Informal explanation	Page
[ ]	given set brackets	29
	hypothesis brackets	59
	generic parameter brackets	93
	schema brackets	102
	renaming list brackets	144
( )	parentheses for general punctuation	
;	semicolon separating declarations	30
	semicolon for sequence of commands	195
:	colon separating names from sets in declarations	29
|	declaration-constraint separator	
	in set comprehension	42
	in existential quantification	51
	in universal quantification	54
	in unique existential quantification	56
	in lambda abstraction	82
	in definite description	58
	branch separator in data type definition	33, 85
•	heavy dot separating constraint or declaration	
	from term in set comprehension	42
	from term in lambda abstraction	81
	from predicate in existential quantification	51
	from predicate in universal quantification	54
	from predicate in unique existential quantification	56
	from predicate in definite description	58
,	comma separates names in a list, renaming items and members of a tuple	
{ }	set enumeration braces	31
	set comprehension braces	42

Sym	Informal explanation	Page
$\emptyset$	any empty set	32
$=$	equality of terms	31, 36
$\neq$	inequality of terms	31, 36
$\cap$	intersection	40, 46
$\cup$	union	39, 45
$\setminus$	difference	41, 46
$\subseteq$	subset	34
$\in$	membership	32
$\notin$	non-membership	33
$\mathbb{P}$	power set	34
$\lll \ \ggg$	disjoint union brackets	85
#	cardinality	37
::=	data type definition	33, 85
==	syntactic equivalence	35
$\mathbb{Z}$	integers	35
$\mathbb{N}$	natural numbers	35
$<$	less than	36
$>$	greater than	36
$\leq$	less than or equal	36
$\geq$	greater than or equal	36
..	subrange	36
$\neg$	negation	43
$\wedge$	conjunction	46
$\vee$	disjunction	44
$\Rightarrow$	implication	47
$\Leftrightarrow$	equivalence	49
$\forall$	universal quantifier	53
$\exists$	existential quantifier	51
$\exists_1$	unique existential quantifier	56

Sym	Informal explanation	Page
λ	lambda abstraction	81
μ	definite description	58
$\vdash$	theorem	59
$\times$	Cartesian product	71
$\mapsto$	maplet in an ordered pair	71
$\leftrightarrow$	relation	73
dom	domain	73
ran	range	74
$^{-1}$	inverse	74
;	fat semicolon for relation composition	76
$\lhd$	domain restriction	77
$\unlhd$	domain subtraction	77
$\rhd$	range restriction	78
$\unrhd$	range subtraction	78
$\nrightarrow$	function	80
$\rightarrow$	total function	83
$\rightarrowtail\!\!\!\!\!\!+$	injection	84
$\rightarrowtail$	total injection	84
$\oplus$	overriding	87
$(\!\mid\ \mid\!)$	relational image	99
seq	sequence	89
$\langle\ \rangle$	sequence brackets	90
head	head of sequence	90
tail	tail of sequence	90
last	last of sequence	90
front	front of sequence	90
rev	reverse of sequence	90
$\frown$	concatenation	91
$\widehat{=}$	schema definition	102

Sym	Informal explanation	Page
$'$	dash in name decoration	109
$?$	input name	109
$!$	output name	109
Δ	Delta	115
Ξ	Xi	118
$\vee$	schema disjunction	119
$\wedge$	schema conjunction	121
pre	precondition	123
θ	binding	131
.	dot notation	130
$\exists$	schema existential quantification	128
$\forall$	schema universal quantification	128
$\Rightarrow$	schema implication	127
$\Leftrightarrow$	schema equivalence	127
$\neg$	schema negation	127
$\backslash$	hiding	133
$/$	renaming	144
$\fatsemi$	very fat semicolon for schema composition	145
$\gg$	piping	142
do ***od***	iteration	197
if fi	alternation	196
$\Box$	guarded command separator	196
$\rightarrow$	guard arrow	196
$\sqsubseteq$	is refined by	198, 200
skip	skip	194
abort	abort	194
$:=$	assignment	195

B.2 Equivalent predicates

The following pairs of predicates are logically equivalent. The page references are to pages where this equivalence, and any restrictions on it, are stated.

Table B.2 Equivalent predicates.

$(P \lor Q) \lor R$	$P \lor (Q \lor R)$	45
$(P \land Q) \land R$	$P \land (Q \land R)$	46
$P \Leftrightarrow Q$	$(P \Rightarrow Q) \land (Q \Rightarrow P)$	49
$P \lor Q$	$Q \lor P$	45
$P \land Q$	$Q \land P$	46
$P \land (Q \lor R)$	$(P \land Q) \lor (P \land R)$	47
$P \lor (Q \land R)$	$(P \lor Q) \land (P \lor R)$	47
$P \Leftrightarrow Q$	$Q \Leftrightarrow P$	49
$\neg(P \lor Q)$	$(\neg P) \land (\neg Q)$	67
$\neg(P \land Q)$	$(\neg P) \lor (\neg Q)$	67
$(\neg P) \lor Q$	$P \Rightarrow Q$	67
$P \Rightarrow Q$	$(\neg Q) \Rightarrow (\neg P)$	67
$\neg(P \Rightarrow Q)$	$Q \land (\neg P)$	265
$\neg(\neg P)$	P	265
$P \Rightarrow (Q \Rightarrow R)$	$(P \Rightarrow Q) \Rightarrow (P \Rightarrow R)$	67
$\exists D \mid P \bullet Q$	$\exists D \bullet (P \land Q)$	52
$\forall D \mid P \bullet Q$	$\forall D \bullet (P \Rightarrow Q)$	54
$\neg(\forall D \mid P \bullet Q)$	$\exists D \mid P \bullet (\neg Q)$	57
$\neg(\exists D \mid P \bullet Q)$	$\forall D \mid P \bullet (\neg Q)$	57
$\exists D \mid P \bullet (Q \lor R)$	$(\exists D \mid P \bullet Q) \lor (\exists D \mid P \bullet R)$	57
$\forall D \mid P \bullet (Q \land R)$	$(\forall D \mid P \bullet Q) \land (\forall D \mid P \bullet R)$	58
$\exists D_1 \bullet (\exists D_2 \bullet P)$	$\exists D_2 \bullet (\exists D_1 \bullet P)$	53
$\forall D_1 \bullet (\forall D_2 \bullet P)$	$\forall D_2 \bullet (\forall D_1 \bullet P)$	55
$\exists x\colon T \bullet (x = E \land P(x))$	$P(E)$	65

B.3 Tautologies

The following is a selection of predicates that are tautologies.

Table B.3 Tautologies.

	Page
$\mathbf{P} \vee (\neg \mathbf{P})$	67
$\mathbf{P} \Rightarrow (\mathbf{Q} \Rightarrow \mathbf{P})$	50
$\mathbf{P} \Rightarrow (\mathbf{P} \vee \mathbf{Q})$	67
$(\mathbf{P} \wedge \mathbf{Q}) \Rightarrow \mathbf{P}$	67
$(\mathbf{P} \wedge (\mathbf{P} \Rightarrow \mathbf{Q})) \Rightarrow \mathbf{Q}$	67
$((\neg \mathbf{P}) \wedge (\mathbf{P} \vee \mathbf{Q})) \Rightarrow \mathbf{Q}$	67
$\mathbf{P} \Rightarrow (\mathbf{Q} \Rightarrow (\mathbf{P} \wedge \mathbf{Q}))$	67
$((\mathbf{P} \Rightarrow \mathbf{Q}) \wedge (\mathbf{Q} \Rightarrow \mathbf{R})) \Rightarrow (\mathbf{P} \Rightarrow \mathbf{R})$	67

B.4 Proof obligations for specification and data design

To state the proof obligations for the implementability of specifications and the correctness of data designs we shall use certain schema names in a conventional way as follows:

Table B.4 Schemas used in stating proof obligations.

Schema	Explanation
AS	Abstract state
AI	Abstract initial state; includes *AS*'
AO	Typical operation on the abstract state; includes Δ*AS*, input declarations **Di** and output declarations **Do**
CS	Concrete state
CI	Concrete initial state; includes *CS*'
CO	Typical operation on the concrete state corresponding to *AO*; includes Δ*CS*, inputs and outputs
FS	Forward simulation; includes *AS* and *CS*

Table B.5 Proof obligations for specification and data design.

Rule	Explanation	Sample
$\vdash \exists AS' \bullet AI$	Consistency of the abstract state	116
$\vdash \exists AS; AS'; \mathbf{Di}; \mathbf{Do} \bullet AO$	Implementability of the abstract operations	125
$\vdash \exists CS' \bullet CI$	Consistency of the concrete state	165
$CI \vdash \exists AS' \bullet (AI \wedge FS')$	Correctness of concrete initial state	165
$(\mathbf{pre}\ AO) \wedge FS \vdash \mathbf{pre}\ CO$	Safety rule for operations	169
$(\mathbf{pre}\ AO) \wedge FS \wedge CO \vdash \exists AS' \bullet (AO \wedge FS')$	Liveness rule for operations	169

B.5 Proof obligations for algorithm design – refinement

To assert that

$$Spec \sqsubseteq Ref$$

show the following:

Table B.6 Proof obligations for algorithm design – refinement.

$\mathbf{pre}\ Spec \vdash \mathbf{pre}\ Ref$	Safety
$(\mathbf{pre}\ Spec) \wedge Ref \vdash Spec$	Liveness

B.6 Proof obligations for algorithm design – sequence

To assert that

$$S \sqsubseteq A_1; A_2$$

show the following:

Table B.7 Proof obligations for algorithm design – sequence.

$\textit{pre}\ S \vdash \textit{pre}\ A_1$	First safety condition
$(\textit{pre}\ S) \wedge A_1 \vdash \textit{pre}\ A_2$	Second safety condition
$(\textit{pre}\ S) \wedge A_1 \wedge A_2' \vdash S[\_''/\_]$	Liveness condition

B.7 Proof obligations for algorithm design – alternation

To assert that

$$S \sqsubseteq \textit{if}\ \mathbf{B}_1 \rightarrow A_1 \ \square\ \mathbf{B}_2 \rightarrow A_2\ \textit{fi}$$

show the following.

Table B.8 Proof obligations for algorithm design – alternation.

$\textit{pre}\ S \vdash B_1 \vee B_2$	Safety condition
$S \wedge B_1 \sqsubseteq A_1$	First liveness condition
$S \wedge B_2 \sqsubseteq A_2$	Second liveness condition

B.8 Proof obligations for algorithm design – initialized do-while

Suppose S is an operation defined on a state X. To assert that

$$S \sqsubseteq \textit{Init};\ \textit{do}\ \mathbf{B} \rightarrow \textit{Body}\ \textit{od}$$

with invariant *Invar* relating X to X', bound function *bf* defined on X with integral number values, and while-test B defined on X representing the boolean expression **B**, show the following.

Table B.9 Proof obligations for algorithm design – initialized do-while.

$\textit{pre Spec} \vdash \textit{pre Init}$	Safety of the initialization
$(\textit{pre Spec}) \wedge \textit{Init} \vdash \textit{Invar}$	Liveness of the initialization

$(\textit{pre Spec}) \wedge \textit{Invar} \wedge \neg B' \vdash \textit{Spec}$	Final condition
$(\textit{pre Spec}) \wedge \textit{Invar} \wedge B' \vdash \textit{bf}\,\theta X' > 0$	First termination condition
$(\textit{pre Spec}) \wedge \textit{Invar} \wedge B' \wedge \textit{Body}'$ $\vdash \textit{bf}\,\theta X'' < \textit{bf}\,\theta X'$	Second termination condition
$(\textit{pre Spec}) \wedge \textit{Invar} \wedge B' \wedge \textit{Body}'$ $\vdash \textit{Invar}\,[\,\_''\,/\,\_'\,]$	Preservation condition
$(\textit{pre Spec}) \wedge \textit{Invar} \wedge B' \vdash (\textit{pre Body})'$	Liveness of the body

B.9 Derived rules of refinement

Table B.10 Derived rules of refinement.

Premisses	Conclusions
none	$S \sqsubseteq S$
$A_1 \sqsubseteq A_2$ $A_2 \sqsubseteq A_3$	$A_1 \sqsubseteq A_3$
$S \sqsubseteq A_1;\ A_2$ $A_2 \sqsubseteq A_3$	$S \sqsubseteq A_1; A_3$
$S \sqsubseteq A_1;\ A_2$ $A_1 \sqsubseteq A_3$	$S \sqsubseteq A_3; A_2$
none	$A_1 \vee A_2 \sqsubseteq$ $\textbf{\textit{if pre}}\ A_1 \rightarrow A_1 \;\square\; \textbf{\textit{pre}}\ A_2 \rightarrow A_2\ \textbf{\textit{fi}}$
$S \sqsubseteq \textbf{\textit{if}}\ \mathbf{B}_1 \rightarrow A_1 \;\square\; \mathbf{B}_2 \rightarrow A_2$ $\textbf{\textit{fi}}$	$S \sqsubseteq$ $\textbf{\textit{if}}\ \mathbf{B}_1 \rightarrow A_1 \;\square\; (\mathbf{B}_2 \wedge (\neg \mathbf{B}_1)) \rightarrow A_2\ \textbf{\textit{fi}}$
none	$A_1 \vee A_2 \sqsubseteq$ $\textbf{\textit{if pre}}\ A_1 \rightarrow A_1 \;\square\; \neg(\textbf{\textit{pre}}\ A_1) \rightarrow A_2\ \textbf{\textit{fi}}$
$S \sqsubseteq \textbf{\textit{if}}\ \mathbf{B}_1 \rightarrow A_1 \;\square\; \mathbf{B}_2 \rightarrow A_2$ $\textbf{\textit{fi}}$ $A_1 \sqsubseteq A_3$	$S \sqsubseteq$ $\textbf{\textit{if}}\ \mathbf{B}_1 \rightarrow A_3 \;\square\; \mathbf{B}_2 \rightarrow A_2\ \textbf{\textit{fi}}$

Premisses	Conclusions
$PartState \mathrel{\widehat=} A \wedge B$	$OpA \wedge OpB \sqsubseteq OpAx; OpBx$
A and B have no declarations in common.	$OpA \wedge OpB \sqsubseteq OpBx; OpAx$
$PartA$ is an operation on A	
$PartB$ is an operation on B	
$OpAx \mathrel{\widehat=} \Delta PartState \wedge OpA \wedge \Xi PartB$	
$OpBx \mathrel{\widehat=} \Delta PartState \wedge \Xi PartA \wedge OpB$	
x is of type X, and is not in the program space of operation A.	$A \sqsubseteq$ $x: X$ $[A; x, x': X]$
$P \mathrel{\widehat=} [x: T; Others]$ x is not in the declaration part of $Others$.	$[\Delta P; \Xi Others \mid x' = \mathbf{E}] \sqsubseteq$ $x := \mathbf{E}$

Sample solutions to selected exercises

The reader should note that the following solutions are samples only, and that many of the problems have other solutions that differ from those given in style. The possible variations in the presentation of specifications using Z are great, and acceptability of specifications is something to be determined by its audience. Some of the exercises have no solution given, and are marked 'For discussion'. The author believes that these exercises have solutions, and readers are encouraged to find a group of people with which to discuss their proposals.

Chapter 3

(3.1) The type of *Student* is $\mathbb{P}$ *Student*, since *Student* is a set whose members are all of type *Student*.

(3.2) The types of the expressions are as follows:

(a) x is of type $\mathbb{Z}$

(b) $x + y$ is of type $\mathbb{Z}$

(c) $\{x, y\}$ is of type $\mathbb{P}\mathbb{Z}$

(d) $\{\{x\}, \{y\}\}$ is of type $\mathbb{P}\mathbb{P}\mathbb{Z}$

(e) $\{on\_shelves\}$ is of type $\mathbb{P}\mathbb{P}Book$

(f) $on\_shelves \cup \{b\}$ is of type $\mathbb{P}Book$

(3.3) The given expressions are of the following kinds:

(a) $x > y$ is a well-formed predicate.

(b) $x \in on\_shelves$ is not well-formed, since x is of type $\mathbb{Z}$ while *on_shelves* is of type $\mathbb{P}Book$.

(c) $a \in on\_shelves$ is not well-formed, since a is of type *Author* while *on_shelves* is of type $\mathbb{P}Book$.

(d) $a \in novelists$ is a well-formed predicate.

(e) $on\_shelves \subseteq novelists$ is not well-formed, since the type of *on_shelves* is $\mathbb{P}Book$, while the type of *novelists* is $\mathbb{P}Author$.

(f) $on\_shelves \subseteq Book$ is a well-formed predicate.

(g) $\{a\}$ is a well-formed term.

(h) $\{a, b\}$ is not well-formed, since a and b are not of the same type.

(i) $\{on\_shelves\}$ is a well-formed term.

(j) $\{on\_shelves, novelists\}$ is not well-formed, since *on_shelves* and *novelists* are of different types.

(3.4) $A \setminus B$ and $B \setminus A$ are equal if and only if A and B are equal.

(3.5) The truth tables are as follows:

(a)

P	**¬P**	**¬(¬P)**
true	false	true
false	true	false

That **P** and **¬(¬P)** have the same truth table is the law of **double negation**.

(b)

P	**Q**	**¬P**	**¬Q**	**(¬P) ∨ (¬Q)**
true	true	false	false	false
true	false	false	true	true
false	true	true	false	true
false	false	true	true	true

(c)

P	**¬P**	**P ∧ (¬P)**
true	false	false
false	true	false

A predicate like **P ∧ (¬P)** that is false whatever the value of its constituent predicates is called a **contradiction**.

(d)

P	**Q**	**¬Q**	**P ∧ (¬Q)**
true	true	false	false
true	false	true	true
false	true	false	false
false	false	true	false

From this we see that **P ∧ (¬Q)** is the negation of **P ⇒ Q**.

(e)

P	Q	R	$P \Rightarrow Q$	$Q \Rightarrow R$	$(P \Rightarrow Q) \wedge (Q \Rightarrow R)$
true	true	true	true	true	true
true	true	false	true	false	false
true	false	true	false	true	false
true	false	false	false	true	false
false	true	true	true	true	true
false	true	false	true	false	false
false	false	true	true	true	true
false	false	false	true	true	true

(3.6) Demonstrating that the predicates are tautologies can be done by truth tables as follows, but see the solution to (3.19) for an alternative approach.

(a)

P	$\neg P$	$P \vee (\neg P)$
true	false	true
false	true	true

That $P \vee (\neg P)$ is a tautology is the law ***tertium non datur***.

(b)

P	Q	$P \vee Q$	$P \Rightarrow (P \vee Q)$
true	true	true	true
true	false	true	true
false	true	true	true
false	false	false	true

(c)

P	Q	$P \wedge Q$	$(P \wedge Q) \Rightarrow P$
true	true	true	true
true	false	false	true
false	true	false	true
false	false	false	true

(d)

P	**Q**	**P ∧ Q**	**Q ⇒ (P ∧ Q)**	**P ⇒ (Q ⇒ (P ∧ Q))**
true	true	true	true	true
true	false	false	true	true
false	true	false	false	true
false	false	false	true	true

(e)

P	**Q**	**P ⇒ Q**	**P ∧ (P ⇒ Q)**	**(P ∧ (P ⇒ Q)) ⇒ Q**
true	true	true	true	true
true	false	false	false	true
false	true	true	false	true
false	false	true	false	true

(f)

P	**Q**	**¬P**	**P ∨ Q**	**(¬P) ∧ (P ∨ Q)**	**((¬P) ∧ (P ∨ Q)) ⇒ Q**
true	true	false	true	false	true
true	false	false	true	false	true
false	true	true	true	true	true
false	false	true	false	false	true

(g)

P	**Q**	**R**	**P ⇒ R**	**(P ⇒ Q) ∧ (Q ⇒ R)**	**((P ⇒ Q) ∧ (Q ⇒ R)) ⇒ (P ⇒ R)**
true	true	true	true	true	true
true	true	false	false	false	true
true	false	true	true	false	true
true	false	false	false	false	true
false	true	true	true	true	true
false	true	false	true	false	true
false	false	true	true	true	true
false	false	false	true	true	true

The truth table for $((\mathbf{P} \Rightarrow \mathbf{Q}) \wedge (\mathbf{Q} \Rightarrow \mathbf{R}))$ was calculated in Exercise (3.5e).

(h) This result follows from truth tables in the text, namely Table 3.9 on p. 45 and Table 3.11. on p. 47.

(3.7) We construct a truth table for $\neg(\mathbf{P} \wedge \mathbf{Q})$ as follows:

P	**Q**	$\mathbf{P} \wedge \mathbf{Q}$	$\neg(\mathbf{P} \wedge \mathbf{Q})$
true	true	true	false
true	false	false	true
false	true	false	true
false	false	false	true

Now we compare the result solution (3.5b) above to establish the result.

(3.8)

P	**Q**	$\mathbf{P} \vee \mathbf{Q}$	$\neg(\mathbf{P} \vee \mathbf{Q})$	$\neg\mathbf{P}$	$\neg\mathbf{Q}$	$(\neg\mathbf{P}) \wedge (\neg\mathbf{Q})$
true	true	true	false	false	false	false
true	false	true	false	false	true	false
false	true	true	false	true	false	false
false	false	false	true	true	true	true

Columns $\neg(\mathbf{P} \vee \mathbf{Q})$ and $(\neg\mathbf{P}) \wedge (\neg\mathbf{Q})$ are the same.

(3.9)

P	**Q**	$\neg\mathbf{Q}$	$\neg\mathbf{P}$	$(\neg\mathbf{Q}) \Rightarrow (\neg\mathbf{P})$
true	true	false	false	true
true	false	true	false	false
false	true	false	true	true
false	false	true	true	true

(3.10)

P	Q	R	Q ⇒ R	P ⇒(Q ⇒ R)
true	true	true	true	true
true	true	false	false	false
true	false	true	true	true
true	false	false	true	true
false	true	true	true	true
false	true	false	false	true
false	false	true	true	true
false	false	false	true	true

P	Q	R	P ⇒ Q	P ⇒ R	(P ⇒ Q) ⇒ (P ⇒ R)
true	true	true	true	true	true
true	true	false	true	false	false
true	false	true	false	true	true
true	false	false	false	false	true
false	true	true	true	true	true
false	true	false	true	true	true
false	false	true	true	true	true
false	false	false	true	true	true

(3.11)

P	Q	P ◇ Q
true	true	false
true	false	true
false	true	true
false	false	true

(a)

P	P ◇ P
true	false
false	true

(b)

P	Q	P ◇ Q	(P ◇ Q) ◇ (P ◇ Q)
true	true	false	true
true	false	true	false
false	true	true	false
false	false	true	false

(c)

P	Q	P ◇ P	Q ◇ Q	(P ◇ P) ◇ (Q ◇ Q)
true	true	false	false	true
true	false	false	true	true
false	true	true	false	true
false	false	true	true	false

(d)

P	Q	Q ◇ Q	(Q ◇ Q) ◇ P
true	true	false	true
true	false	true	false
false	true	false	true
false	false	true	true

(3.12)

P	Q	P ◆ Q
true	true	false
true	false	false
false	true	false
false	false	true

(a)

P	P ◆ P
true	false
false	true

(b)

P	Q	P ♦ P	Q ♦ Q	(P ♦ P) ♦ (Q ♦ Q)
true	true	false	false	true
true	false	false	true	false
false	true	true	false	false
false	false	true	true	false

(c)

P	Q	P ♦ Q	(P ♦ Q) ♦ (P ♦ Q)
true	true	false	true
true	false	false	true
false	true	false	true
false	false	true	false

(d)

P	Q	P ♦ Q	(P ♦ Q) ♦ Q	((P ♦ Q) ♦ Q) ♦ ((P ♦ Q) ♦ Q)
true	true	false	false	true
true	false	false	true	false
false	true	false	false	true
false	false	true	false	true

(3.13) $[AcctNo]$

(3.14) $active, overdrawn, depositors, current: \mathbb{P} AcctNo$

(3.15) The predicates are as follows:

(a) $overdrawn \subseteq active$

(b) $overdrawn \subseteq current$

(c) $depositors \cup current = active$

(d) $depositors \cap current = \varnothing$

(e) $depositors \cap overdrawn = \varnothing$

(3.16) For discussion. Observe that Venn diagrams are not always adaptable to giving a precise view of the relationships among a number of sets. They are, however, good as informal illumination as long as their limitations are recognized.

(3.17)

(a) The proof of

$$[A, B: \mathbb{P}\ X \mid A = B] \vdash A \subseteq B$$

might be documented as follows:

(1)	$A = B$	From the hypothesis
(2)	$\forall x: X \bullet (\ x \in A \Leftrightarrow x \in B\ )$	From (1) by definition of set equality
(3)	$\forall x: X \bullet (\ x \in A \Rightarrow x \in B\ )$	From (2) by truth tables for $\Rightarrow$ and $\Leftrightarrow$
(4)	$A \subseteq B$	From (3) by the definition of the subset relation

(b) The proof of

$$[A, B: \mathbb{P}\ X \mid A = B] \vdash A \setminus B = \varnothing$$

might be documented as follows:

(1)	$\exists x: X \bullet x \in A \setminus B$	Negation of the conclusion
(2)	$\exists x: X \bullet (\ x \in A \wedge x \notin B\ )$	From (1) by definition of set difference
(3)	$\neg(\ \forall x: X \bullet (\ x \notin A \vee x \in B\ )\ )$	From (2) by negation rule for the universal quantifier
(4)	$\neg(\ \forall x: X \bullet (\ x \in A \Rightarrow x \in B\ )\ )$	From (3) by the truth tables for $\vee$ and $\Rightarrow$
(5)	$\neg(A \subseteq B)$	From (4) by the definition of the subset relation
(6)	$A = B$	From the hypothesis
(7)	$A \subseteq B$	From (7) by the previous theorem, contradicting (5)

(c) The proof of

$$[A, B, C: \mathbb{P}\ X] \vdash A \cap (B \setminus C) = (A \cap B) \setminus C$$

might be documented as follows:

(1)	$A \cap (B \setminus C) =$ $\{x: X \mid x \in A \wedge (x \in B \wedge x \notin C)\}$	Definition of intersection and difference
(2)	$\{x: X \mid x \in A \wedge (x \in B \wedge x \notin C)\}$ $=$ $\{x: X \mid (x \in A \wedge x \in B) \wedge x \notin C\}$	By the associativity of conjunction
(3)	$\{x: X \mid (x \in A \wedge x \in B) \wedge x \notin C\} =$ $(A \cap B) \setminus C$	By definition of intersection and difference

The required conclusion follows from (1), (2) and (3).

(d) The proof of

$$[A: \mathbb{P}\ X] \vdash \varnothing \setminus A = \varnothing$$

can be done by *reductio ad absurdum* as follows.

Suppose that the conclusion is false, so that the difference is not empty, then we can say that

$$\exists x: X \bullet (x \in \varnothing \wedge x \notin A)$$

But $x \in \varnothing$ is false, so the conjunction must be false, and so the quantification must be false.

(3.18) In the set comprehension term

$$\{x: \mathbb{N} \mid x^2 \leq 5 \bullet x^2\}$$

the variable x is bound.

(3.19) The appropriate tautology is

$$(((\mathbf{P} \wedge \mathbf{Q}) \Rightarrow \mathbf{R}) \wedge (((\neg \mathbf{P}) \wedge \mathbf{Q}) \Rightarrow \mathbf{R}))$$
$$\Rightarrow (\mathbf{Q} \Rightarrow \mathbf{R})$$

To demonstrate that this is a tautology we use the method of *reductio ad absurdum*. We suppose that there is a way of assigning the values true and false to **P**, **Q** and **R**, so that the whole predicate becomes false. We hope to establish a contradiction and proceed as follows. To save space we use T for true and F for false.

	1	2	3	4	5	6	7	8	9	10	11	12	13	14	15	16
((	(**P**	∧	**Q**)	⇒	**R**)	∧((	(¬	**P**)	∧	**Q**)	⇒	**R**))	⇒	(**Q**	⇒	**R**)
(a)													F			
(b)						T									F	
(c)				T							T			T		F
(d)			T		F					T		F				
(e)		F							F							
(f)	F						F									
(g)	F							T								

The explanation of the entries in the rows is as follows.

(a) We suppose that the implication 13 is false.

(b) This can only be the case if the antecedent 6 (a conjunction) is true and the consequent 15 (an implication) is false.

(c) To make 6 true we mark the implications 4 and 11 both true, and to make 15 false we mark 14 true and 16 false.

(d) Now we have values for **Q** and **R**, so we copy these to the other occurrences of these symbols.

(e) To make 4 true we mark 2 false, since 5 is already false. To make 11 true we mark 9 false, since 12 is already false.

(f) To make 2 false, 1 must be false, since 3 is true. To make 9 false, 7 must be false, since 10 is true.

(g) To make 7 false, 8 must be true, but 8 and 1 are both **P**, so we have a contradiction.

(3.20) An axiom for set equality might be as follows:

$$[A, B: \mathbb{P}\ T] \vdash A = B \Leftrightarrow (\ \forall t: T \bullet (\ t \in A \Leftrightarrow t \in B\ )\ )$$

An axiom for set union might be as follows:

$$[A, B: \mathbb{P}\ T] \vdash A \cup B = \{t: T \mid t \in A \vee t \in B\}$$

An axiom for set intersection might be as follows:

$$[A, B: \mathbb{P}\ T] \vdash A \cap B = \{t: T \mid t \in A \wedge t \in B\}$$

An axiom for set difference might be as follows:

$$[A, B: \mathbb{P}\ T] \vdash A \setminus B = \{t: T \mid t \in A \wedge t \notin B\}$$

An axiom for subset might be as follows:

$$[A, B: \mathbb{P}\ T] \vdash A \subseteq B \Leftrightarrow (\forall t: T \bullet (t \in A \Rightarrow t \in B))$$

Chapter 4

(4.1) The domain is $\{V, A, C, L, Vy, E, Aa, D\}$.
The range is $\{Vy, E, Aa, D, W, G, N\}$.

(4.2) $\exists g: Phenomenon \bullet \mathbf{dom}\ cause\_of \setminus \mathbf{ran}\ cause\_of = \{g\}$.
The Venn diagram in Figure S4.1 illustrates the theorem.

(4.3) $\{V \mapsto Vy, V \mapsto E, E \mapsto G\}$

(4.4) $\{V \mapsto Vy,\ A \mapsto Vy,\ Vy \mapsto W,\ C \mapsto Aa,\ L \mapsto Aa,\ C \mapsto D,\ L \mapsto D,\ D \mapsto N\}$

(4.5)

(a) $Man \times Occasion = D$

(b) $\forall m: Man;\ o: Occasion \bullet m\ D\ o$

(c) $\exists m: Man;\ o: Occasion \bullet \neg\ m\ D\ o$

(4.6) The following predicates are equivalent, and correspond to what the writer of the sentence probably meant.

$$\mathbf{dom}\ loves = NiceGirl$$

$$\forall n: NiceGirl \bullet (\exists s: Sailor \bullet n\ loves\ s)$$

Another meaning is exposed by the following predicate:

$$\exists s: sailor \bullet (\forall n: NiceGirl \bullet n\ loves\ s)$$

It says that there is one sailor who is loved by all the nice girls.

(4.7) The library books on loan to person p are denoted by the expression

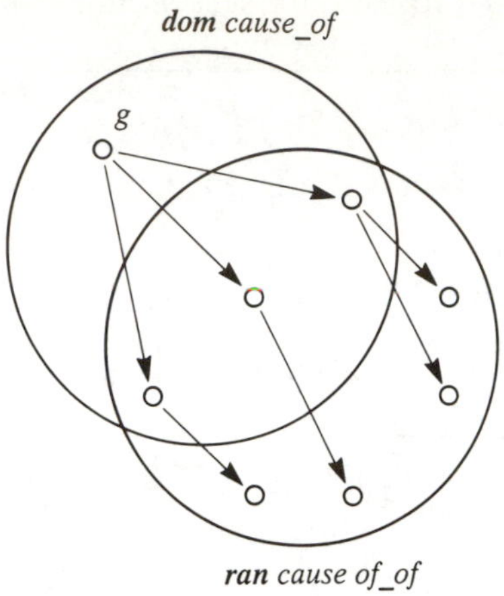

Figure S4.1 Theorem of Saint Thomas Aquinas illustrated.

$$\textbf{dom}\ (lent\_to \rhd \{p\})$$

If $p \notin borrowers$, this denotes the empty set of books. The requirement that nobody should be allowed to have more than eight books on loan is formalized by the following predicate:

$$\forall p: Person \bullet \#\ \textbf{dom}\ (lent\_to \rhd \{p\}) \leq 8 \qquad (29)$$

(4.8)

(a) $acno \mapsto 1000$ is of type $AcctNo \times \mathbb{Z}$.

(b) $balance\ acno$ is of type $\mathbb{Z}$.

(c) $\textbf{dom}\ balance$ is of type $\mathbb{P} AcctNo$.

(d) $\textbf{ran}\ balance$ is of type $\mathbb{P}\mathbb{Z}$.

(e) $depositors \lhd balance$ is of type $\mathbb{P}(AcctNo \times \mathbb{Z})$.

(f) $balance \ntriangleright \mathbb{N}$ is of type $\mathbb{P}(AcctNo \times \mathbb{Z})$.

(4.9) $active = \textbf{dom}\ balance$

(4.10) $overdrawn = \{a: \textbf{dom}\ balance \mid balance\ a < 0\}$

(4.11) $\textbf{dom}(balance \rhd \{b: \mathbb{Z} \mid b > 10000\}) \cap depositors$

(4.12) $active = \textbf{dom}\ details$

(4.13) $\{a: AcctNo \mid a \in \mathbf{dom}\ details \wedge details\ a = c\}$
or
$\mathbf{dom}(details \rhd \{c\})$

(4.14)

$$\begin{array}{ll} Account ::= & \\ special \mid mo \langle\!\langle Mortgage \rangle\!\rangle & (98) \\ \mid de \langle\!\langle Deposit \rangle\!\rangle \mid hi \langle\!\langle HighInterest \rangle\!\rangle & (98, 98) \end{array}$$

(4.15) We shall prove the theorem

$$\vdash \forall s: \mathbf{seq}\ X \bullet s^{-1} \in X \rightarrowtail\!\!\!\!\!\!\rightarrow \mathbb{N} \Rightarrow \# s = \# \mathbf{ran}\ s$$

by using mathematical induction on the length of the sequence s.

The basis of the induction is the case when s is an empty sequence. In this case we have to show that

$$[s: \mathbf{seq}\ X \mid s = \langle\rangle] \vdash$$
$$s^{-1} \in X \rightarrowtail\!\!\!\!\!\!\rightarrow \mathbb{N} \Rightarrow \# s = \# \mathbf{ran}\ s$$

The consequent is true since the length of s is zero, and the range of s is an empty set. Thus the implication is true since its consequent is true.

For the induction hypothesis we suppose that for all sequences of length k

$$[s: \mathbf{seq}\ X; k: \mathbb{N} \mid \# s = k] \vdash$$
$$s^{-1} \in X \rightarrowtail\!\!\!\!\!\!\rightarrow \mathbb{N} \Rightarrow \# s = \# \mathbf{ran}\ s$$

Suppose t is a sequence of length $k+1$, and

$$t = s \mathbin{\char`^} \langle x \rangle$$

for some x of type X. If

$$t^{-1} \in X \rightarrowtail\!\!\!\!\!\!\rightarrow \mathbb{N}$$

then we show that x cannot be in $\mathbf{ran}\ s$ by *reductio ad absurdum* as follows: Suppose x were in $\mathbf{ran}\ s$; then

$$\exists i: 1..\#s \bullet i \mapsto x \in s$$

But this means that

$$(x \mapsto i) \in t^{-1} \wedge (x \mapsto (\#s + 1)) \in t^{-1}$$

contrary to the hypothesis that t^{-1} was a partial function. The deduction proceeds as follows:

$x \notin \mathbf{ran}\ s$

$t = s \frown \langle x \rangle$

$\# t = \# s + 1$

$\# \mathbf{ran}\ t = \# \mathbf{ran}\ s + 1$

$\# \mathbf{ran}\ t = \# s + 1$

$\# \mathbf{ran}\ t = \# t$

(4.16)

$$sum\_of: (AcctNo \pfun \mathbb{Z}) \rightarrow \mathbb{Z} \qquad (271)$$

$$sum\_of\ \varnothing = 0$$

$$(\forall b, b_1: AcctNo \pfun \mathbb{Z};\ a: AcctNo;\ z: \mathbb{Z} \qquad (271, 271)$$
$$\bullet (b = b_1 \cup \{a \mapsto z\} \Rightarrow sum\_of\ b = z + sum\_of\ b_1))$$

(4.17) $sum\_of (\mathbf{dom}(details \rhd \{c\}) \lhd balance)$

(4.18) The following definitions of *min* are possible.

(a)

$$min: \mathbb{Z} \times \mathbb{Z} \rightarrow \mathbb{Z}$$

$$\forall m, n: \mathbb{Z} \bullet ((m \leq n \land min(m, n) = m) \lor (n \leq m \land min(m, n) = n))$$

(b)

$$min == \{m, n, p: \mathbb{Z} \mid m \geq p \land n \geq p \land (m = p \lor n = p) \bullet (m \mapsto n) \mapsto p\}$$

(4.19) The definition of *mins* is as follows.

$$
\begin{array}{|l}
mins: \mathbb{P}\ \mathbb{N} \twoheadrightarrow \mathbb{N} \\
\hline
(\ \forall n: \mathbb{N};\ sn: \mathbb{P}\ \mathbb{N} \mid sn \neq \varnothing \\
\bullet\ (\ mins\ \{n\} = n \\
\quad \wedge\ mins\ \{n\} \cup sn = min\ (n, mins\ sn)\ )\ )
\end{array}
$$

(4.20) The definition of distributed union and distributed intersection is as follows.

$$
\begin{array}{|l}
[X] \\
\hline
duni, dint: \mathbb{P}\ (\mathbb{P}\ X) \rightarrow \mathbb{P}\ X \\
\hline
(\ \forall sosx: \mathbb{P}\ (\mathbb{P}\ X) \bullet \\
\quad (\ duni\ sosx = \{x: X \mid (\ \exists sx: sosx \bullet x \in sx\ )\} \\
\quad \wedge\ dint\ sosx = \{x: X \mid (\ \forall sx: sosx \bullet x \in sx\ )\}\ )\ ) \\
\hline
\end{array}
$$

(4.21) A definition of the notion of one sequence being a permutation of another is as follows.

$$
\begin{array}{|l}
[X] \\
\hline
isperm: \mathbf{seq}\ X \leftrightarrow \mathbf{seq}\ X \\
\hline
(\ \forall s, t: \mathbf{seq}\ X \\
\bullet\ (\ s\ isperm\ t \Leftrightarrow \\
\quad (\ \#\ s = \#\ t \\
\quad \wedge\ (\ \exists f: 1..\#\ s \rightarrowtail 1..\#\ s \bullet \\
\qquad (\ \forall n: 1..\#\ s \bullet s\ (f\ n) = t\ n\ )\ )\ )\ )\ ) \\
\hline
\end{array}
$$

Informally we note that the permutation property is only possible for sequences of the same length, and there is a $1-1$ function that relates indexes of s to indexes of t in such a way that corresponding indexes address the same element of the sequence.

(4.22) A definition of distributed concatenation is as follows.

$$
\begin{array}{l}
[X] \\
\hline
dcat: \mathbf{seq}\ (\mathbf{seq}\ X) \rightarrow \mathbf{seq}\ X \\
\hline
(\ \forall ssx: \mathbf{seq}\ (\mathbf{seq}\ X) \\
\quad \bullet (\ (\ ssx = \langle\rangle \wedge dcat\ ssx = \langle\rangle\ ) \\
\quad\quad \vee (\ ssx \neq \langle\rangle \wedge dcat\ ssx = \mathbf{head}\ ssx \frown dcat\ (\mathbf{tail}\ ssx)\ )\ )
\end{array}
$$

(4.23) The set of all palindromes of values of type X might be defined as follows.

$$palin\ X == \{s: \mathbf{seq}\ X \mid \mathbf{rev}\ s = s\}$$

(4.24) A definition of relational image is as follows.

$$
\begin{array}{l}
[X, Y] \\
\hline
\_\ (\!|\ \_\ |\!)\ : ((X \leftrightarrow Y) \times \mathbb{P}\ X) \rightarrow \mathbb{P}\ Y \\
\hline
(\ \forall f: X \leftrightarrow Y; A: \mathbb{P}\ X \\
\quad \bullet f\ (\!| A |\!) = \mathbf{ran}\ (A \lhd f)\ )
\end{array}
$$

Chapter 5

(5.1) The following is only a sample of an approach that might be adopted.

(Here there should be some explanation of the given sets and the chosen state components, as in the exercises to previous chapters.) The type of responses to the operations is as follows:

BSResponse ::=
account_opened
| *account_closed*
| *deposit_stated_amount*
| *transaction_complete*
| *overdrawn_not_allowed*
| *no_more_account_numbers*
| *bad_account_number*
| *overdrawn_balance_not_allowed*

Bank

$active, depositors: \mathbb{P}\ AcctNo$	(271)
$current, overdrawn: \mathbb{P}\ AcctNo$	(271)
$balance: AcctNo \nrightarrow \mathbb{Z}$	(271)

$$current \cup depositors = active$$
$$current \cap depositors = \varnothing$$
$$active = \mathbf{dom}\ balance$$
$$overdrawn = \{a: current \mid balance\ a < 0\}$$
$$\forall a: depositors \bullet balance\ a \geq 0$$

Every active account is either a deposit account or a current account. No account can be both a deposit account and a current account. The active accounts are those for which we have a record of the balance. The overdrawn accounts are those with negative balances. Every deposit account has a balance that is not negative.

The initial value of the bank is specified next.

Initial_bank

$Bank'$	(281)

$$balance' = \varnothing$$

Initially there are no accounts.

(5.2) For discussion

(5.3) When a deposit account is to be opened there is one input, *amt?*, which is the amount to be invested. The output *a!* is the new account number, and the output *r!* is the response.

Open_a_deposit_account_ok

$\Delta Bank$ (281)
$amt?: \mathbb{Z}$
$a!: AcctNo$ (271)
$r!: BSResponse$ (280)

$a! \notin active$
$amt? \geq 0$
$active' = active \cup \{a!\}$
$depositors' = depositors \cup \{a!\}$
$balance' = balance \oplus \{a! \mapsto amt?\}$
$current' = current$
$r! = account\_opened$

The new account number will be one that is not in use. The input amount must not be negative, but it can be zero. The new account number becomes active, and it is made the number of a deposit account. The new account number is associated with the input amount as the account balance. The current accounts are unchanged. The response is 'Account opened'.

When a current account is to be opened there is one input, *amt?*, which is the amount to be invested, if positive, or to be overdrawn, if negative. The output *a!* is the new account number, and the output *r!* is the response.

Open_a_current_account_ok

$\Delta Bank$ (281)
$amt?: \mathbb{Z}$
$a!: AcctNo$ (271)
$r!: BSResponse$ (280)

$a! \notin active$
$active' = active \cup \{a!\}$
$current' = current \cup \{a!\}$
$balance' = balance \oplus \{a! \mapsto amt?\}$
$depositors' = depositors$
$r! = account\_opened$

The new account number will be one that is not in use. The new account number becomes active, and it is made the number of a current account. The new account number is associated with the input amount as the account balance. The deposit accounts are unchanged. The response is 'Account opened'.

When a bank account is to be closed, the account number *a?* is supplied as an input. The outputs are *amt!*, the amount to be withdrawn to close, and *r!* the response.

$$
\begin{array}{|ll}
\multicolumn{2}{l}{\textit{Close\_a\_bank\_account\_ok}} \\
\Delta Bank & (281) \\
a?: AcctNo & (271) \\
amt!: \mathbb{Z} & \\
r!: BSResponse & (280) \\
\hline
a? \in active & \\
balance\ a? \geq 0 & \\
balance' = \{a?\} \ntriangleleft balance & \\
(\ (\ depositors' = depositors & \\
\quad \wedge\ current' = current \setminus \{a?\}\ ) & \\
\vee\ (\ depositors' = depositors \setminus \{a?\} & \\
\quad \wedge\ current' = current\ )\ ) & \\
amt! = balance\ a? & \\
r! = account\_closed & \\
\hline
\end{array}
$$

The input account number must be active. The associated balance must not be negative. The account is removed from the *balance* relation. The account number is removed from the deposit accounts or the current accounts as appropriate. The balance is output. The response is 'Account closed'. (Note that the following predicates could have appeared, but need not appear, since they can be deduced from those given:

$$active' = active \setminus \{a?\}$$

$$overdrawn' = overdrawn$$

Whether they are included depends on the taste of the reader of the specification.)

The operation must behave differently if the account to be closed is overdrawn. Again *a?* is the number of the account to be closed, and there are two outputs, *amt!*, an amount of money, and *r!*, the response.

$$\begin{array}{|l}
\textit{Close_overdrawn} \\
\hline
\Xi Bank \quad (281) \\
a?: AcctNo \quad (271) \\
amt!: \mathbb{N} \\
r!: BSResponse \quad (280) \\
\hline
a? \in overdrawn \\
amt! = -(balance\ a?) \\
r! = deposit_stated_amount \\
\hline
\end{array}$$

The account is overdrawn. The balance is displayed and the response is 'Deposit the stated amount to clear'.

The general transaction for deposit or withdrawal has an amount *amt?* and an account number *a?* as inputs, and a response *r!* as output. The input amount is positive for a deposit, and negative for a withdrawal.

$$\begin{array}{|l}
\textit{Transaction_ok} \\
\hline
\Delta Bank \quad (281) \\
a?: AcctNo \quad (271) \\
amt?: \mathbb{Z} \\
r!: BSResponse \quad (280) \\
\hline
a? \in active \\
a? \in depositors \Rightarrow balance\ a? + amt? \geq 0 \\
current' = current \\
depositors' = depositors \\
balance' = \\
(balance \oplus \{a? \mapsto ((balance\ a?) + amt?)\}) \\
r! = transaction_complete \\
\hline
\end{array}$$

The account number must be active. If this is a deposit account, then the input amount must leave a balance that is not negative. There is no change to the account numbers of deposit and current accounts. The balance of the account is adjusted by the amount. The response is 'Transaction complete'. (Again there are predicates that could have been made explicit that can be deduced from those appearing in the predicate part of the schema.)

It is an error to try to withdraw too much money from a deposit account.

$$
\begin{array}{|ll}
\multicolumn{2}{l}{\textit{Too\_much\_from\_deposit}} \\
\hline
\Xi Bank & (281) \\
a?: AcctNo & (271) \\
amt?: \mathbb{Z} & \\
r!: BSResponse & (280) \\
\hline
a? \in depositors & \\
balance\ a? + amt? < 0 & \\
r! = overdrawn\_not\_allowed & \\
\hline
\end{array}
$$

The input account number is the number of a deposit account. The amount to be withdrawn would make the balance negative. The response is 'Overdrawn balance not allowed'.

Not much can be done if there are no more account numbers.

$$
\begin{array}{|ll}
\multicolumn{2}{l}{\textit{No\_more\_account\_numbers}} \\
\hline
\Xi Bank & (281) \\
r!: BSResponse & (280) \\
\hline
active = AcctNo & (271) \\
r! = no\_more\_account\_numbers & \\
\hline
\end{array}
$$

There are no more account numbers. The response is 'No more account numbers'.

Only active account numbers can be processed.

$$
\begin{array}{|ll}
\multicolumn{2}{l}{\textit{Bad\_account\_number}} \\
\hline
\Xi Bank & (281) \\
a?: AcctNo & (271) \\
r!: BSResponse & (280) \\
\hline
a? \notin active & \\
r! = bad\_account\_number & \\
\hline
\end{array}
$$

The account number is not active. The response is 'Not an active account number'.

Attempts to overdraw deposit accounts are not allowed. There are two cases to consider. The first is concerned with attempts to open a deposit account with a negative amount.

```
_Overdrawn_at_open_____________________________
| ΞBank                                    (281)
| amt?: ℤ
| r!: BSResponse                           (280)
|______________
| amt? < 0
| r! = overdrawn_balance_not_allowed
|_______________________________________________
```

The amount is negative. The response is 'Overdrawn balance not allowed'.

The second case is when an attempt is made to overdraw an existing balance. In this case the account number is also an input.

```
_Overdraw_at_withdrawal________________________
| ΞBank                                    (281)
| a?: AcctNo                               (271)
| amt?: ℤ
| r!: BSResponse                           (280)
|______________
| a? ∈ depositors
| balance a? + amt? < 0
| r! = overdrawn_balance_not_allowed
|_______________________________________________
```

The account number is active. The amount to be withdrawn exceeds the present balance. The response is 'Overdrawn balance not allowed'.

The final forms of the operations are as follows. First, to open a deposit account.

```
Open_deposit ≙
  Open_a_deposit_account_ok                (282)
  ∨ No_more_account_numbers                (285)
  ∨ Overdrawn_at_open                      (286)
```

Next, to open a current account.

```
Open_current ≙
  Open_a_current_account_ok                (282)
  ∨ No_more_account_numbers                (285)
```

Next, to close an account.

$$Close\_account \mathrel{\widehat=}$$
$$Close\_a\_bank\_account\_ok \quad (283)$$
$$\lor\ Close\_overdrawn \quad (284)$$
$$\lor\ Bad\_account\_number \quad (285)$$

Finally, to make a withdrawal or a deposit.

$$Transaction \mathrel{\widehat=}$$
$$Transaction\_ok \quad (284)$$
$$\lor\ Too\_much\_from\_deposit \quad (285)$$
$$\lor\ Bad\_account\_number \quad (285)$$

(5.4) For discussion

(5.5) Amendments to the informal requirements are left for discussion. We replace the definition of the responses as follows, adding one new value *not_enough_cash*.

BSResponse ::=
account_opened
| *account_closed*
| *deposit_stated_amount*
| *transaction_complete*
| *overdrawn_not_allowed*
| *no_more_account_numbers*
| *bad_account_number*
| *overdrawn_balance_not_allowed*
| *not_enough_cash*

We introduce a new component into the schema *Bank* with the following declaration.

$$liquidity: \mathbb{Z}$$

This component is to be the amount by which the sum of the positive balances exceeds the sum of the negative balances. We need the definition of *sum_of* from the exercises in Chapter 4, and add two predicates to the predicate part of *Bank*.

$$liquidity = sum\_of\ balance$$

$$liquidity \geq 0$$

None of the other schemas describing partial operations needs amending, since the values of *liquidity'* can be calculated from the other predicates. If you wish, you could add

$$liquidity' = liquidity + amt?$$

to *Transaction_ok*, *Open_a_current_account_ok* and *Open_a_deposit_account_ok*, and add

$$liquidity' = liquidity - amt!$$

to *Close_account_ok*, but it would be better to prove these predicates as consequences of the others.

A new error has to be specified to report attempts to break the bank. There are two cases. The first is all cases except closing an account.

```
┌─ Not_enough_cash_noclose ──────────────
│ ΞBank                               (281)
│ amt?: ℤ
│ r!: BSResponse                      (287)
├──────────
│ liquidity + amt? < 0
│ r! = not_enough_cash
└────────────────────────────────────────
```

The proposed transaction would break the bank. The response is 'Not enough cash'.

The second case is for closing an account.

```
┌─ Not_enough_cash_close ────────────────
│ ΞBank                               (281)
│ a?: AcctNo                          (271)
│ r!: BSResponse                      (287)
├──────────
│ a? ∈ active
│ liquidity − balance a? < 0
│ r! = not_enough_cash
└────────────────────────────────────────
```

The account number is active. The proposed transaction would break the bank. The response is 'Not enough cash'.

(5.6) A specification is given in full in Appendix A. The reader will find there some supplementary exercises on interpreting specifications.

(5.7) For discussion

(5.8) For discussion

(5.9) The signature of X is the same as its declaration part. The property is $x \in \mathbb{Z}$.

The signature of Y is

$$x: \mathbb{Z}$$
$$y: \mathbb{Z}$$

and its property is

$$x \in \mathbb{Z} \wedge y \in \mathbb{Z} \wedge y \geq 0$$

The signature of RBQ is

$$rbqueue: \mathbb{P}(\mathbb{Z} \times RB)$$

and its property is

$$rbqueue \in \mathbf{seq}\ RB \wedge \#\, rbqueue > 0$$

(5.10) For discussion

(5.11) For discussion

(5.12) The following preliminary definitions are needed:

$$ZfbTestok \mathrel{\widehat{=}} Testok \wedge ZfbOperation \qquad (17, 132)$$

$$ZfbLeaveok \mathrel{\widehat{=}} Leaveok \wedge ZfbOperation \qquad (18, 132)$$

$$ZfbAlreadyTested \mathrel{\widehat{=}}$$
$$AlreadyTested \wedge ZfbOperation \qquad (21, 132)$$

$$ZfbNotEnrolled \mathrel{\widehat{=}}$$
$$NotEnrolled \wedge ZfbOperation \qquad (21, 132)$$

Now we specify the operations of the interface that affect 'Z for Beginners'.

$$ZfbTest \mathrel{\widehat{=}}$$
$$(\ ZfbTestok \vee ZfbAlreadyTested \qquad (289, 289)$$
$$\vee\ ZfbNotEnrolled\ ) \qquad (289)$$
$$\setminus (enrolled, tested, enrolled', tested')$$

$ZfbLeave \mathrel{\widehat=}$
$(ZfbLeaveok \lor ZfbNotEnrolled)$ (289, 289)
$\setminus (enrolled, tested, enrolled', tested')$

$ZfbEnquire \mathrel{\widehat=}$
$(Enquire \land ZfbOperation)$ (19, 132)
$\setminus (enrolled, tested, enrolled', tested')$

The operations on 'Z Advanced' are built in the same way, starting with the following schema:

ZaOperation

$\Delta TwoClasses$ (130)
$\Delta Class$ (14)

$z\_for\_beginners' = z\_for\_beginners$
$z\_advanced = \theta Class$ (14)
$z\_advanced' = \theta Class'$ (14)

The informal documentation is left for discussion. It should describe eight operations, four on 'Z for Beginners', and four on 'Z Advanced'.

(5.13) It is an error to attempt to add a class with a name that is already in use.

DupClass

$\Xi ClassSystem$ (136)
$cname?: ClassName$ (136)
$csr!: CSResponse$

$cname? \in \mathbf{dom}\ classmap$
$csr! = dupclass$

It is an error to attempt to delete a class with a name that is not the name of an existing class – see the schema *UnknownClass* on p. 138.

It is an error to attempt to delete a class that has students enrolled.

$$\begin{array}{|l}
\hline \textit{ClassNotEmpty} \\
\Xi \textit{ClassSystem} \quad (136) \\
\textit{cname?}: \textit{ClassName} \quad (136) \\
\textit{csr!}: \textit{CSResponse} \\
\hline
\textit{cname?} \in \mathbf{dom}\ \textit{classmap} \\
(\textit{classmap}\ \textit{cname?}).\textit{enrolled} \neq \varnothing \\
\textit{csr!} = \textit{classnotempty} \\
\hline
\end{array}$$

The operations can be made robust as follows:

$$MakeClass \mathrel{\widehat=} MakeClassok \lor DupClass \qquad (137, 290)$$

$$\begin{array}{lr}
DropClass \mathrel{\widehat=} DropClassok & (290) \\
\qquad \lor\ UnknownClass & (138) \\
\qquad \lor\ ClassNotEmpty & (291)
\end{array}$$

(5.14)

$$\begin{array}{l}
CSResponse ::= classadded \\
\quad\quad \mid classdeleted \\
\quad\quad \mid classfound \\
\quad\quad \mid unknownclass \\
\quad\quad \mid dupclass \\
\quad\quad \mid classnotempty
\end{array}$$

Chapter 6

(6.1) First we consider the case in which the student is enrolled but not tested.

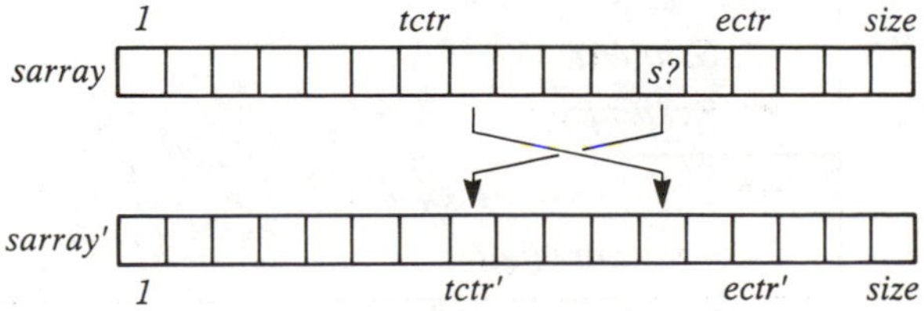

Figure S6.1 Testing a student – direct design.

$$
\begin{array}{|ll}
\multicolumn{2}{l}{\textit{DTestok}} \\
\hline
\Delta DClass & (163) \\
s?: Student & (14) \\
r!: Response & (14) \\
\hline
(\exists i: (tctr'..ectr) & \\
\quad \bullet (sarray\ i = s? & \\
\qquad \land sarray' = sarray \oplus \{i \mapsto (sarray\ tctr'), & \\
\qquad\qquad tctr' \mapsto (sarray\ i)\}\ )\ ) & \\
tctr' = tctr + 1 & \\
ectr' = ectr & \\
r! = success & \\
\hline
\end{array}
$$

There is an array element between $tctr+1$ and $ectr$ that contains the input student. This student is exchanged with the one at $tctr+1$, and the $tctr$ is increased by one. This operation is illustrated in Figure S6.1.

Next we consider the case when the student is already tested.

$$
\begin{array}{|ll}
\multicolumn{2}{l}{\textit{DAlreadyTested}} \\
\hline
\Xi DClass & (163) \\
s?: Student & (14) \\
r!: Response & (14) \\
\hline
\exists i: 1..tctr \bullet sarray\ i = s? & \\
r! = alreadytested & \\
\hline
\end{array}
$$

In this case there is an occurrence of $s?$ in the segment $1..tctr$ of the array.

Lastly we consider the case when the student is not enrolled.

$$
\begin{array}{|ll}
\multicolumn{2}{l}{\textit{DNotEnrolled}} \\
\hline
\Xi DClass & (163) \\
s?: Student & (14) \\
r!: Response & (14) \\
\hline
\forall i: 1..ectr \bullet s? \neq sarray\ i & \\
r! = notenrolled & \\
\hline
\end{array}
$$

In this case there is no occurrence of *s?* in the segment *1..ectr* of the array.

Now we can build up the specification of the concrete form of testing a student.

$$DTest \mathrel{\widehat{=}} DTestok \lor DNotEnrolled \qquad (292, 293)$$
$$\lor\ DAlreadyTested \qquad (292)$$

(6.2) First we consider the case in which the student has done the exercises.

DLeaveCert

$\Delta DClass$ (163)
$s?: Student$ (14)
$r!: Response$ (14)

$ectr' + 1 = ectr$
$tctr' + 1 = tctr$
$r! = cert$
$(\exists i: 1..tctr \bullet$
$\quad (s? = sarray\ i$
$\quad \land sarray' = sarray \oplus \{i \mapsto (sarray\ tctr),$
$\qquad tctr \mapsto (sarray\ ectr)\}))$

The counters *ectr* and *tctr* must both be decremented. There is an occurrence of the input student in the *1..tctr* segment of the array, and this is overwritten by the student at *tctr*. The *tctr* cell is refilled with the student at *ectr*. This operation is illustrated in Figure S6.2.

Next we consider the case in which the student has not done the exercises.

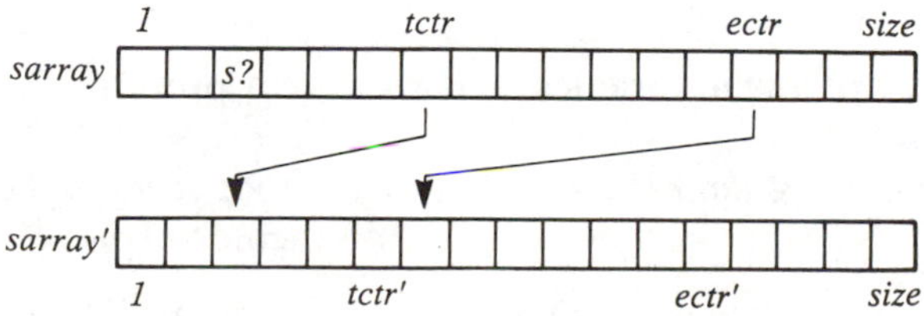

Figure S6.2 Discharging a tested student – direct design.

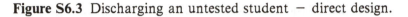

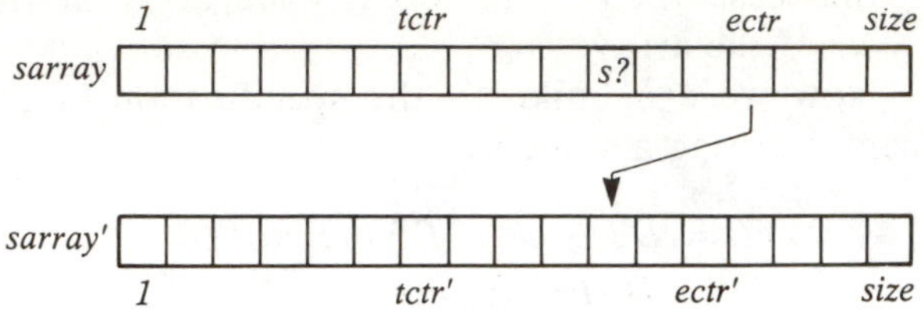

Figure S6.3 Discharging an untested student – direct design.

DLeaveNocert

$\Delta DClass$	(163)
$s?: Student$	(14)
$r!: Response$	(14)

$$ectr' + 1 = ectr$$
$$tctr' = tctr$$
$$r! = nocert$$
$$(\exists i: tctr + 1 .. ectr \bullet$$
$$(s? = sarray\ i$$
$$\wedge\ sarray' = sarray \oplus \{i \mapsto (sarray\ ectr)\}))$$

There is an occurrence of the input student *s?* in the segment *tctr* + *1..ectr*, and this must be replaced by the student at *ectr*. The counter *ectr* is decremented. This operation is illustrated in Figure S6.3.

The case of a student not being enrolled was covered above, so the concrete form for *Leave* is as follows:

$DLeave \mathrel{\widehat=}$
$DLeaveCert \vee DLeaveNocert$ (293, 294)
$\vee\ DNotEnrolled$ (293)

(6.3) For discussion

(6.4) For discussion

(6.5) The following predicates constitute a proof of the theorem.

(1)	$nil\_pointer \notin \mathbf{dom}\ block\_at'$	From *Add_to_head*, since it includes *Queue'*
(2)	$block\_at' = block\_at \oplus \{new\_pointer? \mapsto \theta Block\}$	From *Add_to_head*

(3)	$new\_pointer? \in$ $\mathbf{dom}\ block\_at'$	From (2) and the properties of **dom**, and $\oplus$
(4)	$new\_pointer? \neq nil\_pointer$	From (1) and (3)

(6.6) The theorem to be proved can be stated as follows:

$$Add\_to\_head \vdash next = head \qquad (177)$$

and we consider two cases. First when there are no blocks on the queue to start with.

(1)	$pointers = \langle\rangle$	Hypothesis for this case
(2)	$pointers' =$ $\langle new\_pointer?\rangle \frown pointers$	From *Add_to_head*
(3)	$pointers' = \langle new\_pointer?\rangle$	From (1) and (2)
(4)	$\mathbf{last}\ pointers' = new\_pointer?$	From (3)
(5)	$(block\_at'\ (\mathbf{last}\ pointers')).next$ $= nil\_pointer$	From *Add_to_head*, since it includes *Queue'*
(6)	$(block\_at'\ (new\_pointer?)).next$ $= nil\_pointer$	From (4) and (5)
(7)	$block\_at' = block\_at \oplus$ $\{new\_pointer? \mapsto \theta Block\}$	From *Add_to_head*
(8)	$block\_at' =$ $\{new\_pointer? \mapsto \theta Block\}$	From (7) and case hypothesis
(9)	$(block\_at'\ new\_pointer?).next =$ $next$	From (8)
(10)	$next = nil\_pointer$	From (6) and (9)
(11)	$pointers = \langle\rangle \Leftrightarrow$ $head = nil\_pointer$	From *Add_to_head*, since it includes *Queue*
(12)	$next = head$	From (1), (10) and (11)

In the second case we suppose that there are already blocks on the queue. In this case we can make freer use of the predicate part of *Queue*, since neither *pointers* nor *pointers'* is empty.

(1)	$pointers \neq \langle\rangle$	Hypothesis for this case

(2)	$block\_at' = block\_at \oplus \{new\_pointer? \mapsto \theta Block\}$	From *Add_to_head*
(3)	$next = (block\_at'\ new\_pointer?).next$	From (2)
(4)	$pointers' = \langle new\_pointer? \rangle \frown pointers$	From *Add_to_head*
(5)	$next = (block\_at'\ (pointers'\ 1)).next$	From (3) and (4)
(6)	$(\forall i: 1..(\#pointers' - 1) \bullet (block\_at'\ (pointers'\ i)).next = pointers'\ i+1)$	From *Add_to_head*, since it includes *Queue'*
(7)	$(block\_at'\ (pointers'\ 1)).next = pointers'\ 2$	From (6)
(8)	$next = pointers'\ 2.$	From (5) and (7)
(9)	$pointers' = \langle new\_pointer? \rangle \frown pointers$	From *Add_to_head*
(10)	$pointers'\ 2 = pointers\ 1$	From (9)
(11)	$pointers\ 1 = \textbf{head}\ pointers$	From the definition of ***head***
(12)	$\textbf{head}\ pointers = head$	From *Add_to_head*, since it includes *Queue*
(13)	$next = head$	From (8), (10), (11) and (12)

(6.7) A specification of adding a block to the end of the queue is as follows.

Add_to_end

$\Delta Queue$ (176)
$Block$ (176)
$new\_pointer?: Pointer$ (175)
$data?: Data$ (175)

$new\_pointer? \notin \textbf{dom}\ block\_at$
$data = data?$
$pointers' = pointers \frown \langle new\_pointer? \rangle$
$block\_at' = block\_at$
$\oplus \{new\_pointer? \mapsto \theta Block\}$ (176)

The new pointer must not be one that already addresses a block in the queue. The new block contains the input data. The new block is attached to the end of the queue, and added to the storage map.

(6.8) Deleting by pointer can be specified as follows.

Delete_by_pointer

$\Delta Queue$ (176)
$old\_pointer?: Pointer$ (175)

$old\_pointer? \in \mathbf{dom}\ block\_at$
$pointers' = squash\ (pointers \rhd \{old\_pointer?\})$
$block\_at' = \{old\_pointer?\} \lhd block\_at$

The pointer must be one addressing a block in the list. The pointer is removed from the sequence, and from the storage map.

(6.9) For discussion

(6.10) The concrete form of the enquire operation is as follows:

IEnquire

$\Xi IClass$ (181)
$s?: Student$ (14)
$r!: Response$ (14)

$(\ (\ s? \notin yes.ss \wedge s? \notin no.ss \wedge r! = notenrolled\ )$
$\vee\ (\ s? \in no.ss \wedge r! = alreadyenrolled\ )$
$\vee\ (\ s? \in yes.ss \wedge r! = alreadytested\ )\ )$

If the input student is in neither set, the response is *notenrolled.* If the student is in the no-set, the response is *alreadyenrolled.* If the student is in the yes-set, the response is *alreadytested.*

(6.11) To specify testing a student we use the same cases as in the abstract specification. First, when all goes well:

$$
\begin{array}{|ll}
\multicolumn{2}{l}{\_ ITestok \_\_\_\_\_\_\_\_\_\_\_\_\_\_\_\_\_\_\_\_} \\
\Delta IClass & (181) \\
s?: Student & (14) \\
r!: Response & (14) \\
\hline
s? \in no.ss & \\
yes'.max = yes.max & \\
no'.max = no.max & \\
yes'.ss = yes.ss \cup \{s?\} & \\
no'.ss = no.ss \setminus \{s?\} & \\
r! = success & \\
\hline
\end{array}
$$

The student must be in the no-set. The student is removed from the no-set and added to the yes-set. The response is *success*.

If the student is not enrolled, we must do something else.

$$
\begin{array}{|ll}
\multicolumn{2}{l}{\_ INotEnrolled \_\_\_\_\_\_\_\_\_\_\_\_\_\_\_\_\_\_\_\_} \\
\Xi IClass & (181) \\
s?: Student & (14) \\
r!: Response & (14) \\
\hline
s? \notin yes.ss & \\
s? \notin no.ss & \\
r! = notenrolled & \\
\hline
\end{array}
$$

The student is in neither the yes-set nor the no-set. The response is *notenrolled.*

The last case is as follows.

$$
\begin{array}{|ll}
\multicolumn{2}{l}{\_ IAlreadyTested \_\_\_\_\_\_\_\_\_\_\_\_\_\_\_\_\_\_\_\_} \\
\Xi IClass & (181) \\
s?: Student & (14) \\
r!: Response & (14) \\
\hline
s? \in yes.ss & \\
r! = alreadytested & \\
\hline
\end{array}
$$

The student is already in the yes-set. The response is *alreadyenrolled.*

Now we put them together.

$$ITest \mathrel{\hat=} ITestok \lor INotEnrolled \qquad (298, 298)$$
$$\lor IAlreadyTested \qquad (298)$$

(6.12) To discharge a student we first look at the case where there is a student to discharge.

ILeaveok

$Delta.IClass$ (181)
$s?: Student$ (14)
$r!: Response$ (14)

$$\begin{aligned}
&((\, s? \in yes.ss \\
&\quad \land yes'.ss = yes.ss \setminus \{s?\} \\
&\quad \land no'.ss = no.ss \\
&\quad \land r! = cert\,) \\
&\lor (\, s? \in no.ss \\
&\quad \land no'.ss = no.ss \setminus \{s?\} \\
&\quad \land yes'.ss = yes.ss \\
&\quad \land r! = nocert\,)) \\
&yes'.max = yes.max \\
&no'.max = no.max
\end{aligned}$$

If the student is in the yes-set, the student is removed, and the response is *cert*. If the student is in the no-set, the student is removed, and the response is *nocert*.

The other case was specified in an earlier exercise.

$$ILeave \mathrel{\hat=} ILeaveok \lor INotEnrolled \qquad (299, 298)$$

Chapter 7

(7.1)

(a)

$$\begin{aligned}
&\textbf{if}\ x < y \rightarrow \\
&\quad t: \mathbb{N} \\
&\quad t := x \\
&\quad x := y \\
&\quad y := t \\
&\Box\ x \geq y \rightarrow \textbf{skip} \\
&\textbf{fi}
\end{aligned}$$

Prog1a

$x, x', y, y': \mathbb{N}$

$x' = max(x, y)$
$y' = min(x, y)$

(b)

```
if x < y →
  | t: ℕ
  | t := x
  | x := y
  | y := t
□ x > y → skip
fi
```

```
┌─ Prog1b ──────────────
│ x, x', y, y': ℕ
├────────────
│ x ≠ y
│ x' = max(x, y)
│ y' = min(x, y)
└───────────────────────
```

(c)

```
z := 0
do z < x ∧ z < y →
  | z := z+1
od
```

```
┌─ Prog1c ──────────────
│ x, x', y, y', z, z': ℕ
├────────────
│ x' = x
│ y' = y
│ z' = min(x, y)
└───────────────────────
```

(d)

```
z := 0
do z < x → z := z+1
□ z < y → z := z+1
od
```

```
┌─ Prog1d ──────────────
│ x, x', y, y', z, z': ℕ
├────────────
│ x' = x
│ y' = y
│ z' = max(x, y)
└───────────────────────
```

(7.2)

(a)

```
┌─ Prog2a ──────────────
│ x, x', y, y': ℕ
├────────────
│ x' = y+1
│ y' = y
└───────────────────────
```

```
x := y+1
```

(b)

Prog2b

$x, x', y, y' : \mathbb{Z}$

$x' \geq 0$
$y' = y$
$x' = y \lor x' = -y$

$\textit{if } y \geq 0 \rightarrow x := y$
$\square\ y \leq 0 \rightarrow x := -y$
fi

(c)

$limit : \mathbb{N}$

$limit > 0$

$p := 1$
$\textbf{do } (ar\ p) \neq 0 \rightarrow$
$\quad p := p + 1$
od

Prog2c

$ar, ar' : (1..limit) \rightarrow \mathbb{Z}$
$p, p' : (1..limit)$

$\exists i : 1..limit \bullet (ar\ i) = 0$
$ar' = ar$
$(ar\ p') = 0$

(7.3) We note that

$$\textbf{pre } S \vdash \textbf{pre } S$$

and that

$$(\textbf{pre } S) \land S \vdash S$$

and these are sufficient to establish the required result.

(7.4) We are to prove that the refinement relation is transitive.

(1)	$\textbf{pre } A_1 \vdash \textbf{pre } A_2$	Since A_1 is refined by A_2
(2)	$(\textbf{pre } A_1) \land A_2 \vdash A_1$	Since A_1 is refined by A_2
(3)	$\textbf{pre } A_2 \vdash \textbf{pre } A_3$	Since A_2 is refined by A_3
(4)	$(\textbf{pre } A_2) \land A_3 \vdash A_2$	Since A_2 is refined by A_3
(5)	$\textbf{pre } A_1 \vdash \textbf{pre } A_3$	From (1) and (3)

(6) $(\textbf{pre } A_1) \wedge A_3 \vdash (\textbf{pre } A_2) \wedge (\textbf{pre } A_1) \wedge A_3$ From (1)

(7) $(\textbf{pre } A_1) \wedge A_3 \vdash (\textbf{pre } A_1) \wedge A_2$ From (6) and (4)

(8) $(\textbf{pre } A_1) \wedge A_3 \vdash A_1$ From (6), (4) and (2)

The required conclusions are (5) and (8).

(7.5) The preconditions of the specification and the assignment are the same, namely $x > 0$, so the safety condition is satisfied. For the liveness we must show that

$$[x, x' : 0..5 \mid x > 0 \wedge x' = x - 1] \vdash x' < x$$

which follows from the properties of the natural numbers.

(7.6) Since the precondition of the assignment statement is true, the safety condition is met at once. For the liveness condition we have to show that

$$[\Xi DirectClass \mid ectr = size \wedge r! = noroom] \quad (163)$$
$$\vdash \theta DirectClass = \theta DirectClass' \quad (163, 163)$$
$$\wedge\ r! = noroom$$

and all the predicates in the conclusion are in the hypothesis.

(7.7) The first safety condition is

$$\textbf{pre } S \vdash \textbf{pre } A_1$$

and this is valid since S and A_1 are both total. Similarly, the second safety condition

$$(\textbf{pre } S) \wedge A_1 \vdash (\textbf{pre } A_2)'$$

is valid since

$$[x, y, x', y' : \mathbb{N} \mid x' = x + y \wedge y' = y] \vdash x' \geq y'$$

The liveness condition is

$$[x, y, x', y', x'', y'' : \mathbb{N} \mid x' = x + y \wedge y' = y \wedge x'' = y' \wedge y'' = x - y] \vdash x'' = y \wedge y'' = x$$

and the conclusions are easily derived from the hypothesis.

(7.8) The first safety condition is

$$[x, y: \mathbb{N} \mid x \geq y] \vdash x \geq y$$

which is valid. The second safety condition is

$$[x, y, x', y': \mathbb{N} \mid x \geq y \wedge y' = x - y \wedge x' = x]$$
$$\vdash x' \geq y'$$

which is valid. The liveness condition is

$$[x, y, x', y', x'', y'': \mathbb{N}$$
$$\mid x' = x \wedge y' = x - y \wedge x'' = x' - y' \wedge y'' = y']$$
$$\vdash x'' = y \wedge y'' = x - y$$

Again the conclusions follow easily from the hypothesis.

(7.9) S is total, but A_1 has a precondition

$$[x, y: \mathbb{N} \mid x + y \leq maxnat]$$

(7.10) To prove the replacement rule for the first part of a sequence we proceed as follows:

(1)	$\textbf{pre } S \vdash \textbf{pre } A_1$	First safety rule
(2)	$(\textbf{pre } S) \wedge A_1 \vdash (\textbf{pre } A_2)'$	Second safety rule
(3)	$(\textbf{pre } S) \wedge A_1 \wedge A_2' \vdash S[\_''/\_']$	Liveness rule
(4)	$\textbf{pre } A_1 \vdash \textbf{pre } A_3$	Safety rule
(5)	$(\textbf{pre } A_1) \wedge A_3 \vdash A_1$	Liveness rule
(6)	$\textbf{pre } S \vdash \textbf{pre } A_3$	From (1) and (4)
(7)	$(\textbf{pre } S) \wedge A_3$ $\vdash (\textbf{pre } S) \wedge (\textbf{pre } A_1) \wedge A_3$	From (1)
(8)	$(\textbf{pre } S) \wedge A_3 \vdash (\textbf{pre } S) \wedge A_1$	From (5) and (7)
(9)	$(\textbf{pre } S) \wedge A_3 \vdash (\textbf{pre } A_2)'$	From (2) and (8)
(10)	$(\textbf{pre } S) \wedge A_3 \wedge A_2'$ $\vdash (\textbf{pre } S) \wedge (\textbf{pre } A_1) \wedge A_3 \wedge A_2'$	From (1)
(11)	$(\textbf{pre } S) \wedge A_3 \wedge A_2'$ $\vdash (\textbf{pre } S) \wedge A_1 \wedge A_2'$	From (5) and (10)
(12)	$(\textbf{pre } S) \wedge A_3 \wedge A_2' \vdash S[\_''/\_']$	From (5) and (10)

(7.11) The safety rule is

$$\textit{\textbf{pre}}\ [PosDiff \mid y \geq z] \vdash \textit{\textbf{pre}}\ Assign\_ymx \qquad (207, 207)$$

and this is true because the predicate parts of the hypothesis and the conclusion are both $y \geq x$. The liveness rule is

$$\textit{\textbf{pre}}\ [PosDiff \mid y \geq z] \wedge Assign\_ymx \qquad (207, 207)$$
$$\vdash PosDiff \wedge y \geq z \qquad (207)$$

and this is true because the predicate parts of the hypothesis and the conclusion are the same, namely

$$y \geq x \wedge z' = y - x \wedge y' = y \wedge x' = x$$

(7.12) The following are given:

$$\textit{\textbf{pre}}\ S \vdash B_1 \vee B_2$$

$$S \wedge B_1 \sqsubseteq A_1$$

$$S \wedge B_2 \sqsubseteq A_2$$

$$A_1 \sqsubseteq A_3$$

The safety condition to be proved is

$$\textit{\textbf{pre}}\ S \vdash B_1 \vee B_2$$

which is the first thing given. The first liveness condition is

$$S \wedge B_1 \sqsubseteq A_3$$

which follows from the second and fourth givens. The second liveness condition is

$$S \wedge B_2 \sqsubseteq A_2$$

which is the third thing given.

(7.13) By throwing away unwanted conjuncts we have

$$\textit{\textbf{pre}}((A_1 \vee A_2) \wedge \textit{\textbf{pre}}\ A_1) \wedge A_1 \vdash (\textit{\textbf{pre}}\ A_1) \wedge A_1$$

Adding a disjunct to the conclusion allows us to deduce

$$\textit{\textbf{pre}}((A_1 \vee A_2) \wedge \textit{\textbf{pre}}\ A_1) \wedge A_1$$
$$\vdash ((\textit{\textbf{pre}}\ A_1) \wedge A_1) \vee ((\textit{\textbf{pre}}\ A_1) \wedge A_2)$$

whence we can deduce

$$\textbf{\textit{pre}}((A_1 \vee A_2) \wedge \textbf{\textit{pre}}\ A_1) \wedge A_1 \vdash (A_1 \vee A_2) \wedge \textbf{\textit{pre}}\ A_1$$

(7.14) We have to show that

$$A_2 \wedge \neg(\textbf{\textit{pre}}\ A_1) \sqsubseteq A_2$$

The safety condition is proved as follows:

$$\textbf{\textit{pre}}(A_2 \wedge \neg(\textbf{\textit{pre}}\ A_1)) \vdash \textbf{\textit{pre}}\ A_2 \wedge \neg(\textbf{\textit{pre}}\ A_1)$$

since ***pre*** A_1 contains only undashed variables. Hence

$$\textbf{\textit{pre}}(A_2 \wedge \neg(\textbf{\textit{pre}}\ A_1)) \vdash \textbf{\textit{pre}}\ A_2$$

by dropping a conjunct. The liveness condition is proved as follows:

$$\textbf{\textit{pre}}(A_2 \wedge \neg(\textbf{\textit{pre}}\ A_1)) \vdash (\textbf{\textit{pre}}\ A_2) \wedge \neg(\textbf{\textit{pre}}\ A_1)$$

as before, then adding A_2 to both hypothesis and conclusion, and simplifying $A_2 \wedge (\textbf{\textit{pre}}\ A_2)$ we have

$$\textbf{\textit{pre}}(A_2 \wedge \neg(\textbf{\textit{pre}}\ A_1)) \wedge A_2 \vdash A_2 \wedge \neg(\textbf{\textit{pre}}\ A_1)$$

(7.15) The refinement of *DEnoughRoom* is verified as follows. For the first safety condition we must show that

$$\textbf{\textit{pre}}\ DEnoughRoomX \vdash \textbf{\textit{pre}}\ Search \qquad (216, 217)$$

but ***pre*** *Search* is just the invariant on the concrete state, which is all in ***pre****DEnoughRoomX*.

For the second safety condition, we must show that

$$\textbf{\textit{pre}}\ DEnoughRoomX \wedge Search \qquad (216, 217)$$
$$\vdash (\textbf{\textit{pre}}\ Decide)' \qquad (217)$$

The relevant predicates are as follows. (Note that some quantifications and set comprehension terms have been abbreviated with the help of the relational image notation.)

(1)	$(ectr < size$ $\vee s \in sarray(\!|1..ectr|\!))$	From ***pre*** *DEnoughRoomX*
(2)	$s' = s$	From *Search*
(3)	$sarray' = sarray$	From *Search*
(4)	$ectr' = ectr$	From *Search*
(5)	$tctr' = tctr$	From *Search*

The essential predicate of (**pre** *Decide*)' is

$$ectr' < size \lor s' \in sarray'(\!|1..ectr'|\!)$$

which is easily deduced from the five predicates above.

The liveness condition is as follows:

(**pre** *DEnoughRoomX*) $\land$ *Search*	(216, 217)
$\land$ *Decide*'	(217)
$\vdash$ *DEnoughRoomX* [_''/_']	(216)

The hypothesis is as follows.

(1)	$(ectr < size$ $\lor s \in sarray(\!|1..ectr|\!))$	From **pre** *DEnoughRoomX*
(2)	$((sarray\ where' = s$ $\land where' \in 1..ectr)$ $\lor (s \notin sarray(\!|1..ectr|\!)$ $\land where' = ectr + 1))$	From *Search*
(3)	$s' = s$	From *Search*
(4)	$sarray' = sarray$	From *Search*
(5)	$ectr' = ectr$	From *Search*
(6)	$tctr' = tctr$	From *Search*
(7)	$(where' \leq ectr'$ $\Leftrightarrow s' \notin sarray'(\!|1..ectr'|\!))$	From *Decide*'
(8)	$((s' \notin sarray'(\!|1..ectr'|\!)$ $\land r'' = success$ $\land ectr'' = ectr' + 1$ $\land tctr'' = tctr'$ $\land sarray'' = sarray'$ $\oplus \{ectr'' \mapsto s'\})$ $\lor (s' \in sarray'(\!|1..ectr'|\!)$ $\land r'' = alreadyenrolled$ $\land ectr'' = ectr'$ $\land tctr'' = tctr'$ $\land sarray'' = sarray'))$	From *Decide*'

The predicate part of *DEnoughRoomX* [_'' / _'] is as follows.

$$
\begin{array}{l}
(\ ectr < size \lor s \in sarray(\!| 1..ectr |\!)\ ) \\
(\ (\ s'' \notin sarray''(\!| 1..ectr'' |\!) \\
\quad \land r'' = success \\
\quad \land ectr'' = ectr + 1 \\
\quad \land tctr'' = tctr \\
\quad \land sarray'' = sarray \\
\qquad \oplus \{ectr'' \mapsto s\}\ ) \\
\lor\ (\ s'' \in sarray''(\!| 1..ectr'' |\!) \\
\quad \land r'' = alreadyenrolled \\
\quad \land ectr'' = ectr \\
\quad \land tctr'' = tctr \\
\quad \land sarray'' = sarray\ )\ )
\end{array}
$$

The deduction of this from the hypotheses is straightforward.

(7.16) The precondition of *Addup_init* is just the predicate part of *SumSpace*, and this is also the precondition of *Addup_invar*. Thus the safety condition

$$\textbf{pre } Addup\_invar \vdash \textbf{pre } Addup\_init \qquad (222, 222)$$

is satisfied. The liveness condition is

$$
\begin{array}{ll}
\textbf{pre } Add\_invar \land Addup\_init & (222, 222) \\
\vdash Addup\_invar & (222)
\end{array}
$$

and this is valid because of the following implications.

$$intarr' = intarr \Rightarrow intarr' = intarr$$

$$ctr' = 0 \Rightarrow ctr' \leq n$$

$$ctr' = 0 \land s' = 0 \Rightarrow s' = sumseq((1..ctr') \lhd intarr')$$

(7.17) *Addup_init* is

$$
\begin{array}{|l}
\hline
\textit{Addup\_init} \\
\Delta SumSpace \qquad\qquad (220) \\
ctr, ctr' : 0..n \\
\hline
intarr' = intarr \\
s' = 0 \\
ctr' = 0 \\
\hline
\end{array}
$$

and we observe that the state can be partitioned so that *s* and *ctr* are in separate partitions, so the two assignments can be treated separately.

(7.18) To prove that

$$\begin{aligned} &\mathit{Addup\_body} \sqsubseteq \\ &\quad \mathit{ctr} := \mathit{ctr} + 1; \\ &\quad s := s + \mathit{intarr}(\mathit{ctr}) \end{aligned} \qquad (224)$$

we begin by proving the first safety condition

$$\mathbf{pre}\ \mathit{Addup\_body} \vdash \mathit{ctr} < n \qquad (224)$$

which is immediate.

The second safety condition is

$$\begin{aligned} &[\Xi \mathit{SumSpace};\ \mathit{ctr}, \mathit{ctr}': 0..n \\ &\mid \mathit{ctr} < n \wedge \mathit{ctr}' = \mathit{ctr} + 1] \vdash \mathit{ctr}' \leq n \end{aligned} \qquad (220)$$

and the correctness of this is obvious from the laws of arithmetic.

The liveness condition is

$$\begin{aligned} &[\mathit{intarr}, \mathit{intarr}', \mathit{intarr}'': 1..n \rightarrow \mathbb{Z}; \\ &\ s, s', s'': \mathbb{Z}; \\ &\ \mathit{ctr}, \mathit{ctr}', \mathit{ctr}'': 0..n \\ &\mid (\ \mathit{ctr} < n \\ &\quad \wedge s = \mathit{sumseq}((1..\mathit{ctr}) \lhd \mathit{intarr}) \\ &\quad \wedge \mathit{ctr}' = \mathit{ctr} + 1 \\ &\quad \wedge s' = s \\ &\quad \wedge \mathit{intarr}' = \mathit{intarr} \\ &\quad \wedge s'' = s' + \mathit{intarr}'(\mathit{ctr}') \\ &\quad \wedge \mathit{ctr}'' = \mathit{ctr}' \\ &\quad \wedge \mathit{intarr}'' = \mathit{intarr}'\ )] \\ &\vdash \\ &\quad (\ \mathit{ctr} < n \\ &\quad \wedge s = \mathit{sumseq}((1..\mathit{ctr}) \lhd \mathit{intarr}) \\ &\quad \wedge s'' = \mathit{sumseq}((1..\mathit{ctr}'') \lhd \mathit{intarr}'') \\ &\quad \wedge \mathit{ctr}'' \leq n \\ &\quad \wedge \mathit{intarr}'' = \mathit{intarr} \\ &\quad \wedge \mathit{ctr}'' = \mathit{ctr} + 1\ ) \end{aligned}$$

The deduction of the predicates of the conclusion from the hypothesis is straightforward.

(7.19) We have to prove that

$$\mathit{Search} \sqsubseteq \qquad (217)$$
$$\mathit{if}\ \mathit{ectr} = 0 \rightarrow \mathit{where} := 1$$
$$\square\, \mathit{ectr} > 0 \rightarrow \mathit{Search1} \qquad (225)$$
$$\mathit{fi}$$

The safety condition is

$$\mathbf{pre}\ \mathit{Search} \vdash \mathit{ectr} \geq 0 \qquad (217)$$

and this is a consequence of an implicit predicate in ***pre*** *Search*. The first liveness condition is

$$[\mathit{Search} \mid \mathit{ectr} = 0\,] \sqsubseteq \mathit{where} := 1 \qquad (217)$$

The second liveness condition is

$$[\mathit{Search} \mid \mathit{ectr} > 0\,] \sqsubseteq \mathit{Search1} \qquad (217, 225)$$

but the hypothesis is just the definition of *Search1*, so the proof is immediate.

(7.20) We have to show that

$$\mathit{Search1} \sqsubseteq \mathit{Search2};\ \mathit{Search3} \qquad (225, 225, 226)$$

The first safety condition is

$$\mathbf{pre}\ \mathit{Search1} \vdash \mathbf{pre}\ \mathit{Search2} \qquad (225, 225)$$

and this is valid since the preconditions are the same. The second safety condition is

$$\mathbf{pre}\ \mathit{Search1} \wedge \mathit{Search2} \qquad (225, 225)$$
$$\vdash (\mathbf{pre}\ \mathit{Search3})' \qquad (226)$$

pre *Search1* provides $ectr > 0$ and *Search2* provides $where' \leq ectr \wedge ectr' = ectr$. From these, the conclusion $ectr' > 0 \wedge where' < ectr'$ is easily drawn. The liveness condition is

$$\mathbf{pre}\ \mathit{Search1} \wedge \mathit{Search2} \wedge \mathit{Search3}' \qquad (225, 225, 226)$$
$$\vdash \mathit{Search1}[\,\_'' \,/\, \_'\,] \qquad (225)$$

and the hypothesis is as follows. (Note that some quantifications and set comprehension terms have been abbreviated with the help of the relational image notation.)

(1)	$ectr > 0$	From *pre Search1*
(2)	$ectr > 0$	From *Search2*
(3)	$((sarray\ where' = s \wedge where' \in 1..(ectr-1)) \vee (s \notin sarray(\!|1..(ectr-1)|\!) \wedge where' = ectr))$	From *Search2*
(4)	$s' = s$	From *Search2*
(5)	$sarray' = sarray$	From *Search2*
(6)	$ectr' = ectr$	From *Search2*
(7)	$tctr' = tctr$	From *Search2*
(8)	$ectr' > 0$	From *Search3'*
(9)	$where' \leq ectr'$	From *Search3'*
(10)	$((sarray\ where' = s' \wedge where'' = where') \vee (sarray\ where' \neq s' \wedge where'' = where' + 1))$	From *Search3'*
(11)	$s'' = s'$	From *Search3'*
(12)	$ectr'' = ectr'$	From *Search3'*
(13)	$tctr'' = tctr'$	From *Search3'*
(14)	$sarray'' = sarray'$	From *Search3'*

The predicate part of the conclusion is as follows:

$$
\begin{array}{l}
ectr > 0 \\
sarray'' = sarray \\
ectr'' = ectr \\
tctr'' = tctr \\
((s \notin sarray(\!|1..ectr|\!) \\
\quad \wedge where'' = ectr + 1) \\
\vee (sarray\ where'' = s \\
\quad \wedge where'' \in 1..ectr)) \\
s'' = s
\end{array}
$$

The deduction of the conclusion from the hypothesis is straightforward.

(7.21) We have to show that

$$\begin{array}{ll}
\mathit{Search3} \sqsubseteq & (226)\\
\mathbf{if}\ \mathit{sarray}(\mathit{where}) \neq s \rightarrow & \\
\quad \mid\ \mathit{where} := \mathit{where} + 1 & \\
\square\ \mathit{sarray}(\mathit{where}) = s \rightarrow \mathbf{skip} & \\
\mathbf{fi} &
\end{array}$$

The safety condition is

$$\begin{array}{ll}
\mathbf{pre}\ \mathit{Search3} & (226)\\
\vdash \mathit{sarray}(\mathit{where}) \neq s \vee \mathit{sarray}(\mathit{where}) = s &
\end{array}$$

which is certainly valid.

The liveness conditions are left for discussion.

(7.22)

$$\begin{array}{ll}
\mathit{DEnrolProg} \sqsubseteq & (204)\\
\mathit{where}: \mathbb{N} & \\
\mathit{Search}; & (217)\\
\mathbf{if}\ \mathit{where} \leq \mathit{ectr} \rightarrow & \\
\quad \mid\ \mathit{DAlreadyEnrolledProg} & (168)\\
\square\ \mathit{where} > \mathit{ectr} \wedge \mathit{ectr} = \mathit{size} \rightarrow & \\
\quad \mid\ \mathit{DNoRoomProg} & (168)\\
\square\ \mathit{where} > \mathit{ectr} \wedge \mathit{ectr} < \mathit{size} \rightarrow & \\
\quad \mid\ \mathit{DEnrolokProg} & (166)\\
\mathbf{fi} &
\end{array}$$

(7.23) For discussion

(7.24) The program strategy appears to be to increase z until it becomes x or y, halting at the first match. The invariant for this strategy is as follows:

Prog1c_invar

$x, y, z, x', y', z': \mathbb{N}$

$x' = x$
$y' = y$
$z' \leq x$
$z' \leq y$

Since z is being increased in the loop body, the bound function could be $x-z$. (It could also be $y-z$, but one will do.) The initialization program certainly implements the invariant. The negation of the while-test is

$$z = x \vee z = y$$

and this makes the invariant the same as the specification.

(7.25) The program strategy appears to be to increase z until it becomes x or y, halting only when it is not less than either of them. The invariant for this strategy is as follows:

Prog1d_invar

$$x, y, z, x', y', z' : \mathbb{N}$$

$$x' = x$$
$$y' = y$$
$$z' \leq x \vee z' \leq y$$

Since z is being increased in the loop body, we will take $(x+y)-z$ as the bound function.

The initialization program certainly implements the invariant. The negation of the while-test is

$$z \geq x \wedge z \geq y$$

and this makes the invariant the same as the specification.

(7.26) The specification to be refined is as follows:

Prog2c

$$ar, ar' : (1..limit) \rightarrow \mathbb{Z}$$
$$p, p' : (0..limit)$$

$$\exists i : 1..limit \bullet (ar\ i) = 0$$
$$ar' = ar$$
$$(ar\ p') = 0$$

The proposed program is

```
p := 1;
do (ar p) ≠ 0 →
| p := p+1
od
```

The strategy appears to be to search up the array stopping as soon as the counter p finds a zero. We do not have to consider what happens if there is no zero, because the precondition promises that there will be one. The following invariant seems possible.

```
┌─Prog2c_invar────────────────────────────
│ ar, ar': (1..limit) → ℤ
│ p, p': (0..limit)
├─────────────
│ ar' = ar
│ ∀i: 1..(p'−1) • ar' i ≠ 0
└─────────────────────────────────────────
```

For the bound function $limit - p$ will serve.

The initial program implements the invariant, and the predicate

$$ar\ p' = 0$$

turns the invariant into the specification, agreeing with the proposed while-test. The body calculated from the invariant, while-test and bound function is

```
┌─Prog2c_body─────────────────────────────
│ ar, ar': (1..limit) → ℤ
│ p, p': (0..limit)
├─────────────
│ ar p ≠ 0
│ ar' = ar
│ ∀i: 1..(p−1) • ar i ≠ 0
│ ∀i: 1..(p'−1) • ar' i ≠ 0
│ p' = p + 1
└─────────────────────────────────────────
```

and this is implemented by the proposed body.

(7.27) For discussion

(7.28) The following specification is proposed:

```
┌─Setzeros────────────────────────────────
│ intarr, intarr': 1..n → ℤ
├─────────────
│ ∀i: 1..n • intarr' i = 0
└─────────────────────────────────────────
```

We first introduce a counter:

$$Setzeros \sqsubseteq \quad (313)$$
$$ctr: 0..n$$
$$SetzerosExt \quad (314)$$

where *SetzerosExt* is defined as follows:

$$SetzerosExt \mathrel{\widehat{=}} [Setzeros; ctr, ctr': 0..n] \quad (313)$$

The following invariant is suggested:

```
┌─Setzeros_invar──────────────────────
│ intarr, intarr': 1..n → ℤ
│ ctr, ctr': 0..n
├──────────
│ ∀i: 1..ctr' • intarr' i = 0
└─────────────────────────────────────
```

The invariant is illustrated in Figure S7.1.

The bound function will be $n - ctr$.

For an initial program we will choose

$$ctr := 0$$

but see below for an alternative initialization.

The while-test must be $ctr \neq n$.

The specification of the body is as follows.

```
┌─SetzerosBody────────────────────────
│ intarr, intarr': 1..n → ℤ
│ ctr, ctr': 0..n
├──────────
│ ctr ≠ n
│ ∀i: 1..ctr' • intarr' i = 0
│ ∀i: 1..ctr • intarr i = 0
│ ctr' = ctr + 1
└─────────────────────────────────────
```

and this is refined by

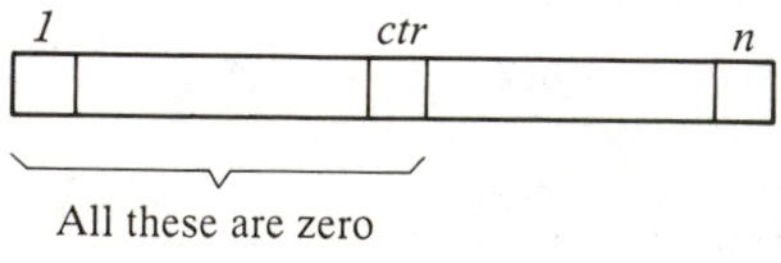

Figure S7.1 Invariant for zeroing an array.

ctr := *ctr* + *1*

A different initialization would be

ctr := *1*;
intarr(*1*) := *0*

and the rest of the algorithm design would be the same.

(7.29) A suggested strategy is to search the array from the beginning, using *ctr* to keep track of where we have got to, and using *pos* to note an occurrence of the least integer so far encountered. This strategy is made more precise by the following invariant.

Findmin_invar

$\Delta Pstate$ (242)

$intarr' = intarr$
$pos' \leq ctr'$
$\forall i: 1..ctr' \bullet intarr\ i \geq intarr\ pos'$

Each time the while-test is made, the array must not have changed. *pos* will not be greater than *ctr*, and will index an array entry that is not greater than any so far encountered. The invariant is illustrated in Figure S7.2.

The initialization proposed is as follows:

$Findmin\_init \mathrel{\widehat{=}} [Findmin\_invar \mid ctr' = 1]$ (315)

The value of *pos*' is forced to be *1*.

To make the invariant an implementation of the specification we need the following guard:

$Findmin\_guard \mathrel{\widehat{=}} [Pstate \mid ctr \neq size]$ (242)

An appropriate bound function is *size* − *ctr*.

The specification of the body is as follows.

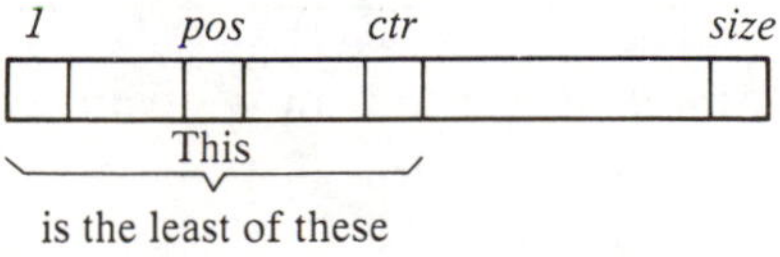

Figure S7.2 Invariant for finding a minimum.

Findmin_body_0

$$\begin{array}{l} \Delta Pstate \\ \hline ctr < size \\ intarr' = intarr \\ pos \leq ctr \\ pos' \leq ctr' \\ \forall i: 1..ctr \bullet intarr\ i \geq intarr\ pos \\ \forall i: 1..ctr' \bullet intarr\ i \geq intarr\ pos' \\ ctr' > ctr \end{array} \qquad (242)$$

We finalize our strategy by adding $ctr' = ctr + 1$ to the body and make some substitutions.

Findmin_body_1

$$\begin{array}{l} \Delta Pstate \\ \hline ctr < size \\ intarr' = intarr \\ pos \leq ctr \\ pos' \leq ctr + 1 \\ \forall i: 1..ctr \bullet intarr\ i \geq intarr\ pos \\ \forall i: 1..(ctr + 1) \bullet intarr\ i \geq intarr\ pos' \end{array} \qquad (242)$$

Now this schema can be simplified:

Findmin_body_2

$$\begin{array}{l} \Delta Pstate \\ \hline ctr < size \\ intarr' = intarr \\ pos \leq ctr \\ pos' \leq ctr + 1 \\ ((\ intarr\ (ctr + 1) < intarr\ pos \\ \quad \wedge\ pos' = ctr + 1\ ) \\ \vee\ (\ intarr\ (ctr + 1) \geq intarr\ pos \wedge pos' = pos\ )\ ) \end{array} \qquad (242)$$

An appropriate program is now given:

Findmin $\sqsubseteq$ (242)
ctr := *1*;
pos := *1*;
do *ctr* $\neq$ *size* $\rightarrow$
| *Findmin_body_2* (316)
od

The refinement of *Findmin_body_2* is as follows:

Findmin_body_2 $\sqsubseteq$ (316)
ctr := *ctr* + *1*;
if *intarr ctr* < *intarr pos* $\rightarrow$
| *pos* := *ctr*
□ *intarr ctr* $\geq$ *intarr pos* $\rightarrow$
| **skip**
fi

(7.30) The informal notation can be made precise as follows. First we give two schema definitions:

NoOperation

no, no': *StudentSet*	(179)
Δ*StudentSet*	(179)
no = θ*StudentSet*	(179)
no' = θ*StudentSet'*	(179)

RemoveStudentNo

RemoveStudent	(180)
NoOperation	(317)
s, s': *Student*	(14)
s? = *s*	

Now we make the operation precise with the following schema expression:

∃Δ*StudentSet* • (*RemoveStudentNo* \ *s?*) (179, 317)

(7.31) For discussion

Appendix A

(A.1) The predicate

$$\textbf{ran } waiting \cap \textbf{dom } docked = \varnothing$$

expresses the fact that a tanker cannot be both in the queue and in a berth (1).

The predicate

$$\# \, waiting = \# \, (\textbf{ran } waiting)$$

expresses the fact that the tankers queueing will all be different (2).

The predicate

$$\# \, waiting > 0 \Rightarrow \textbf{ran } docked = berths$$

expresses the fact that no tanker will be queueing unless all the berths are full (3).

The declaration

$$docked\colon Tanker \rightarrowtail\!\!\!\!\!\!\!\!\;\;+ \; Berth \qquad (244, 244)$$

expresses the fact that the tankers in the berths will all be different since the relation is a function (4), and the fact that two tankers cannot occupy the same berth since the function is an injection (5).

(A.2) *known* is the set of tankers that are either occupying berths or queueing for them.

(A.3) The relation between tankers and the berths they occupy is introduced by the following:

$$docked\colon Tanker \rightarrowtail\!\!\!\!\!\!\!\!\;\;+ \; Berth \qquad (244, 244)$$

(A.4) 'In the initial state there are no tankers queueing and all the berths are free.'

(A.5) The set *known* is initially empty.

(A.6) No. We get a state in which there is a queue and free berths, which is not allowed.

(A.7) Yes. The berths are presented in the output list in the same order as the corresponding tankers in the input list.

(A.8) The predicates

$$\textbf{ran } docked \neq berths$$

and

$$\mathbf{ran}\ docked \subseteq berths$$

or the predicate

$$b! \in berths \setminus \mathbf{ran}\ docked$$

indicate that there is at least one free berth.

(A.9) The predicates

$$\mathbf{ran}\ docked \neq berths$$

and

$$\#\, waiting > 0 \Rightarrow \mathbf{ran}\ docked = berths$$

indicate that there will be no queue of waiting tankers.

(A.10) No. The berth *b!* is an output parameter.

(A.11) The new tanker *a?* is added to the set *known*.

$$known' = known \cup \{a?\}$$

(A.12) The tanker *a?* is removed from the set *known*.

(A.13) $waiting = \langle\rangle$

(A.14) No. *Leaveq* applies only when

$$waiting \neq \langle\rangle$$

i.e. when

$$\#\, waiting > 0$$

and we know that

$$\#\, waiting > 0 \Rightarrow \mathbf{ran}\ docked = berths$$

(A.15) Nothing changes, but the output response *known_tanker* is produced.

(A.16) The system frees the berth and removes the tanker. The output response is *ok*.

(A.17) Not at all.

(A.18) Not very much. The operator can use *Leave*, and this will give *r!*=*not_at_berth*, indicating that the tanker intending to leave is not in fact berthed. The *Queryq* operation will reveal that it is a queueing tanker. At this stage the best the operator can do is to write down the details of the departing tanker so that when its turn to be allocated a berth arrives the *Leave* operation can be run again.

Bibliography

The following annotated list includes all the works referred to in this book. The index item 'References' will lead the reader to the places in the text where a reference is made. It also includes other works about Z, and a selection of works on the wider theme of formal methods for software development. For these last two categories, no index entries will be found.

Not all these works are currently in print, but can be found in libraries.

Collins, B. P., Nicholls, J. E. and Sørenson, I. H. (1987). Introducing formal methods: the CICS experience with Z. *IBM Hursley technical report* TR12.260.

Describes the introduction of Z and its use in the development of software at IBM's Hursley laboratory.

Denvir, T. (1986). *An introduction to discrete mathematics for software engineering.* Macmillan, Basingstoke

A good introduction to discrete mathematics, including several topics outside the scope of this book.

Dijkstra, E. W. (1975). Guarded commands, nondeterminacy and formal derivation of programs. *Communications of the ACM*, **18**(8).

Proposes the guarded command language as a basis for programming.

Diller, A. (1990). *Z – an introduction to the use of formal methods.* John Wiley, Chichester.

An introduction to the mathematics used in specifications, and the Z schema calculus.

Fagan, M. E. (1976). Design and code inspections to reduce errors in program development. *IBM Systems Journal*, **15**, 182 – 211.

Discusses the use of inspections of product documentation.

Fagan, M. E. (1986). Advances in software inspections. *IEEE Transactions on Software Engineering* **12**(7), 44 – 51.

Reviews the progress made in inspection techniques since 1976.

Gravell, A. (1991). What is a good formal specification? In *Z User Workshop, Oxford 1990* (ed. J. E. Nicholls). Springer, Berlin.

Lists some principles for choosing among models and notations in constructing effective specifications.

Gries, D. (1981). *The science of programming*. Springer, Berlin.

Develops the use of Dijkstra's guarded command language as a practical language for understanding and recording programs.

Hayes, I. J. (ed.) (1987). *Specification case studies*. Prentice-Hall, Englewood Cliffs NJ.

A collection of Z specifications in various styles. An early classic that did much to promote interest in Z.

Houston, I. S. C. and Wordsworth, J. B. (1990). A Z specification of part of the CICS file control API. *IBM Hursley technical report* TR12.272.

Describes an application programming interface for data access in a transaction processing system.

Jones, C. B. (1980). *Software development – a rigorous approach*. Prentice-Hall, Englewood Cliffs NJ.

A thorough classical exposition of the Vienna Development Method and its application to specification and design.

Jones, C. B. (1986). *Systematic software development using VDM*. Prentice-Hall, Englewood Cliffs NJ.

Less forceful in its approach than Jones (1980), but covering similar ground.

King, S. (1990a). Z and the refinement calculus. *Oxford University Computing Laboratory*, PRG-79.

Explains the differences between Z and Morgan's refinement calculus (Morgan (1990)), and shows how they might be combined in software development.

King, S. (1990b). The CICS application programming interface: Program control. *IBM Hursley technical report* TR12.302.

One of the publications of a project to discover the semantics of an existing programming interface (see Wordsworth (1991)). This specification contains an example of a promotion to a stack.

King, S., Sørensen, I. H. and Woodcock, J. C. P. (1988). Z: Grammar and concrete and abstract syntaxes. *Oxford University Computing Laboratory*, PRG-68.

A syntax for Z produced early in the drive for a standard, it includes proposals for a syntax for importing one specification into another.

McMorran, M. A. and Nicholls, J. E. (1989). Z User Manual. *IBM Hursley technical report* TR12.274.

A summary of the Z notation based on the practice of IBM's development laboratory.

Morgan, C. C. (1990). *Programming from Specifications.* Prentice-Hall, Englewood Cliffs NJ.

A textbook based on Morgan *et al.* (1989).

Morgan, C. C., Robinson, K. A. and Gardiner, P. H. B. (1989). On the refinement calculus. *Oxford University Computing Laboratory* PRG-70.

An approach to specification and refinement based on the guarded command language.

Potter, B., Sinclair, J. and Till, D. (1991). *An introduction to formal specification and Z.* Prentice-Hall, Englewood Cliffs NJ.

An introduction to the Z notation, use of proof, and the development of specifications into programs.

Spivey, J. M. (1987). *Understanding Z: A specification language and its formal semantics.* Cambridge University Press, Cambridge.

Mathematical semantics of Z.

Spivey, J. M. (1989). *The Z notation: A reference manual.* Prentice-Hall. Englewood Cliffs NJ.

Good summary of the mathematical notation. Excellent but very brief exposition of its use for software development.

Woodcock, J. C. P. (1991). *A primer on proof in Z.* ZIP – a unification initiative for Z standards, methods, and tools, ZIP/RAL/91/004, July.

This work contains a complete basis for a proof system for Z. It can be obtained from Jim Woodcock, Oxford University Computing Laboratory, 11 Keble Road, Oxford OX1 3QD.

Woodcock, J. C. P. and Loomes, M. (1988). *Software Engineering Mathematics.* Pitman, London.

Strong on the mathematical foundations useful for software development, carefully introduced. Larger examples than in Spivey (1989).

Wordsworth, J. B. (1989). Practical experience of formal specification: a programming interface for communications. In *Proceedings of ESEC '89*, Springer, Berlin.

Describes some Z features useful in building large, multi-level specifications, and describes a method for specifying certain kinds of concurrency with Z schemas.

Wordsworth, J. B. (1991). The CICS application programming interface definition. In *Z User Workshop, Oxford 1990* (ed. J. E. Nicholls). Springer, Berlin.

A report on the use of Z to capture the semantics of an existing programming interface. Includes a list of IBM technical reports that contain specifications of the interface.

Wordsworth, J. B. (1992). Formal methods and product documentation. In *Proceedings of FM '91*, Springer, Berlin.

Describes the kind of product documentation that formal methods make possible, and its exploitation as a business asset.

Single copies of the IBM technical reports described above can be obtained by writing to the Communications Department, IBM United Kingdom Laboratories Ltd, Hursley Park, Winchester, Hants SO21 2JN, UK.

Index

D

T

U

V

W

X

Numerics

Special characters